The Social Worker & Psychotropic Medication

Toward Effective Collaboration with Mental Health Clients, Families, and Providers

Kia J. Bentley

Joseph Walsh

Virginia Commonwealth University

Brooks/Cole Publishing Company
I(T)P™ *An International Thomson Publishing Company*

Pacific Grove • Albany • Bonn • Boston • Cincinnati • Detroit • London
Madrid • Melbourne • Mexico City • New York • Paris • San Francisco
Singapore • Tokyo • Toronto • Washington

Sponsoring Editor: *Lisa Gebo*
Marketing: *Jean Thompson*
Production Coordinator: *Fiorella Ljunggren*
Production: *Greg Hubit Bookworks*
Manuscript Editor: *Molly D. Roth*
Permissions: *Cathleen S. Collins*
Interior Design: *John Edeen*
Cover Design: *Vernon T. Boes*
Typesetting: *ColorType, Inc.*
Cover Printing: *Color Dot Graphics, Inc.*
Printing and Binding: *Quebecor Printing, Fairfield*

For more information contact:

Brooks/Cole Publishing Company
511 Forest Lodge Road
Pacific Grove, CA 93950
USA

International Thomson Publishing Europe
Berkshire House 168-173
High Holborn
London WC1V 7AA
England

Thomas Nelson Australia
102 Dodds Street
South Melbourne, 3205
Victoria, Australia

Nelson Canada
1120 Birchmount Road
Scarborough, Ontario
Canada M1K 5G4

International Thomson Editores
Campos Eliseos 385, Piso 7
Col. Polanco
11560 México D. F. México

International Thomson Publishing GmbH
Königswinterer Strasse 418
53227 Bonn
Germany

International Thomson Publishing Asia
221 Henderson Road
#05-10 Henderson Building
Singapore 0315

International Thomson Publishing Japan
Hirakawacho Kyowa Building, 3F
2-2-1 Hirakawacho
Chiyoda-ku, Tokyo 102
Japan

Printed in the United States of America
10 9 8 7 6 5 4 3 2 1

Library of Congress Cataloging-in-Publication Data

Bentley, Kia J.
The social worker & psychotropic medication : toward effective collaboration with mental health clients, families, and providers / Kia J. Bentley, Joseph Walsh.
p. cm.
Includes bibliographical references and index.
ISBN 0-534-34004-0 (casebound: 0-534-34101-2)
1. Psychiatric social work—United States. 2. Mental Illness–
–Chemotherapy—United States. 3. Psychopharmacology—United States.
I. Walsh, J. Michael (Joseph Michael), [date]. II. Title.
HV689.B46 1996
362.2'0425'0973—dc20 95-36303
CIP

THIS BOOK IS PRINTED ON ACID-FREE RECYCLED PAPER

Contents

CHAPTER 5

Intervention Concerns with Special Populations 105

PART THREE

Knowledge and Skills for Psychosocial Interventions 121

CHAPTER 6

Medication Education for Clients and Families 123

CHAPTER 7

Medication Adherence and Refusal 136

CHAPTER 8

Medication Monitoring and Management 152

PART FOUR

Future Directions 171

CHAPTER 9

Future Directions for Psychopharmacology: Implications for Social Workers 173

Preface

We hope that *The Social Worker & Psychotropic Medication* will be a practical and useful resource for social work students and practitioners as they fulfill their daily roles in medication management in mental health settings. We also hope that the book will contribute to the conceptualization and clarification of the social worker's role in psychopharmacology. We are referring here not only to the expansion of the social worker's roles in this area but also to a shift toward a "partnership" model of practice. Ideally, the book will be recognized as one that begins to fill the acknowledged gap between current practice in mental health and current curriculum materials.

Our three specific goals for our readers are that, when they have finished the book, (1) they will be *aware* of the relevant facts and fictions about psychotropic medications, as well as the historical, political, and ethical context of their administration; (2) they will be *articulate* regarding the basics of psychopharmacology and the language of the field; and (3) using a range of techniques and strategies in collaboration with clients, families, and other providers, they will be *active* with regard to their clients' medication-related concerns. In essence, we hope that our book will help social workers be more responsive to the comprehensive needs of their clients.

The area of social work and medication management has piqued our interest because it seems to be a place where many interesting and even controversial issues are played out. Some of these issues include turf battles between psychiatrists and other providers, ethical issues between clients and their families, policy issues—from the state department to the local agencies—and power issues between the client and the clinician. It is, however, also an area in which social workers have long been involved but have either not had the knowledge or skills necessary to act or been reluctant to use what they did know. We hope that our book will equip social workers with up-to-date knowledge and suggest values and skills needed to better fulfill their professional roles in mental health and related fields of practice.

We believe the two most salient features of the book are that it is profession-specific to social work and a practice-focused treatment of the topic. Despite the fact that social workers are the number-one mental health professional providers in the country and the fact that treatment with psychotropic medication is at least part of the treatment of choice for most mental illnesses, no book has ever addressed the role of social workers in medication management. This book is intended to be primarily a major text for social work courses in psychopharmacology or a required supplemental text in clinical practice, human behavior, or mental health courses at either the BSW or the MSW level. No academic preparation or work experience is absolutely necessary to understand the book, although a basic course in biology or an introduction to social work practice might help.

The book is divided into four parts. Part One, "Social Work Roles in Medication Management," provides the context and foundation for the rest of the text. The first chapter, on the "History and Overview of Social Work Roles in Medication Management," begins with four case scenarios in which the social worker is faced with the question of how to intervene appropriately in client situations that involve medication issues. We introduce our perspective on interdisciplinary collaboration, based on an appreciation of the stress/diathesis model of mental illness, and then trace the history of the social work profession with regard to issues of medication use by clients. Then we review the social worker's six roles as they are or should be practiced today.

Chapter 2, "Defining Effective Collaboration," presents the three basic themes of partnership, balance, and integration, which provide a consistent foundation for the book. With regard to the *partnership* model of practice, we articulate the need to form relationships with clients and their families based on an appreciation of their strengths and viewpoints, on a view of the helping relationship as active and mutual, and on a perception of the social worker's role as an equal problem-solving partner. Another theme that pervades the book is that of *balance.* Social workers must often help their clients reach a balance between the costs and the benefits of using psychotropic medications. This entails balancing the rights of individuals with those of society, as well as balancing the need to expand their role with that of understanding the legitimacy and uniqueness of the physicians' and nurses' roles. The theme of *integration* centers on the social workers' need to better integrate psychopharmacology issues and traditional psychosocial treatments. It is a combination of approaches that is often the most powerful.

Part Two, "A Primer on Psychopharmacology," is the most technical part of the book. The intent here is to provide social workers with information about the science of medication that is relevant to their practice of the six roles outlined in Chapter 1.

Chapter 3, "Basic Principles: Neurotransmission, Pharmacokinetics, and Pharmacodynamics," reviews the central nervous system, the brain, the properties of nerve cells, neurotransmitters, the way the body handles drugs, and the effects of drugs on the body. We also introduce the four classes of medication that are the focus of the book: antipsychotic, antidepressant, mood-stabilizing, and anti-anxiety drugs. Chapter 4, "Specific Medications for Specific Disorders," looks more closely at these four classes of medication. We discuss in some detail the side effects of the medications, with emphasis on adverse psychological, social, and physical effects. We then discuss the many types of drugs within each class, and the symptoms and disorders they are intended to treat. We feature three case examples for each class of medication, drawn from our own practice, to illustrate how social workers become involved in medication issues. In Chapter 5, "Intervention Concerns with Special Populations," we go a step further to discuss how each class of medication may have different effects on different clients. We consider differences in effects with regard to gender, age, racial and ethnic background, and persons who have a dual diagnosis of mental illness and substance abuse.

Part Three, "Knowledge and Skills for Psychosocial Interventions," includes chapters on psychoeducation, adherence, and monitoring. Chapter 6, "Medication Education for Clients and Families," discusses the rationale for providing medication education to clients and their families and reviews issues that are likely to arise in the implementation and evaluation of education programs. Chapter 7, "Medication Adherence and Refusal," addresses both the conceptual and the interventive knowledge needed to address these specific issues with clients and families. To that effect, we present a model for understanding adherence based on the client's characteristics, aspects of treatment, and the social environment, as well as illness itself. We address legal and ethical issues, with an emphasis on client self-determination. Finally, we provide an overview of interventions commonly used by social workers to increase adherence to the regimen of psychotropic medications. Chapter 8, "Medication Monitoring and Management," articulates specific psychosocial roles for social workers as they help clients manage their medication. This includes monitoring the effects of medications, dealing effectively with bothersome side effects, and approaching difficult decisions and problems productively, as well as negotiating with physicians and other health care providers. The chapter concludes with a definition of advocacy in psychopharmacology and with a discussion of clients' medication rights and steps in self-advocacy.

Part Four, "Future Directions," looks ahead to developments in psychopharmacology, including new drugs on the horizon, the movement by psychology and other health professions to obtain prescription privileges, and the increased public scrutiny that now surrounds psychotropic medications. For example, what will managed care mean for clients' access to medication? What do expanded roles for social workers imply with regard to their liability? The book closes with an easy-to-read glossary, which provides social work students and working professionals with demystifying definitions (and pronunciations) of the terms commonly used in this ever-expanding field.

A note about language. We have chosen to use the term *client* throughout the book, even though some recipients of mental health care prefer to be called *consumers, patients, psychiatric survivors, customers,* or other descriptive terms. Since our book's main focus is the social worker's interaction with service recipients, we believe that *client* is the most appropriate, nonstigmatizing term. Also, we use the term *physician* to refer to both psychiatrists and nonpsychiatrist M.D.s, because it is the most broadly descriptive of today's medication providers.

Our aim is to provide rich and relevant information. By "rich," we mean information that is sufficiently detailed, yet simple enough to grasp, and rooted in a foundation of basic knowledge that leads to real understanding. By "relevant," we mean information that social workers need to know because of their *own* roles and responsibilities in mental health. Whether we met that aim is for the reader to decide.

Acknowledgments

I am indebted and grateful to those who in some way shaped and stimulated my thinking about, and interest in, psychopharmacology and social work, especially the mental health consumers and families I have met through Alliance for the Mentally Ill activities in Louisiana and Virginia and during my tenure on the Virginia State Mental Health Planning Council. I am grateful especially to Marilyn Rosenson, Tib and Maizie Thibeaux, June Poe, Bob Trusdell, Mary Ann Beall, Luanne Holsinger, Linda Powell, and Shela Silverman. I am also grateful to colleagues Ursula Gerhart and Harriette Johnson for their encouragement and groundbreaking writing on the topic, and colleagues a little closer to home like Mary K and Stephen, who make VCU a great place to work and play. Major thanks, too, to my Dean Frank Baskind for his continuing unambiguous support, and to Elsie Smithers for typing and managing all the references. And, of course, to Marti for thinking I am terrific no matter how many copies this book sells.

My doctoral student John Bricout is largely responsible for compiling the glossary and deserves considerable kudos. He welcomed his assigned task with enviable eagerness and enthusiasm, and I am grateful. Perhaps the biggest thanks should go to my colleague, coauthor, and friend, Joe, who made the project a genuine pleasure and who everyday finds a way to make me glad to be a social worker and teacher. ***K. J. B.***

Back in 1974 I had the good fortune to literally "stumble" into a career in the human services field at a key transition period in my life. I knew at the time that I had found my niche, and over the years have come to feel even more strongly that my career as a social worker is the most satisfying I could have hoped for. I have worked with many fine professionals from various disciplines who have contributed to my professional growth. Trying to name them all would make for an overly long list, and still I would inadvertently omit the names of some of my important influences. Instead, I would like to recognize the organizations for which I have had the pleasure of working. These include Harding Hospital in Worthington, Ohio; Columbus Area Community Mental Health Center, the Bridge Counseling Center, and North Community Counseling Centers in Columbus, Ohio; the Mental Health Association of Franklin County, Ohio; and the Daily Planet, Marshall Center, and Virginia Alliance for the Mentally Ill in Richmond, Virginia.

I would also like to thank a few individuals: First, my colleague and friend Kia Bentley for inviting me to work on this project and for always being so pleasant and helpful as I was adjusting to academic life. Second, Ellen Netting for her excellent role modeling and mentoring of my academic development. Finally I wish to dedicate this book to my wife, Margaret, and our children, Brian, Nathan, and Robyn, who remind me every day that one's commitment to family is the most important of all. *J. W.*

We wish to express our gratitude to several people who have greatly contributed to this book in all its phases of development and production. Lisa Gebo, our editor at Brooks/Cole, has been a delight, and we appreciate her involvement in and care of our project. We also deeply appreciate the thoroughness and flair of manuscript editor Molly D. Roth, and the considerable efforts and production management skills of both Greg Hubit of Bookworks and Fiorella Ljunggren of Brooks/Cole. Special thanks go to the reviewers of the manuscript, who critiqued honestly and gently and thoroughly; the book is better because of them. They are William Berg, University of Wisconsin; Patricia B. Higgins, Western State Hospital; Harriette C. Johnson, University of Connecticut; Mary Fran Libassi, University of Connecticut; Jill Littrell, Georgia State University; Thomas F. McGovern, Texas Tech University Health Sciences Center; John Salamone, University of Connecticut; and Edward H. Taylor, University of North Carolina at Chapel Hill. ***K. J. B. & J. W.***

PART ONE

Social Work Roles in Medication Management

CHAPTER 1

History and Overview of Social Work Roles in Medication Management

CHAPTER 2

Defining Effective Collaboration

CHAPTER 1

History and Overview of Social Work Roles in Medication Management

Introduction

Four Case Scenarios

A social worker employed at a Midwestern public mental health agency provides a range of psychosocial interventions for clients with mental illness. At the present time she is faced with the following dilemmas involving four clients on her caseload:

1. Mark is a 31-year-old white male diagnosed with schizophrenia who lives with his parents and is primarily supported by public entitlements for mental disability. His active symptoms (delusions, hallucinations, and scattered thinking) are well controlled with antipsychotic medications, which he receives from the agency psychiatrist. However, the side effects of these medications are severe: Mark experiences persistent and uncontrollable spasms in his neck, arms, and back. He cannot sit still and continuously flails his arms and neck about. Because these spasms are both unsightly and disruptive to his physical coordination, he is reluctant to leave his house. Puzzled by the severity of these side effects, his psychiatrist wonders if their origin is psychosomatic. Still, the paradox is clear: Mark can either maintain mental stability and experience physically disabling spasms or experience psychotic symptoms and feel more comfortable physically. Mark's parents, who can rarely reach the part-time agency psychiatrist by phone, frequently call the social worker to seek advice on resolving this apparently no-win situation. However, the social worker has no quick answers to the problem. Further, she cannot engage Mark in any rehabilitative activities because of his reluctance to be out in public, where his jerking motions in fact become worse.

2. Carla, age 33, has been diagnosed with schizo-affective disorder (including elements of thought and mood disorder), which her paranoid perspective manifests the most dramatically. She lives alone and receives disability benefits but, unlike Mark, likes to be around people and even looks for jobs. She takes antipsychotic and mood-stabilizing medications willingly, which clarify her thoughts and calm her. However, the social worker has come to understand that Carla is by nature very forgetful. She often forgets to

take her medications and even occasionally forgets her doctor's appointments. When Carla does not take her medications for a week or more, she becomes agitated and paranoid, tending to direct her distorted thoughts at people in her immediate environment. One day Carla calls her social worker in crisis. She is convinced that the downstairs neighbor is planning to murder her, and she is considering physical retaliation. Carla admits that she is out of medication, having misplaced her most recent supply. She asks if the social worker can get some medication to her immediately, because she fears losing control of herself. The physician, who works only ten hours per week at the agency, is not available, but the social worker knows Carla's type and dosage of medication and that it is available in the small stock supply of the agency's medication room.

3. John is a 34-year-old single unemployed white male, living with his sister and brother-in-law, who experiences dysthymia and demonstrates dependent personality traits. Though he is highly intelligent, cares about others, and has a notable self-deprecating wit, John shows extreme anxiety in all social situations and has a very poor self-image. For several months, the social worker has intervened to help John reach his goal of self-sufficiency as he sought better social skills, employment, and junior college enrollment. Making significant strides, John applies for jobs, attends interviews, and visits a regional college campus. However, with each initiative, he becomes almost incapacitated with anxiety and fear of failure. The social worker decides to refer him to an agency physician who will evaluate medication that can help John deal with his depressed mood through this difficult time.

John impresses the physician as someone working hard to overcome his problems. He decides to prescribe amitriptyline, which may alleviate John's depression, help him sleep better at night, and reduce his anxiety. The medication seems effective and is gradually raised until John is taking and responding well to 350 milligrams (mg) daily. During their weekly sessions, the social worker helps Jim monitor the effects of his medication. Several months later, John begins working. He seems committed to make the experience a success, but the stress of his job responsibilities and his need to interact regularly with co-workers overwhelm him. One evening, John abruptly quits. In a panic, fearing that he has blown a rare opportunity to work, he takes a serious overdose of his medications. He survives but is hospitalized for one night for observation.

Learning of the overdose, the physician becomes angry and tells the social worker that he will no longer prescribe medications for John. He states that doing so would constitute irresponsible practice because the client is a suicidal risk. However, the social worker continues to see John, who seems truly remorseful about his action. He recovers from the crisis and states that he wants to continue focusing on the same goals. Further, because the medication has helped him move forward, John hopes that he can resume taking an antidepressant drug. The social worker feels placed in a difficult bind. She tends to agree with John, but the physician will not see him again. The social worker will violate agency policy and put her reputation as a team player in jeopardy if she arranges to transfer John's psychiatric care to another agency physician.

4. Darlene, age 22, single, and unemployed, lives with her older sister in an apartment. Though she has maintained a stable mood for one year, she has been hospitalized twice in the past three years for manic episodes. Symptoms of her bipolar disorder respond well to a combination of antipsychotic and mood-stabilizing medications. The social worker who provides Darlene with counseling has referred her to clubhouse and vocational training programs for additional service. Darlene, who comes from a highly successful and socially prominent family, at present depends on her parents for financial resources. Over the course of one week, Darlene calls her social worker daily, which is highly unusual, and complains of anxiety, inability to sleep, and a vague fearfulness that some harm may come to her from intruders. The social worker arranges for her to be seen on an emergency basis by the agency psychiatrist. During this appointment, which the social worker also attends, it is determined that Darlene is decompensating into a psychosis and requires hospitalization. The entire family, known by the social worker and involved in her treatment planning, becomes understandably upset but also furious with agency staff. Until now they have expressed satisfaction with the treatment. But now they wonder why the agency staff did not know that Darlene had consciously stopped taking her medication. While in the hospital, Darlene eventually confides to the social worker that she stopped taking her medication in order to prompt a regression because she was afraid to assume increased responsibility for herself. However, the family is so upset that, before Darlene is discharged from the hospital, her parents convince her to transfer to another agency for follow-up care. The social worker understands from contacts with various family members that they are divided over this issue, but the wishes of the parents have prevailed.

These actual case scenarios exemplify the dilemmas a social worker may face in situations involving clients who take psychotropic medication. In the first example, the social worker seems to be in a no-win situation as she tries, with the client and family, to decide whether or not the client's use of psychotropic medication is appropriate. In the second example, the social worker needs to wrestle with the temptation to move out of his legal boundaries and dispense medication, especially because the act appears to be safe and in the client's (and possibly the neighbor's) best interest. In the third situation, the social worker has become entangled in a conflict between her client and a physician/colleague. The fourth scenario represents an instance of the social worker's mistaken assumptions about the extent to which collaborative treatment has been implemented with her client's family. During a crisis she has found that there are issues of trust that have not been fully addressed. How can the worker effectively advocate for the client in any of these four circumstances? How much priority should she place on maintaining cooperative interdisciplinary roles? How can the social worker implement what seems to be best for the clients in light of complicating medication concerns?

The Changing Roles of Social Workers

Professional practice in social work is based on biopsychosocial theories of assessment and intervention. In mental health treatment settings, both assessing mental status and monitoring medication should be included as a significant part of the person-in-environment assessment because they are so relevant to this client population's capacity for social functioning. Though medications affect functioning at a biochemical level, they equally impact the psychological and social concerns of clients and their significant others. In this chapter, we will attempt to outline the range of roles that social workers should be prepared to assume in working with clients who use or who consider the use of psychotropic medications. Traditionally, social workers have not emphasized a knowledge of medications as a key component of their professional training or continuing education; however, continued ignorance of this topic will only result in disservice to clients.

One model that attempts to explain the interplay between biological and environmental influences in mental health is the *stress-diathesis* (or stress vulnerability) model of mental illness (Falloon, Boyd, & McGill, 1984; Yank, Bentley, & Hargrove, 1993). This model asserts that though the cause of mental illness is apparently associated with genetic factors and abnormalities in brain chemistry and structure, the course of disorders is partly related to environmental factors. Liberman (1988b, p. 9) writes that "vulnerability and stressors are moderated in their impact . . . by the presence of protective factors," such as skills in coping and competence, medication, and social support. If social workers can help build up protective factors, they can decrease the impairments and handicaps experienced by mental health clients and their families. Though the model was originally developed to explain the course of schizophrenia, social workers will find it useful because it clarifies how they can contribute, particularly through medication management, to improved psychosocial functioning in clients and their families. This model suggests that though social workers most likely will not influence genes, chromosomes, or the size of frontal lobes, they surely can help build protective factors and, through psychosocial interventions, can help clients maximize the benefits of their psychotropic medication.

All social workers, particularly those in health and mental health service settings, work at least occasionally with clients who use medications as part of their overall intervention plans. However, social workers have only recently begun to elaborate a range of specific professional roles with regard to medication issues. Historically, they have functioned as physician's assistants, supporting client compliance with medications according to the physician's recommendations. Still, as indicated in the four case examples, the range of service delivery modalities for some client populations has expanded to a point where clients and families occasionally ask social workers, regardless of their level of competence in the area, to make difficult decisions about the use of psychotropic medication. Crisis situations, which demand immediate action by clients and their families, do not always allow social workers to postpone intervention in deference to the physician's expertise.

Social workers must possess a sound knowledge of medications and their consequences for clients' lives, but not merely to complement the physician's role. To medication issues, the social work profession brings a unique perspective based on its appreciation of client self-determination, its perspective that medication is only one part of comprehensive psychosocial intervention, and its view of the person-in-environment as the basis for assessment and intervention. Social work also promotes a partnership model of practice, which bases the relationships with clients and families on an appreciation of their strengths and viewpoints and on the assumption that the helping relationship is active and mutual.

There are four reasons for these developments within the social work profession during the past 20 years. First, the presence of social workers in public mental health service settings of all types has increased in proportion to other professional disciplines (Manderscheid & Sonnenschein, 1990). The number of full-time equivalent social work staff in all mental health organizations in the United States rose from 17,687 in 1972 to 40,951 in 1986. Of the four main mental health professions (psychiatry, psychology, social work, and nursing), only nursing outnumbered social work in 1986. However, in outpatient mental health centers, social workers comprised 46% of client care staff (and 30.4% of total agency staff). Psychiatrists fell from 9.2% of all staff in 1972 to 5.2% in 1986. Likewise, nursing dropped from 3.3% to 2.1%. These statistics indicate that more social workers than before are providing services to clients, with fewer psychiatrists and nurses available for client care.

Second, because national public policy emphasizes deinstitutionalization and community care, which has been facilitated by the increased use of intensive case management and other psychosocial rehabilitation programs, the use of psychiatric hospitals has decreased, while the number of persons in the community with mental illnesses has increased (Solomon, 1992). Many people with mental illness have limited social functioning skills, frequently find themselves in crisis situations, and require continuous mental-status monitoring by social workers. Treatments including psychosocial rehabilitation and case management, largely associated with the social work profession, have been found to be effective in helping persons with mental illness adjust to community living (Anthony, 1993). Thus, social workers are coming into broader contact with these client populations. Psychiatrists and nurses cannot assess clients under controlled conditions as regularly as when clients were more frequently hospitalized.

Berg and Wallace (1987) support the idea that the increased presence of people with mental illness in the community has complicated the role of the social worker in medication management. They found differences in knowledge and roles between inpatient and outpatient social workers. Inpatient social workers showed more knowledge about medications and subscribed more closely to the medical model than outpatient social workers. Outpatient social workers were more likely than inpatient social workers to consider issues about clients' rights, record clients' negative experiences with medications, and report their assessment of the physician's screening. They also tended to more actively encourage clients to take medications and work with families on related issues. Therefore, it appears from this study that outpatient social workers, perhaps because of their less-controlled interactions with other members of the treatment team, develop greater autonomy in monitoring medication and have more influence on clients who depend on them for input about medications.

A third reason for the expanded demand for social workers involves the profession's increasing emphasis on collaborative approaches with consumers and family members (Bentley & Harrison, 1989). Social workers are often the first point of contact for significant others who develop concerns about the mental status of their loved ones. The implications of this spirit of collaboration, which we call the partnership model of practice, are developed extensively in the next chapter.

Finally, new types of psychotropic medications (antipsychotic, antidepressant, mood-stabilizing, and anti-anxiety drugs), introduced into the market since the 1980s, have proliferated. A broad range of issues has also arisen for consumers to consider: symptomatic indications for use, choices among drug types and classes, side effects, special precautions, the use of generic versus brand name drugs, and input into decisions of compliance and refusal of medications, to name just a few. The relative benefits and risks of using medication must always be weighed by all professional practitioners. Indeed, many states have only recently required that professionals provide written information about medications to clients at the time of prescription (Ravid & Menon, 1993).

To understand the current challenges to the profession, social workers must also understand the historical forces that have fostered the current practice climate. They must look back at the evolution of medications as treatment resources and the development of social work as a subspecialty within the mental health field.

A Historical Context of Intervention for People with Mental Illness

The Treatment Prior to 1950 of People with Mental Illness

Both psychiatric hospitals and general hospital wards serving persons with mental illness have existed in this country since its inception. Benjamin Franklin founded the Pennsylvania Hospital in Philadelphia in 1751, the nation's first to include services for the mentally ill, or, as Franklin wrote, "Those distempered in mind and deprived of their rational faculties" (Jones, 1976, p. 461). Still in operation, the first state-supported hospital devoted solely to the care of the mentally ill was founded at Williamsburg, Virginia in 1773. During the next 65 years, 15 states established such hospitals, with the number of institutions growing to 123 by 1880.

This era of "moral treatment" emphasized active rehabilitation and structuring inpatients' lives to stabilize their uncontrolled thoughts and emotions. During the second half of the 19th century, however, as the population of the United States increased, these primarily public institutions became vastly overcrowded, so that moral treatment gave way to mere patient management that focused on control of unruly behavior. Though intervention came to include medications in the late 19th century, they were used to control aggressive behavior rather than to implement active treatment.

The concept of medication as restraint fostered a suspiciousness of its use among many social workers and other professionals through the 20th century. During the second half of the 19th century, bromides (sedative medications) were introduced. By the 1874 meeting of the Association of Medical Superintendents, the generic sedative chloral hydrate was established as the most popular drug used by hospital psychiatrists, despite its potentially dangerous side effect of respiratory system paralysis (Caplan, 1969). Few advances were made in medication for hospitalized persons over the next 75 years. Through the 1940s, the leading medical textbooks still listed nonspecific sedative drugs, such as barbiturates, bromides, and chloral hydrate, as well as rest, baths, and hydrotherapy, as primary treatments for psychotic persons. These treatments were assumed to provide no more than temporary relief (Valenstein, 1986). Various other somatic treatments, such as shock therapies and lobotomy, were developed in hospitals between 1900 and 1950, but these have been used to a much lesser degree since the antipsychotic medications were introduced. When these medications came into more widespread use in the 1950s, social workers and other professionals perceived them as a negative alternative to counseling and rehabilitative interventions.

The Rise of Psychiatric Social Work

The now century-old tradition of psychiatric social work was one of several specializations (including medical social work and child welfare) that emerged during the first decade of the 20th century. This specialty emerged because hospital physicians and administrators needed to link their institutions with community treatment environments to ensure better, more responsive ongoing diagnosis and treatment for patients (Lubove, 1965). At that time, crowded institutions and population growth in major American cities caused pressure to discharge mental patients and insure their permanent adjustment to the community. Because medications were not used outside of hospitals at that time, social workers did not become involved in those issues. In fact, not until the second half of this century did the social work profession turn its attention to hospitalized clients with mental illness.

Social psychiatry emerged in the work of America's preeminent psychiatrist of that time, Adolf Meyer, who emphasized a "multiple causation" perspective on treatment (Caplan, 1969). He emphasized the need for close contact with the patient's home and social environment, as well as the crucial role of social workers in facilitating suitable social environments for patients. Meyer emphasized the importance of seeing patients as social beings as well as physical organisms, defining insanity as a disease of social functioning as well as a manifestation of a disturbed mind. Mary Brooks Meyer, his wife, acted as a social worker in 1904 when he asked her to follow up on the progress of some discharged patients from Manhattan State Hospital.

When the New York State Charities Aid Association implemented a statewide aftercare program in 1904, they hired Edith Horton, a graduate of the New York School of Private Philanthropy, as an aftercare agent for two mental hospitals. As the first professional psychiatric social worker, Horton's duties included locating jobs, housing, and community resources for discharged patients. The need to focus on the life history and social environment of each client had in fact first been proposed by the Charities Aid Association in 1894. Interestingly, 100 years later, many states still struggle to develop service systems based on this same model of continuity of care even though its driving idea is so old.

The principles of intervention in psychiatric social work were derived from the model of medical social work developed by the physician Richard Cabot and the social worker Ida Cannon at the Massachusetts General Hospital in 1905 (Callicutt, 1983). With the physician James Putnam, the social worker Edith Burleigh adopted three roles for psychiatric social work: to provide an investigation of the client's social environment prior to discharge, to contribute to diagnostic assessment, and to complement the physician's treatment. In 1913, Mary Jarrett introduced the professional title "psychiatric social worker" and outlined the four practice functions: casework, clinic management, public education, and research (Southard & Jarrett, 1922). French (1940) later presented her own version of these four functions of the social worker in psychiatric settings as (1) analyzing social situations in light of the client's present difficulty, (2) interpreting problems and the psychiatrist's recommendations to the family, (3) helping the family and patient work out a plan for social adjustment, and (4) explaining the diagnosis and plan for treatment to workers at other participating agencies. Although nowhere do they address medication as an issue, Southard and Jarrett also see the social worker's role as complementary to that of the psychiatrist, similar to that of the physician's assistant, still carried out today.

While the field of psychiatric social work grew during the 1900s, few workers sought or found positions in the hospitals that used medications. French (1940) lists the following as reasons for negative professional attitudes: low pay, isolation from community contact, the need in some cases to live at the institutions, large caseloads, and the demands for nonprofessional duties within the institution. Her statistics support the lack of enthusiasm of members of the American Association for Psychiatric Social Work, founded in 1920, for mental hospital work. In 1920, 35% of association members worked in mental hospitals (n = 6), but by 1937, the percentage had dropped to 13.5% (n = 55). In her comprehensive volume about the field of psychiatric social work, French does not once mention medication.

The Introduction of Psychotropic Medications

By the 1960s, researchers had discovered drugs from the four major chemical groups, which continue to be used in pharmacology today. These include the antipsychotic or major tranquilizers, the benzodiazepines (anti-anxiety agents), the antidepressants, and lithium, a mood-stabilizer (Kaplan & Sadock, 1993). Thorazine, a brand name for the generic compound chlorpromazine, was introduced in the United States in 1954, and was followed by Haldol (haloperidol) in 1958. Remaining among the most frequently prescribed antipsychotic medications, both are used to clarify a client's thought processes through sedation and the reduction or elimination of hallucinations. Librium, the first benzodiazepine, was marketed in 1957. The first antidepressants introduced were the monoamine oxidase (MAO) inhibitors, which became available in the late 1950s. When the tricyclic antidepressant imipramine appeared in 1958, it became more widely prescribed because, unlike the MAO drugs, it did not require stringent dietary restrictions as a precaution against side effects. The mood stabilizer lithium, effective in treating persons with bipolar disorder, appeared in 1969. With these drugs, psychiatry had at its disposal four classes of medications; the 40 years since have been devoted to clinical studies and the development of related compounds. Four major additions since 1980 include the anticonvulsant drugs (carbamazepine and valporic acid), used as mood stabilizers and also to increase the potency of other medications; the nonbenzodiazepine anti-anxiety agents, which do not present the same potential for physical addiction as benzodiazepines; new classes of antidepressant and anti-obsessive-compulsive drugs; and several new antipsychotic medications, of which clozapine and risperidone are currently the most well known. Though they serve the same clinical functions as the older drugs, these newer medications are derived from different chemical compounds, have somewhat different routes of action, and have fewer negative side effects in some cases (see Chapter 4 for further discussion of medication types).

Many physicians were reportedly reluctant to use the antipsychotic medication chlorpromazine when it was introduced (Johnson, 1990). While this may seem strange in today's age of biological psychiatry, resistance was due in part to the time-honored stance that medications work well for behavioral management but have limited therapeutic use. Physicians expressed concern that the medication would not actively treat the illness but serve only as a sedating agent, as previous medications did. They also feared that it would steer professionals away from active treatment, be inferior to existing somatic therapies, and present too much uncertainty regarding side effects. A nationwide survey of state hospitals in 1956 revealed that only 19% of patients used chlorpromazine (or reserpine, a related sedative considered innovative at the time) because of professional resistance and the fact that state budgets did not yet include funding for the new medication.

One notable paradox arose: the new emphasis on biological psychiatry, through the increased use of drugs, fostered a compartmentalization of the medical and social approaches to the treatment of mental illness. A sharper distinction evolved between psychiatry on the one hand and social work and related disciplines on the other. Contrary to the vision of Meyer and those who shared his psychosocial perspective, psychiatry would no longer be as concerned with rehabilitation or community support activities. This distinction eventually provided a rationale for social workers to assume more active roles, within a partnership model, in helping clients on psychotropic medication use a variety of interventions in their social adjustment.

Social Work Role Categories

Physician's Assistant

In the role of physician's assistant, the social worker tends to accept unquestionably the physician's decisions about psychotropic drugs and, as such, is limited to helping clients take their medications according to the physician's recommendations. The worker is not expected to offer advice about any decisions involving the prescription and use of medication or any compliance strategy, although he or she does play a role in the assessment process. Psychiatric social workers functioned mainly as physicians' assistants through the 1970s.

For many years, the role of physician's assistant was the most common because of factors that included the relatively limited legal scope of the practice of social work, traditions of authority among the core helping professions, the focus of professional social work education on other areas, and negative attitudes of social workers about the relative appropriateness of medication as a primary means of intervention (Gerhart & Brooks, 1983). Psychiatrists and physicians have traditionally been, and still are, the primary providers of biological interventions for all types of emotional problems and mental disorders. However, deinstitutionalization and the new emphasis on community-based care has prompted social workers over the past three decades to broaden their psychosocial framework to include considering interventions using psychotropic medication. Though social workers are still limited to the role of physician's assistant in many settings, we see this as a move away from this role for the many reasons discussed earlier in this chapter.

Consultant/Collaborator

Much of the professional literature of the past 20 years concerning psychotropic medication discusses the roles that social workers play or ought to play regarding clients' use of medications, thus augmenting the original physician's assistant role. In the late 1970s, McCollum, Margolin, and Lieb (1978) wrote that the social worker needs to be skilled in three areas. First, the worker must be able to assess clients for possible referral to physicians. This involves evaluating the client's current levels of functioning, the intensity of the observed suffering, and the client's capacity to manage his or her suffering. Secondly, the worker must prepare clients for active participation in the process of assessment by the physician. To prepare the clients for referral, the worker's responsibilities include articulating the specific reasons for the referral, reviewing the client's attitude toward psychiatrists, discussing the client's expectations about medications, and closely monitoring the client's subjective experiences of effects after medications have been prescribed. Third, the worker must monitor clients; we will discuss this in a separate section below. Finally, we add another necessary worker skill: assessing the client's ability to pay for medication, the cost of which may be quite high.

Though McCollum et al. focus on the need for a consultative and collaborative relationship between the social worker and client, Miller, Wiedman, and Linn (1980) emphasize the need for the social worker to likewise conceptualize her or his relationship with the physician. Both social workers and physicians need to see themselves as consultants and collaborators with each other. Specifically, they need to specify the range of roles of the social worker in medication management, interpret how important it is for clients to take their medication as instructed, devise systematic procedures to evaluate each medication's effectiveness, and use client files to record relevant data when monitoring a client's response. These authors further call on physicians to provide in-service training to other professionals on such issues as drug categories, side effects, and interviewing techniques. Social workers, in turn, could teach physicians about various aspects of psychosocial intervention. Of course, the activities discussed by Miller et al. imply that disagreements may arise among the physician, social worker, and client over many issues, which they must openly deal with toward constructive resolution.

Another part of the consultant/collaborator role is validation, or working to empower clients to make decisions about the use of medication (Tobias, 1990). The validator "confirms, legitimates, substantiates, or verifies the feelings, ideas, values, or beliefs of the client as well-grounded, correct, or genuine within the client's system" (p. 357). Validation promotes active, effective client participation in rehabilitation planning and intervention. As validator, the social worker seeks to uncover the client's perceptions and experiences, supporting as legitimate those components that can be channeled into action on the client's part. With regard to the use of medication, clearly the validator can assist the client to become a stronger consultant/collaborator in interactions with all helping professionals.

Monitor of Side Effects

To monitor medication, the social worker must observe and help the client observe the positive and negative effects of medication and the appearance or persistence of symptoms in the client. The social worker may also help to check the client's use of medications as prescribed. He or she needs to help evaluate the client's responses to any discomfort, the importance of the physiologically adverse effects (i.e., dry mouth versus impotence), and any impairments in family or social functioning. Finally, the worker conveys information from the monitoring process back to the client, perhaps to the family, and to the physician. Through these activities, the social worker both helps the client monitor medication and serves as a resource to the physician.

Davidson and Jamison (1983) further define this role by delineating three types of side effects for the social worker to monitor: physical, psychological, and social. Through self-study (e.g., use of the annual *Physician's Desk Reference*) and collaboration with medical personnel, the social worker can become educated about physical side effects. Psychological side effects involve any changes in the client's self-image that emerge as a result of using medications. For example, clients may come to view themselves as "sick" people or may become overly dependent on medication as a solution to perceived emotional problems. They may also, as a result of the latter, avoid potentially healthy challenges in the social environment. Estroff (1981) has also written about the psychological side effects of psychotropic medication, noting the paradox that while medicine may help the client think more clearly, clients can also interpret it as a message that they are crazy and cannot get well (see Chapter 7 for a fuller discussion of this issue). Further, the side effects may make them appear even more disturbed to others, so that clients see themselves as marginal, different, and "ill." Social side effects include any potentially negative consequences that go beyond the individual client to consider how medication use affects one's standing with certain social institutions, such as hospitals, the Social Security Administration, or society at large. For example, people may overuse or physicians may overprescribe psychotropic medications to maintain qualifications for disability benefits or facilitate discharge from the hospital before the client's ego strength reaches a level that makes satisfactory community functioning likely. Further, medications initially used for symptom relief so that psychosocial treatments could be initiated can become the complete treatment. To their listing of social side effects, Davidson and Jamison might have added that families have been given the difficult responsibility of monitoring both the client's response to medications and his or her development of additional self-care skills, if the client is dependent on the family. This topic of extraphysical side effects, which we will fully develop in Chapters 4, 7, and 8, merits particularly close attention by social workers because the health professions have largely neglected it.

Advocate

Gerhart and Brooks (1983), in their review of social work literature, state that social workers typically assumed either of the two roles of physician's assistant and consultant/collaborator. While they agree that both roles are useful, Gerhart and Brooks found that social workers do not objectively weigh the benefits and risks of medication with regard to both physical and psychological side effects. They propose the implementation of a third role, that of the client advocate, based on their perception that medical expertise is not always the rule and that medication can have serious negative effects that might outweigh its benefits. They define advocacy as the "representation of mentally ill individuals and groups by social work practitioners in an effort to present the client's expressed desires to those in the mental health system who have the power" to assess how medications are administered (p. 456). The social work advocate ideally has a peer relationship with the physician and participates in all phases of decision making regarding the choices made for medication. Gerhart and Brooks claim that this role is more crucial now than ever because of the emphasis on community care, which makes the responsible monitoring of a client's medication needs and outcomes difficult to maintain for any single person, but particularly for the physician. They also claim that to function as an advocate, the worker must have a good working knowledge of mental illness, psychotropic medications, and laws and regulations about such issues as forced medications and the rights of persons with mental illness. Interestingly, they admit that this role might best be filled by a specialist, such as a client-rights advocate, because he or she may have to oppose the physician and other professionals. However, we believe that social workers can competently carry out the advocacy role when they represent the client's position from a sound base of knowledge and professional values, although this can be difficult at times (see Chapter 9).

Higgins (1995) goes beyond the types of advocacy we have just outlined. She suggests that social workers should function as political advocates for clients who cannot access medications they want to use. This situation developed quite dramatically with the introduction of clozapine in 1991. The medication had demonstrated benefits with some persons with schizophrenia who had not responded to more traditional antipsychotic medications. However, the cost of the medication, coupled with the need to monitor blood counts on a weekly basis, created a very expensive treatment regimen. Because some clients and families who could not afford the drug filed suits to gain access to it, adjustments were made in public insurance policies, helping to broaden its availability (Reid, Pham, & Rago, 1993). Because issues related to the cost of medication are serious, and restrictions on the availability of medication may arise, Higgins argues that social workers need to serve as advocates before not only physicians, but also agencies, funding sources, and government regulators. Further, when funding caps limit a client's access to medication, social workers may need to become involved in decision making about which eligible clients should have access to medications such as clozapine. The relevance of Higgins' perspective is a reminder that medication issues should be considered in their broadest contexts. Bachur (1986) also stresses this point, arguing that considerations of drug use and misuse need to be studied not merely in the context of the individual and family, but also more broadly, including informal helpers such as friends and neighbors, local community agencies, and government policy makers.

Cohen (1988) agrees that, of all professional helpers, social workers have the primary responsibility to be client advocates. He restates the rationale that social workers are involved in all phases of psychiatric treatment and are the most highly represented profession in community mental health centers. Concerned about the negative effects of medication, Cohen is skeptical of psychiatry's willingness to address this issue adequately. He states that adherence to the medical model of treatment tends to result in some abuses in somatic intervention. He proposes that social workers as advocates undertake a greater amount of activity with clients in several areas, including knowledge of prior history of drug reactions; identification of negative physical, psychological, and social effects; and provision of oral and written drug information, perhaps independent of the physician.

Social workers need to be aware that empowerment and advocacy efforts with clients and families may lead them to decide to refuse medication or to negotiate extensively with physicians about the types and dosages of medication the client should take. These situations often give rise to value dilemmas for social workers. For example, Bentley (1993) holds that social workers need to support the right of refusal of medication or any other treatment for legal, empirical, and ethical reasons in light of the profession's mandate to respect each client's dignity, worth, and right to self-determination. A family advocate, Rosenson (1993) disagrees, stating that the professional's decision to proceed with appropriate medications even in the face of refusal is in some cases a prerequisite for the client to recover enough to participate in further decision making about treatment. Thus, social workers may find themselves in an ethical bind when clients or physicians choose strategies the social workers do not believe will work. Such issues are discussed in more detail in Chapter 9.

Educator

The role of educator is crucial to the social work profession's maintenance of collaboration with clients and families. A major force contributing to the family advocacy movement was a perceived lack of efforts by mental health professionals to help clients and families understand the rationale behind decisions about medication and other interventions (Hatfield, 1981). The uses and actions of medication are complicated and confusing for many professionals as well as the general public, and there continues to be a great need for social workers to address the topic by directly providing educational materials and other information. With the widespread development of client and family psychoeducational and medication education programs, this area has seen progress (e.g., Anderson, Reiss, & Hogarty, 1986; Falloon et al., 1984). So that they can provide basic information about relevant medication issues during individual client interventions, social workers should strive to keep up with all ongoing developments in the field. Bentley and Reeves (1990) have outlined six educational units for social work students, which can also apply to practicing professionals as areas of continuing education to be shared with clients and families. These include public and professional attitudes about psychotropic medication, changing social work roles in psychopharmacology, medication content in psychoeducation, ongoing medication-management techniques, ethical and legal issues in client refusal of medications, and current research and resources.

Further, Bentley, Rosenson, and Zito (1990) specify as educational four of their nine roles for social workers in helping clients adhere to appropriate medication schedules. These roles include educating clients and families about the purposes, actions, and effects of medication; teaching clients and families how to monitor positive and negative effects; teaching skills in problem solving regarding medication; and offering practical suggestions to help clients take medication appropriately. In emphasizing psychosocial themes of adjustment, the educator role complements the kinds of information generally provided to clients by physicians and nurses.

Researcher

A recurring theme in discussions of all role categories is the need for social workers to develop their own literature about issues of psychotropic medication to advance the profession's holistic and collaborative perspectives. For example, Davidson and Jamison (1983) recommend that social workers produce more literature on the potentially negative effects of medications, the impact of medicines on self-control and one's sense of personal responsibility for problem resolution, and the engagement of the hard-to-reach client in a comprehensive treatment program that includes medication. These three areas represent aspects of medication usage that other professions have not adequately addressed but that are consistent with social work's psychosocial theoretical framework. Cohen (1988) also calls for social workers to write more about specific case studies and research on the broad range of medication effects, both positive and negative.

Hogarty (1991), who has written extensively for two decades about the relationship of medication to direct social work practice, identifies the potential for social workers to become more productive in research related to mental illness. He points out that there is now a broad professional acceptance of the positive effects of the combined interventions of medication, counseling, and psychosocial rehabilitation for persons with serious mental illnesses. However, because researchers often cannot separate medication side effects from clients' outcomes, the optimal effects of various types of social work intervention have not yet been fully tested. Toward resolving this issue, Hogarty points to recent research indicating that low-maintenance dosages of psychotropic drugs sufficiently stabilize the mental status of many clients. That is, social workers are now in a position to conduct research to ascertain the main effects of drugs and psychosocial interventions, as well as the interactions of these two types of treatment, on clients' outcomes. Through these means they can evaluate the effectiveness of medication in ways that may support more treatment strategies involving low dosages of medication.

SUMMARY

Social Work Roles Restated

The purpose of this chapter has been to outline the range of roles that social workers have assumed in their work with clients who take psychotropic medication. In developing collaborative relationships with clients, families, and professionals, social workers are now involved in all areas of the client's life that impact social functioning. Here are the six roles for social workers discussed in this chapter:

1. The physician's assistant, who merely echoes and supports the recommendations of the client's physician regarding issues of medication.
2. The consultant/collaborator (with the physician *and* client), who performs preliminary screenings to determine clients' possible need for medication, makes referrals to physicians, monitors effects for the physician and client, and regularly consults with physicians and clients on related issues while maintaining a nonadversarial position.
3. The advocate, who supports clients' expressed preferences and presents them to others in the mental health service system without necessarily maintaining a nonadversarial position. Advocates may assist clients and their family members either with physicians and others, in obtaining services directly, or with administrative or political bodies, toward such ends as access to medication, access to funding for medication, or supplementary services related to the use of medication. By substantiating their ideas and feelings as legitimate, the advocate also validates the desires of clients or families to become more involved in their own advocacy efforts.
4. The monitor of medication effects, including both positive and negative physical, psychological, and social effects.
5. The educator of clients, families, and perhaps other human service providers about broad issues relevant to medication, including actions, benefits, risks, and side effects, always from a social work perspective.
6. The researcher, who documents using case reports, single-case design methods, or more elaborate designs to show how medications impact the lives of clients and families, how they interact with other interventions, and how collaborative interprofessional relationships can be maintained to achieve coordination of intervention.

Values

These social work roles and activities reflect the profession's most fundamental values. With their commitment to each client's self-determination and individual dignity, social workers complement the perspectives of related professionals by promoting the interests of clients and families during interactions with the mental health system. Of the core mental health professionals, it falls on social workers to make sure the voices of their clients are heard by all who interact with them. There may be occasions, of course, when competing values take priority, for example in meeting basic needs and preserving life. Though we will amplify on this issue in the next chapter, we want to emphasize here that the social work roles we have discussed are ultimately defined as much by how they are implemented as by their substance.

CHAPTER 2

Defining Effective Collaboration

Besides providing the historical context of social work roles in psychopharmacology, we suggest a philosophy of practice for social workers who seek to fulfill these roles successfully. We believe that the key component for achieving this success is effective collaboration—especially with clients and their families, but also with other mental health care providers, such as psychiatrists, nurses, and psychologists. Specifically, we offer three key strategies that undergird effective collaboration in mental health and related fields of practice. Social workers must (1) hold fast to a partnership model of practice, (2) maintain a balanced perspective in the face of complex issues related to rights and roles, and (3) work toward the successful integration of psychosocial services with psychopharmacology. All the roles and practice strategies we suggest are built on this foundation.

Principles of a Partnership Model of Practice

In a *partnership model* of practice, the social worker genuinely appreciates both the strengths and the limits of clients and their families; considers their perspectives valid and important to the helping process; and views the relationship as active and mutual, in which the helping process is action-oriented and the participants are equal problem-solving partners. Working toward partnership implies working toward a nonthreatening alliance of companions and a mutual sharing of expertise. Readers will notice that it echoes the principle often discussed in relationship to empowerment practice (Lee, 1994; Simon, 1994).

Appreciate Participants' Strengths and Limits

Clinical scholars and researchers at the University of Kansas have developed the *strengths perspective* for social work, which suggests a complete reorientation of practice toward the individual client's unique strengths and aspirations and *away* from pathology, symptoms, or weaknesses (Rapp, 1992). In its fullness, the perspective goes beyond a minor shift in practice emphasis or a simple reframing of client problems into more positive terms. As Rapp (p. 51) states, work with clients should "reek of 'can do' in every stage of the helping process" because *all* clients, including those with mental illnesses, can "learn, grow and change." While Weick, Rapp, Sullivan, and Kisthardt (1989) acknowledge that most social workers are intuitively comfortable with the strengths perspective, they also point to the difficulty many experience in adopting this perspective as their primary orientation. One such difficulty is the widespread reliance in the field of mental health on what some would call a pathology-based classification scheme, such as the DSM-IV, for decisions about treatment and reimbursement. Nevertheless, in this book we will openly struggle with how to reorient social work practice toward clients' strengths, while still responding when the stated need of clients is to reduce problems or so-called deficits directly.

Appreciating the limits of clients is as complex as appreciating their strengths. The key is to avoid automatically defining a client's mental illness, emotional disorder, or resulting handicaps as given limitations (in other words, avoid presuming incompetence or poor judgment). According to Deegan (1992), viewing people with psychiatric problems as automatically irrational, crazy, or unreasonable is fueled by "mentalism" (akin to sex*ism* and rac*ism*). Deegan (p. 12) sees this attitude as a "spirit breaking central attitudinal barrier" that leads to a cycle of disempowerment and despair among people with mental illness. By *limits* we mean any existing barriers to progress, such as a lack of skills or inadequate resources. Social workers need to help clients define realistically their own situational limits and personal challenges (which may or may not be related to symptomatology) just as they would help identify their clients' unique strengths and assets. Ignoring or underplaying the sometimes severe limits that clients have in social functioning can result in exaggerated and harmful expectations on the part of the social worker. Similarly, ignoring or underplaying strengths can contribute to the depersonalization and demoralization that clients often feel in the mental health system.

Appreciate Participants' Perspectives

Another significant dimension of the partnership model of practice is the clinician's own view of the opinions, thoughts, and beliefs of the client and the client's family members. Specifically, we suggest that the social worker view these as valid, valuable, and in general, the most important pieces of information needed to define the direction and pace of practice. As Rapp (1992, p. 53) states, the client's perspective should be the "centerpiece" of work. While some see this as a given in social work, others will recognize it as a call to shift their focus away from preconceived notions of where clients should be headed and truly "begin where the client is."

Clearly a relevant issue, self-determination is perhaps "the most confounding concept in the intellectual underpinnings of social work" because of its "illusive" and "clouded" nature in real-world practice (Rothman, 1989,

p. 598). Rothman describes self-determination as a moral imperative and useful practice tool that fosters change and growth and reviews the potential limits to self-determination that all people experience, such as economic circumstances, resources, agency roles, values, mandates and pressures, and mental acuity and skill. The controversy then arises as to what extent a client's mental illness affects the clinical actualization of his or her self-determination.

For example, several years ago, Belcher and Ephross (1989) suggested that, at least for the homeless mentally ill, social workers may need to move away from "traditional practice models that view all clients as competent and able to make informed decisions" and instead move toward a more realistic view of the "needs, strengths, limitations, and diversity" of this population (pp. 423–424). On the other hand, Sullivan (1992) insists that mental health clients can know what's best and should be able to express their choice. Similarly, Runyan and Faria (1992) state that "treating clients as essentially normal, capable functioning human beings who happen to have a mental disorder" is the key to empowerment (pp. 40–41). As far back as 1963, Soyer argued that the "self-determined aspirations" of the clients should be the focus of practice, even if those aspirations appear unrealistic (p. 77). Soyer offered two provocative reasons to justify the strong stance: (1) the client just might be right and (2) perhaps only by living life can clients "try, test, and temper" their goals (p. 77).

Rapp (1992) points out that the stated *wants* of clients do not differ from their *needs* (and for that matter, they do not seem different from most people's). He says people with mental illness want "a decent place to live and adequate income, friends and opportunities to recreate, an opportunity to contribute (work, family, helping others) and recognition for that contribution" (p. 48). Kisthardt (1992) notes that making the client the "director" of the helping process "breathes new life into the time-honored maxim of self-determination in social work" (p. 63); it also enhances the control clients have over their own lives (Moxley & Freddolino, 1990). The tendencies of social workers to avoid risks or their desire to save clients from failure, as Soyer (1963) states, too often "dampen rather than fire" the aspirations and desires of clients (p. 78). Mosher and Burti (1992) echo the persistent call for a helping process based on clients' needs as clients perceive them, but they also acknowledge that negotiation and compromise may help temper "completely unrealistic wishes" (p. 12). However, social workers still tend to let clients "self-determine" only when they happen to agree with their clients' decisions or direction. Too often they define their own professional perspective as "truth" and relegate clients' "interior knowledge" (Weick & Pope, 1988, p. 13) of self as unreliable or invalid. In later chapters, we will see how concerns about self-determination and clients' strengths and limitations affect medication management.

Just as the client's perspective must be validated, so must that of the family, especially because they often provide expert observations of family interactions and of the client's behavior (Kassis, Boothroyd, & Ben-Dror, 1992). DeChillo's study (1993) of collaboration among 14 social workers and families of 102 psychiatric clients in New York City found that the most significant variable related to the extent of their collaboration was the social workers' attitudes toward family involvement in treatment and care.

View Relationship and Process Actively

The partnership model calls for a dynamic working relationship between the social worker and clients and families that is characterized by mutuality, authenticity, and a sense of being "in process." Partners should constantly seek greater empathy and understanding of each other and clearer communication. Many authors have called for a reconceptualization of the client-clinician relationship in psychiatric social work, specifically that clinicians try to reduce the social distance between them and their clients and families (Libassi, 1992), demystify the relationship and process (Rose, 1990), and reconsider power issues (DeChillo, 1993). Saleeby (1992) summarizes the needed reconceptualization as

> a give-and-take that begins with the demystification of the professional as expert, an operating sense of humility on the part of the helper, the establishment of an egalitarian transaction, the desire to engage clients on their own terms, and a willingness to disclose and share. (p. 42)

With this reconceptualization, social workers seek to redistribute power among themselves, clients, and families. Although the social worker-client relationship clearly has some built-in power differentials related to education and societal sanctions, Mosher & Burti (1992) suggest that by acknowledging them through open and direct discussion, social workers can minimize them. However, like the models of feminist therapy in the 1970s, the partnership model of social work practice calls for clinicians to go beyond a mere acknowledgment of power issues to the actual redistribution of power. Tobias notes that just as clients "must grapple with gaining power, social workers must grapple with the loss of power" (1990, p. 359).

As Kisthardt (1992) points out, the mutual sharing of power in the client-clinician relationship "is both vexing and liberating" (p. 64). Though it may put social workers in the unfamiliar territory of defining roles and boundaries for practice, it also frees each from the pressure to be something other than his or her genuine self (such as an all-knowing, dispassionate expert). Kisthardt notes that because clients may not be familiar with such ideas about the helping relationship, social workers must model mutuality and partnership, especially in the engagement process.

We envision a helping process in which clients and social workers alike are busy and involved, with their work clearly action-oriented. That is, they work primarily to do or change something, or participate to the extent allowed by their particular strengths and weaknesses.

The skills we stress in this book draw heavily from a problem-solving approach to social work, psychiatric rehabilitation, and clinical case management, and less on the techniques of insight-oriented psychotherapy. Even so, purposeful conversation and reflective discussion are still major aspects of the process, as not only the means to establishing relationships, defining goals, and exploring potential strategies of intervention, but also the means to ventilating and sorting out feelings and getting support and validation. For example, listening to the stories of family members (Kassis et al., 1992)—and we would add clients—even repeatedly, will deepen relationships among participants.

Participate Equally in Problem Solving

The final dimension of the partnership model of practice is that the participants in the helping process should play roles based on their own individualized expertise and experience. As long as providers, clients, and families are each seen as experts with rich experiences, unique perspectives, and specialized knowledge, achieving this ideal is realistic.

The role of the social worker, then, is to share knowledge. The social worker teaches the client basic strategies shown to be useful in helping people reach their goals, whether this be problem solving, skills training, psychoeducation, cognitive-behavioral techniques, or other psychosocial and environmental interventions. Everett and Nelson (1992) describe case managers who go even further by sharing not only what they know, but also what they *don't* know. That is, when gaps in their own knowledge base become apparent, these case managers may share with clients their search for answers in the literature, lectures, or workshops. This way their clients can see their clinical processes right before their eyes.

Libassi (1992) describes the purpose of the helping process as building clients' confidence, particularly for those clients with mental illness. The clinician must focus on assessing and clarifying issues to be addressed, teaching new skills, and emphasizing the use of environmental supports and resources. Describing the role of a case manager in mental health, Kisthardt (1992) says she or he should be an advisor, consultant, and educator, one who provides the "conditions, knowledge, and linkages" needed to address the concerns of the client. Corrigan, Liberman, and Engel (1990), who also advocate psychoeducation and skills training, stress that both clinician and client should share information, negotiate, and offer feedback. These activities are no different when issues related to medication management must be addressed. The social worker's role is to help make adjustments in treatment techniques or in conditions in the treatment system to insure that it is client driven.

Freund (1993) also notes the shifting roles of clinicians as mental health clients gain greater "interdependence." The clinician now helps clients learn through experience and ask questions that may point to previously unrecognized issues; she or he also continuously highlights the choices available to the client. As Rapp (1992) notes, a partnership model does not mean that social workers are passive participants or quasi servants. It is *not* "If a client wants a donut, I will run out and get him a donut"; according to Rapp, "this is no more a partnership than when the professional dictates to the client" (p. 56).

The ideal, then, is to bring together the strengths and ideas of the client, the client's family, and the provider to produce the most powerful and productive overall perspective. The client shares her or his experiences and knowledge as an equal participant, offers a perspective that serves as important "data" to be incorporated into every step of the helping process. The role of the client is to make choices and to validate and legitimize the actions of the providers on her or his behalf.

Thus, the partnership model involves the client's family in the helping process to the extent possible, given the client desires. Spaniol, Zipple, and FitzGerald (1984) suggest 15 ways professionals might share power with families, including many of the ideas already discussed in this chapter, such as clinicians' acknowledging their own limits and pointing to family strengths. The core notion is that families be viewed as "collaborative adjuncts" to the rehabilitation process (p. 80). Similarly, DeChillo (1993) offers six components of family collaboration that include recognizing the family as a key resource, involving the family in goal formulation, and providing education and practical advice about coping with mental illness.

However, in spite of a recent marked improvement in the clinician's view of families, the positive potential for family involvement is yet unrealized. Interestingly, in his study of collaboration between social workers and families of people with mental illness, DeChillo (1993) found that both the social workers and the family members surveyed rated the other group *lower* on perceived level of collaboration than either group rated themselves. One of two things seems to have occurred. Either the social workers and families each exaggerated their own level of collaboration, or they each failed to recognize the actual level of collaboration in the other group. Other surveys have shown that families are dissatisfied with their level of participation in decision making and often feel their opinions are not valued (Cournoyer & Johnson, 1991). Interestingly, a follow-up satisfaction-with-services survey of 57 family members of people with mental illness showed that the amount of education about medication issues (or lack thereof) was one of the greatest areas of dissatisfaction (Solomon & Marcenko, 1992).

At the same time, the most recent research shows that families can successfully participate in the care of their relative in ways unthought of only a few years ago. For example, one study in the field of aging shows that family members can be trained to be case managers without increasing the amount of subjective burden they feel or changing the amount of contact with their relative (Seltzer, Litchfield, Kapust, & Mayer, 1992). Social workers in this project provided consultation and information to families to help them deal with inevitable obstacles in carrying out their tasks.

MAINTAINING A BALANCED PERSPECTIVE

A second strategy that undergirds effective collaboration with clients who take psychotropic medication, their families, and mental health providers is cultivating a balanced perspective in the face of complex issues related to clients' rights and professional roles. Specifically, social workers must maintain a proper balance among the rights of individual clients, their families, and society; between the "costs" and "benefits" of using psychotropic medication; and between the social worker's role in medication management and the legitimacy and uniqueness of other helping professions.

Rights of Individual, Family, and Society

The entire court system could be described as an attempt to establish an impartial mechanism to decide the distribution of rights between individuals and society. Determining the appropriate balance between these interests becomes more difficult when the individual has a mental illness or an emotional disorder. Although clients' rights issues gained attention in the 1970s with landmark court battles and passage of a client bill of rights, this struggle for balance is still seen in debates about such issues as involuntary commitment and the right to refuse treatment. Today's constriction of clients' rights seems to be related to many mental health providers' continued presumption that clients are incompetent and the "bureaucratic paternalism" that too often characterizes the mental health system (Bentley, 1991; Winslade, 1981). That is, mental illness and involuntary hospitalization are often seen as synonymous with incompetence. Such attitudes can lead mental health professionals to make inappropriate decisions on behalf of clients and undermine their basic right to self-determination.

At the same time, the enhanced involvement of families in recent years has raised some important questions related to the appropriate role of families in clinical decision making. What does client confidentiality really mean in light of the care-giving family's "need to know"? What voice should family members have when it comes to clinical treatment decisions? As families have pointed out, their lives can be dramatically impacted by the choices clients make. Indeed, an entire body of literature exists about the family's burden of such caregiving. This literature speaks to the frustration, anger, grief, and pain that most families experience as they try to cope with mental illness in their loved ones. Trained to understand the systemic effects of individual choices, social workers must recognize the family's rights to pursue their ideas of what is their own and their loved one's "best interest."

However, the rights of clients, families, and society can and do clash, especially regarding medication management. Social workers can be caught between their desire to collaborate with families and their ethical and legal obligation to honor the decisions and confidence of their clients (Zipple,

Langle, Spaniol, & Fisher, 1990). Zipple et al. offer several helpful strategies for resolving such conflicts, such as sharing nonconfidential information with families, providing them with written information when appropriate, referring them to educational groups in the community, using release-of-information procedures, and using mediators when necessary. While it is true that, in social work, the client's rights hold the preeminent position, effective collaboration is achieved by trying to balance the rights of all who have a stake in the process. Establishing a partnership model of practice is an important factor. While social workers' obligation to hold the client's well-being in highest regard is clear, their obligations to themselves, their agency, and society are also recognized (National Association of Social Workers [NASW], 1980).

Costs versus Benefits of Medications

Bentley and Reeves (1992) argue that "research on the efficacy of psychotropic medication as a therapeutic intervention . . . has affirmed their role as an important aspect of treatment" (p. 41). Bentley (1993) also argues that social workers should stand for balance and common sense. That is, while acknowledging the significant contribution that psychotropic drugs can make toward reducing symptoms and improving the quality of life for many people, social workers should not ignore the disturbing side effects of medications or the sociopolitical aspects of their use.

In his seminal review of the history of social work and drug treatments, Cohen (1988) strongly advocates increased attention to the adverse effects of psychiatric drugs. Urging social workers to avoid repeating the failures of the past, Cohen contends that earlier in the century social workers either ignored or rationalized the negative effects of shock treatments on their clients. According to Cohen, they inappropriately aligned themselves with the psychiatric establishment rather than listening to their clients. He warns that the same thing may happen today with psychotropic drug treatments. Others in this field (Davidson & Jamison, 1983; McCollum et al., 1978) also suggest that social workers should pay more attention to not only the negative physical effects of these medications, but also their negative psychological and social effects. These latter effects include the overuse of medications, their use for social control, and their potential reinforcement of a negative sense of self. Gerhart and Brooks (1983) also urge social workers to be aware of the "seriously substandard" administration of antipsychotics in hospitals and community mental health centers (p. 454).

Responding to Cohen's (1988) essay, Johnson (1989, p. 659) critiques what she believes is his overstatement of the risks of psychotropic medications, calling for a fuller evaluation of both the risks and benefits of drug treatment and the "wrenching dilemmas" that practitioners and clients face in this area. We also disagree with Cohen (1988) on several points. For example, we do not believe that social workers should avoid encouraging psychotropic drugs merely because they have side effects or they bring up issues of authority and coercion. Similarly, Jamison and Davidson (1983) state that psychotropic drugs are a "mixed blessing" (p. 140) and should be cautiously accepted as an ethical, humane alternative to deterioration. As Bentley (1993) states, "When medications are used properly, most clients are helped, families are relieved, and hospital stays are shortened" (p. 104). On the other hand, many authors (e.g., Brown, 1985; Cohen & McCubbin, 1990) caution that the renewed interest in psychiatric drugs is most likely related to the medical profession's desire to remain dominant in the field and for drug companies to reap healthy profits. Clearly the economic and sociopolitical aspects of prescription practices, drug-research budgets, managed care, insurance reimbursements, and the like must be faced head on.

Expanded Roles with Regard for Related Professions

To maintain a balanced perspective of their role, social workers need to understand better the unique contributions to client care made by professionals in fields such as nursing, psychology, and psychiatry, and even nonprofessional helpers such as folk healers. Social workers need to define what is unique about their own professional perspective, what is shared with related disciplines, and what falls outside their purview. As we will demonstrate later, this is a great historical challenge in and of itself. It is even more interesting in an area so closely identified with other professions —psychopharmacology.

The benefits of interdisciplinary collaboration are well articulated. For example, Sands (1989) notes that such collaboration "helps us arrive at a comprehensive understanding of the client" and "solve complex problems" (p. 1). Similarly, Toseland, Zaneles-Palmer, and Chapman, 1986) note how teamwork improves services to the client as well as work satisfaction for professionals.

In mental health, social workers have tended to play key roles on interdisciplinary teams. In the Toseland et al. (1986) survey of 71 team members from 7 disciplines, social workers were reported as having a high degree of influence, second only to psychiatrists. Further, it showed that social workers tended to play a wide range of roles including some that overlapped with other professions. Interestingly, there were strong differences of opinion among the team members in two areas: (1) whether or not team members ought to have equal power, and (2) whether there ought to be a clear differentiation of roles among the professions.

Claims of a unique perspective and expectations about roles may be interrelated. For example, social workers often refer to their unique "holistic perspective" as their profession's strength (Dane & Simon, 1991). However, nurses have also cited a "holistic perspective" as a key distinguishing aspect of their profession. One survey of physicians found that hospital social workers were perceived as having a limited understanding of clients' psychosocial problems and as performing only as discharge planners who arrange for concrete services (Pray, 1991). A large-scale survey of social workers, physicians, and nurses in a medical setting (Cowles & Lefcowitz, 1992) found disagreements among the three regarding professional roles. Unfortunately, other professionals did not think social workers had the ability to assess emotional problems. Overall, however, differences in the way roles were perceived related less to what social workers did than to what they did that was their exclusive domain.

Thus, though social workers see themselves as highly trained and knowledgeable clinicians, they constantly face having to explain and demonstrate who they are, often making a case for their indispensability, especially when in settings not dominated by social workers (Dane and Simon, 1992; Mailick & Jordan, 1977). Because often what they do is influenced by other professions who don't fully understand them, social workers have noted a discrepancy between what they can do, want to do, or were trained to do, and what they actually do (Harrison, Drolen, & Atherton, 1989). For example, Pray (1991) notes that the gatekeeping function of physicians and psychiatrists subtly defines what is deemed an appropriate role for social workers.

Dane and Simon (1991) relate this continued misunderstanding in part to the devaluing of women's work, because women constitute a large majority of social workers. They also note the divergent missions and training of other mental health professions, as well as the poorly defined and stressful roles that exist in many settings. Mizrahi and Abramson (1985), in their analysis of the sources of strain between social workers and physicians, provide insight into the social worker's longstanding struggle to be understood. Specifically, they note that physicians' training stresses hard science knowledge, puts little emphasis on the clinical relationship, and offers little opportunity for them to process their feelings. They also state that physicians are socialized to be the autonomous decision makers and authority figures. In stark contrast to social work training, which emphasizes values, relationship, and "process," the training and socialization of physicians thus leads to differing perspectives in a number of important areas, such as the role and rights of clients/families and the role and function of social work. Similarly, Mailick and Jordan (1977) note how differences among professional knowledge, values, and methods of communication influence collaboration.

Clearly, more training in interprofessional collaboration is needed. Weil (1982) suggests that social workers consider the barriers to collaborative relationships and openly address differences in socialization and status. Avoiding stereotypes is also crucial to prevent negative attitudes toward other professions. Greater interdisciplinary collaboration begins with mutual respect and mandates the bold confrontation of misperceptions and ignorance (Gibelman, 1993). Mailick and Ashley (1981) summarize this view:

> Of utmost importance in working with a collaborative group is the capacity to listen, to be respectful, to understand the implications of other professional opinions, to be willing to recognize and accept areas in which the expertise of colleagues is unique, and to defer to special knowledge when appropriate. (p. 135)

Integrating Psychosocial Interventions and Psychopharmacology

A third strategy that undergirds effective collaboration with mental health clients, families, and providers is the successful integration of psychosocial interventions with psychopharmacology. Social workers need not only to recognize the intrinsic power of combined treatments but also to appreciate the ideological and practical challenges that emerge, especially in managing parallel treatment (in which one professional provides psychosocial treatment at the same time a physician provides medical treatment to the same patient).

Gerard Hogarty, who has devoted much of his career to understanding the interactions between psychotropic drug use and psychosocial treatments among people with schizophrenia, concludes that the most powerful treatment is a *combination* of medication and psychosocial treatments, and the effects of each seem to contribute to the other's effectiveness, or are additive. Others have reached similar conclusions (e.g., Dewan, 1992; Frank & Kupfer, 1986; Glick, Burti, Suzuki, & Sacks, 1992). Beitman and Klerman (1991) show that either solid empirical research or decades of clinical experience support combining treatments in persons diagnosed with such mental illnesses as depression, panic, agoraphobia, obsessive-compulsive disorder, generalized anxiety disorder, anorexia, schizophrenia, and borderline personality disorder. Nonetheless, even though social workers know that it is productive to offer both kinds of treatments to clients, clients too often are not afforded the opportunity.

Competing Ideologies

One important barrier to combining treatments is the ideological conflict stemming from certain schools of thought. For example, those trained in psychoanalytic, interpersonal, or behavioral techniques may place less emphasis on medication than on psychosocial treatment (Klerman, 1984). Those trained in biological psychiatry, on the other hand, place tremendous emphasis on pharmacology. Thus, some professionals conclude that medication merely covers up symptoms and avoids the "real" issue, while others deride psychosocial interventions as "psychobabble" or "soft." Some assert that this split reflects the historical separation of body and mind (Bradley, 1990). Saleeby (1985) speculates that the lack of biological content in social work curriculums is related to a professional suspiciousness of the medical model. Rather than allow biological content to narrow their perspective and contribute to reductionist thinking, he suggests that social workers see how knowledge about human biology and medication allows them to be more holistic. Others have called for a similar integration of biology and psychology in mental health. For example, in describing the treatment of people with bipolar disorder, Jamison and Akiskal (1983) write,

> Although biologic variables underlie the etiology of this disorder, its primary manifestations are behavioral and psychological, with profound changes in perceptions, attitudes, personality, mood and cognition. Psychological interventions can be of unique value to the client. (p. 185)

Similarly, Hoffman (1990) pleads with readers to reject the "two-track" model of treating depression, in which persons receive treatment as if they have two distinct disorders: biological depression (treated with medication) and psychological depression (treated with psychotherapy). He calls for a "unitary approach" that recognizes the complexities of treating disorders that have both biological and psychological components. "We have to take care to keep both the baby and the bath water in the same tub" (p. 371). Since social workers cannot prescribe medication or medically monitor its therapeutic effects, working toward an integrated approach means working toward open and productive partnerships with physicians and the effective management of parallel treatment.

Managing Parallel Treatment

A number of dynamics that deserve attention come up in the management of the relationships among client, prescriber, and social worker. These dynamics include referring to a prescribing physician, accepting referrals from physicians, and managing the coresponsibility for the client's treatment.

Kanter (1989) has written extensively on the "clinical case manager's" role in collaborating with physicians, especially in maintaining effective medication regimens. A number of other authors have also commented on the increased frequency and need for so-called "three-party" treatment relationships. Pilette (1988), for example, attributes this rise to the expansion of the private practice marketplace and the increasing access of social workers and psychologists to insurance reimbursement, among other things. Historically, community mental health centers and HMOs have relied on nonmedical professionals to provide psychosocial treatment and physicians to provide drug consultation. While the client may benefit from the respective strengths of each clinician, and the providers from covering all the clinical bases, the problems inherent to the arrangement raise many difficult questions.

For instance, who has the ultimate authority over and responsibility for the client's treatment? How will disagreements be handled? Who will decide about major changes in treatment? Questions about confidentiality (How much sharing is too much?) also arise. Bradley (1990) contends that the "entry route" of the client is an important factor in answering those questions; that is, how the client came to the three-party relationship. Was she or he a client of a psychiatrist who referred her to a social worker, or vice versa?

Goldberg, Riba, and Tasman (1991) examine psychiatrists' attitudes toward prescribing medications for persons being treated by nonmedical psychotherapists. In this study, of the 60 respondents who prescribed such medication, 73% worked with master's-level social workers (MSWs). Three-fourths of the medication services were initiated by the nonmedical provider. Over two-thirds of the psychiatrists were satisfied with their current level of involvement in the cases; in fact, 25% said they wished they did less with clients, whereas 8% wished they did more. Interestingly, one of the concerns raised most often by the psychiatrists was their need to know more clearly how they were to be available after hours or for emergencies.

Kelly (1992) advises pharmacotherapists (physicians, psychiatrists) to work *only* with people they know and trust and to make it clear they are not just a medication dispenser but a consultant. Kelly says the pharmacotherapist should consider the psychotherapist to be a responsible professional and a reliable informant but "not a medical colleague, supervisee or competitor" (p. 779). According to Kelly, the psychotherapist should also use a pharmacotherapist who appreciates the complexity of parallel treatment and considers herself or himself as a consultant, not a cotherapist or competitor.

Both clinicians need to be aware of the potential influence the psychosocial treatment and the use of medication can have on each other. For example, while psychosocial treatments may actually help a client adhere to a medication regimen, medication may in turn help clients become more cognitively or emotionally "ready" for psychosocial treatment. Though medication may heighten the client's confidence in treatment on the one hand, it could also encourage magical thinking and decrease motivation for treatment on the other (Bradley, 1990).

In addition, both clinicians should be aware of transference and countertransference issues that emerge in the three-party relationships (Dewan, 1992). According to Bradley, these issues can emerge from the client, the psychotherapist, and the pharmacotherapist. Positive transference occurs with the client when she or he views medication as a nurturing act, a "gift-giving acknowledgement of pain" (Bradley, 1990, p. 314). It can symbolize for the client a form of feeding and serve as proof of both clinicians' empathy. On the other hand, the addition of a second therapist can be experienced as either "narcissistic injury" ("I must be sicker than I thought") or evidence of a lack of interest or competence on the part of the referring clinician.

Psychotherapists demonstrate countertransference when making referrals if they distance themselves from clients by devaluing their skills or investment in the client's case. Countertransference also occurs when psychotherapists interpret receiving a referral as an indication of their secondary status (Bradley, 1990). When making referrals to physicians, psychotherapists must face their own discomfort about exposing their work to another, while the physicians who get the referrals have to deal with sharing power and avoiding competition (Busch & Gould, 1993). Likewise, physicians must avoid being "all knowing doctor" or letting clients idealize them, thus devaluing the clients' psychosocial treatment.

Interestingly, while stressing collaboration and frequent communication between the nonmedical provider and the physician, several authors warn against the collaboration becoming *too* close, making role distinctions unclear or skewing appropriate differences in approaches (Busch & Gould, 1993; Kelly, 1992).

Our suggested foundation of partnership, balance, and integration has implications for how and when social workers make referrals to physicians. For example, it seems reasonable to consider referral whenever a client experiences symptoms for which there are known useful drug treatments. This is particularly true when the client has only partially responded to psychosocial interventions. In deciding the timing of the referral, social workers must consider the severity of the client's symptoms and the extent to which the client's life is disrupted. It is important to remember that any referral a social worker makes to a physician is really a referral for an *evaluation* of *possible* treatment with psychotropic medication. Therefore, any discussion with clients about such a referral should begin with an overview of what to expect in the evaluation process, including a review of the pros and cons of merely seeking an evaluation. However, clients will probably also want to discuss what they will do if either offered or denied a prescription. The social worker should therefore share basic knowledge about the costs and benefits of medication in keeping with their clients' particular concerns and circumstances, including any known potential interactive or additive effects with psychosocial treatments. Social workers should use all their clinical skills to help clients practically and emotionally manage decisions to seek a physician's evaluation and treatment, in a spirit of cautious optimism. After the medical evaluation, the client and social worker will continue to address client reactions and responses on a number of levels (see Chapters 1, 7, and 8).

Because few studies exist about the referral process in social work and psychopharmacology, not much is known about it. Littrell and Ashford (1994) have examined the impact of treatment setting on the medication referral practices of social work field instructors. In cases of major depression, they found that the field of practice setting did not affect the sense of obligation to refer. On the other hand, with clients whose symptoms were less severe, those in mental health settings were more likely to make referrals than those in family service settings. How long clients had been in treatment had no effect on the obligation to refer. Perhaps one of the biggest contributions that Littrell and Ashford make is to raise the question, "Are social workers legally and ethically culpable should they fail to raise the possibility of medication referral?" (p. 123). We will revisit this question in our last chapter.

To summarize the challenges inherent in the collaboration between a physician who prescribes medication and a social worker who provides psychosocial interventions and supports, we turn to Bradley:

> To reduce the potential for rivalry, fear, anxiety, idealization, devaluation and splitting, both clinicians must appreciate the power of interpersonal dynamics in any triadic relationship but also resolve themselves the ideologic conflicts that have been inherent in the medication versus psychotherapy debate. (1990, p. 310)

PART TWO

A PRIMER ON PSYCHOPHARMACOLOGY

CHAPTER 3

BASIC PRINCIPLES: NEUROTRANSMISSION, PHARMACOKINETICS, AND PHARMACODYNAMICS

CHAPTER 4

SPECIFIC MEDICATIONS FOR SPECIFIC DISORDERS

CHAPTER 5

INTERVENTION CONCERNS WITH SPECIAL POPULATIONS

CHAPTER 3

BASIC PRINCIPLES: NEUROTRANSMISSION, PHARMACOKINETICS, AND PHARMACODYNAMICS

Social workers may have limited interest in psychopharmacology—indeed, it can make for esoteric reading. Still, a basic knowledge of the chemical processes associated with medications is essential for social workers whose clients use such drugs. Only with this knowledge can the social worker comprehend the nature and significance of changes in the client's physical and mental status, and understand the physician's rationales for dosage and administration. When a client describes or demonstrates the effects of medications, positive or negative, they must be interpreted in terms of their pharmacology. This knowledge directly applies to the social worker/client relationship in four areas:

1. Understanding the effectiveness of medications in symptom reduction
2. Monitoring side effects, including the medication's physical, psychological, and social consequences
3. Educating clients and families about the course of physical and psychological adjustment to medications
4. Communicating with physicians and pharmacists about the present and potential effects of medicine

The social worker's understanding of medication cannot be considered complete if he or she is aware only of its effects on thinking and mood. To promote a safe and effective drug regimen and to inform clients fully, social workers must also know the causes of the biological and psychological changes leading to symptom relief.

In this chapter, we introduce you to the central nervous system and the basic principles of *psychopharmacology*, or the study of drugs that affect a person's thinking, emotions, and behaviors. We describe the structure of the brain and nervous system; the properties of neurons and receptors; the processes by which the human body handles psychotropic drugs; and the effects of drugs on body chemistry. We also introduce some general information about the actions of antipsychotic, antidepressant, mood-stabilizing, and anti-anxiety medications, although we discuss these more fully in Chapter 4. So that the reader can grasp the rationale for medication treatment in a logical, holistic way, we have ordered chapter topics from the most general (nervous system) to the most specific (types of drugs).

The primary sources we used to research this material include Adelman (1987), Arana and Hyman (1991), Devane (1990), Gelenberg, Bassuk, and Schoonover (1990), Grabowski and VandenBos (1992), Kaplan and Sadock (1993), Lawson and Cooperrider (1988), Pirodsky and Cohen (1992), Silverstone and Turner (1988), and Wilson and Claussen (1993).

The Central Nervous System

The social work profession's person-in-environment perspective promotes the worker's focus on transactions within and among systems at all levels (micro, mezzo, and macro). To maintain this perspective, the social worker must acquire and assess broad sources of information about social phenomena. Though no social system can begin to approximate the nervous system's elegance and mystery, a systems perspective will help you appreciate the complexity of the central nervous system's structure and processes. It is a massive and astoundingly intricate information-processing unit consisting of 100 billion nerve cells and even more connectors between these cells. Because psychotropic medications act on the nervous system, an awareness of its geography is an appropriate starting point for understanding how these drugs work. However, much remains to be discovered about the specific biological processes within the nervous system. Its complexity should remind the social worker that, in spite of great gains made each year in knowledge about the human body, scientists have just begun to grasp the nature of routine system processes and the impact of drugs on them.

The Brain and Nervous System

The brain consists of nerve cells, glial cells, and blood vessels. Though *nerve cells,* also called *neurons,* carry out all the brain's functions, they make up only a fraction of its weight. *Glial cells,* which surround the neurons and outnumber them by a 10 to 1 ratio, have the sole function of providing an extensive supporting environment as their source of nourishment and a system for carrying away waste products. The brain is richly supplied with an intricate system of tiny *blood vessels*. Though it makes up only 2% of the body's weight, the brain receives 15% of its blood supply.

All human behaviors, including thoughts and emotions, are the result of neural activity, with changes in such behavior accompanied by corresponding changes in brain chemistry. Chemical processes in the brain are influenced by a range of factors originating both inside and outside the body. For instance, the simple act of greeting a client in the agency's waiting room sets off a complex chain, or pathway, of cellular activities by which the social worker's nervous system interprets verbal and nonverbal messages and initiates responses. A *pathway* is a series of interconnecting neurons working together for some coordinated purpose. Conversations with friends, practice interventions, or psychotropic medications are all prompts for chemical activities within and among neurons, which cause emotional or behavioral changes.

However, this perspective does not assume a purely materialist view of human functioning. Human behavior is always caused by transactions among biological, psychological, social, and even spiritual systems. In fact, biological science remains unclear about many basic processes in brain functioning. Why do people react with strong emotion to a beautiful sunset, work of art, or piece of music? What determines their methods of solving interpersonal problems? How do they come to develop their personal values or decide on ultimate life goals? While the nervous system is highly interactive with the environment, the means by which thoughts, feelings, and behaviors are mediated by the various sources of stimuli is unclear. Whatever your assumptions about identity, will, spirituality, or nature vs. nurture as the source of personality, we wish to emphasize that all human experiences are accompanied by nervous system activities.

The basic function of the brain is to receive information from the outside world, use this information to decide on responsive courses of action, and implement these decisions with commands to various muscles and glands. Though the brain can be divided into sections to differentiate its many activities, its processes are highly interconnected. The brain is generally conceived of as having three sections: hindbrain, midbrain, and forebrain (see Figure 1).

The *hindbrain* consists of the brain stem (including the reticular formation), cerebellum, and pons. Located at the base of the brain, the *brain stem* links the brain with the spinal cord. It is the oldest area of the brain, appearing prior to the evolution of mammals. The brain stem is primarily occupied with the maintenance of unconscious life support functions. It consists of several subsections. At its base, the *medulla oblongata* regulates vital functions, including arousal, heartbeat, respiration, blood flow, muscle tone, and movement of the stomach and intestines. The *pons,* located just under the midbrain, links various areas of the brain with each other and the central nervous system. At the center of the brain stem and traveling its full length is a core of neural tissue known as the *reticular formation.* Nerve fibers from this system extend down the spinal cord and control the position and tension of muscles. The *cerebellum,* located behind the brain stem, receives information from the muscles and joints, the organs of balance, the skin, and the eyes and ears. It controls bodily functions operating below the level of consciousness, including

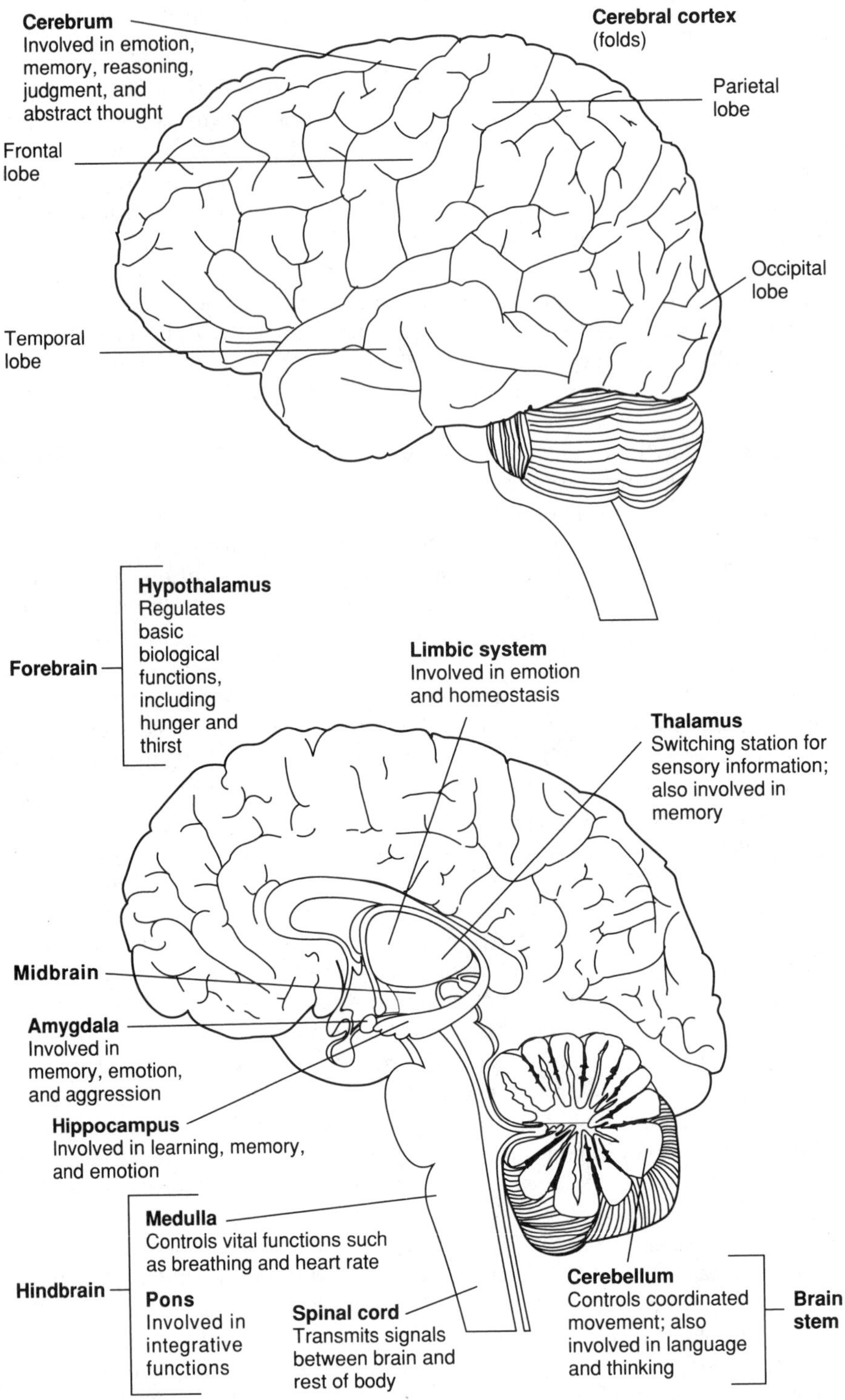

FIGURE 1
Structure of the brain.

posture, balance, and movement through space. Memory for certain kinds of simple learned responses may be stored there as well. Though the hindbrain does not include any targeted sites of action for psychotropic medications, some drugs affect activities there, producing undesired side effects.

The *midbrain* is located just above the brain stem. Though small, it represents a second level of brain evolution, more advanced than the hindbrain. The midbrain monitors and integrates various sensory functions and serves as a center of visual and auditory stimulation. On the upper surface of the midbrain, collections of cells relay specific information from sense organs to higher levels of the brain.

The *forebrain* is the largest section of the brain and consists of many specialized areas. Comprising a group of cell structures in the center of the brain, above the brain stem, the *limbic system* is a center of activities that create emotions. Thus, many psychotropic medications are targeted at neurons in this system. The limbic system also maintains the body's homeostasis, a concept from systems theory that should be familiar to social workers and that refers here to the constancy and stability of the body's physiological functioning. The limbic system permits people to adjust their internal states to maintain a constant climate in spite of external conditions such as extreme heat and cold. It regulates such functions as body temperature, blood pressure, heart rate, and blood-sugar levels. A major component of the limbic system, the *hypothalamus* is a relay station for internal regulatory systems, monitoring information coming from the autonomic nervous system (see p. 42) and influencing the body's behavior through those pathways. The hypothalamus produces *neurohormones,* or chemicals manufactured in the brain, as one means of maintaining the body's homeostasis. Specialized neurons release neurohormones into surrounding capillaries, where the blood transports them into the pituitary gland. From this "master gland," or regulatory site, they are eventually carried to target cells to regulate such things as temperature, balance, and appetite. They also influence motivation, sexual arousal, eating and drinking, sleeping, waking, certain chemical balances, and emotions important to survival.

The limbic system includes other activity centers. The *thalamus,* located near the center of the forebrain, relays sensory information from the body to the brain. Because all sensory fibers extending into the cortex must first pass through it, the thalamus is a major integrating center. It helps initiate consciousness and makes preliminary classifications of external information. An important center of learning, the *hippocampus* converts information from short-term to long-term memory. Located on both sides of the limbic system, the *basal ganglia* connect the cerebral cortex to other parts of the brain and help regulate skeletal muscle movements. Like the cerebellum, these nerve fibers are concerned with movement and control, particularly the initiation of movements. When the basal ganglia are unintentionally affected by certain psychotropic medications, adverse side effects result. This is the site at which dopamine is depleted in Parkinson's disease and one of the sites at which stimulant drugs act.

The *cerebrum* is the largest portion of the human brain and facilitates its highest intellectual functions. The center of emotion, memory, reasoning, abstract thought, and judgment, it integrates highly diverse brain activities. The cerebrum allows people to organize, remember, communicate, understand, appreciate, and create. The cerebrum is divided into two halves, each of which controls the opposite side of the body. On the surface of each hemisphere is an intricately folded layer of nerve cells known as the *cerebral cortex.* Characterized visually by its many folds, the cortex is an evolutionary product by which humans can accommodate a much larger area for the cortex than their skull size would otherwise allow. The cortex is composed of four sets of lobes, each with distinct functions. The *frontal lobes,* the largest, govern personality, emotion, reasoning and learning, and speech. Their primary function is motor control, including fine motor control, gross motor control, control of eye movements, motoric aspects of speech, and motor learning and planning. The frontal lobes are also involved in decision making and purposeful behavior. The *temporal lobes* affect gross motor skills and the integration of sensory input. Their functions include hearing, perception, and the storage of memory. Centers of long-term memory and information processing, the *parietal lobes* receive sensory information from the body. Finally, the *occipital lobes* are entirely devoted to processing visual input.

The *spinal cord,* which runs from the brain stem to the base of the spine, is a part of the central nervous system but is also associated with two other systems. First, the *autonomic nervous system* consists of neuron chains that extend from the medulla oblongata and spinal cord into the body's organs. These neurons regulate the unconscious and involuntary activities of the internal organs and blood vessels. The autonomic system includes two subsystems: the *sympathetic system* functions during the expenditure of energy; the *parasympathetic system* is more prominent in the body's buildup of energy reserves. For example, the sympathetic system acts to speed up one's heart rate during exercise, and the parasympathetic system slows it down during rest. Because its site of integration is the hypothalamus, the autonomic system is affected by some psychotropic medications.

Second, the *peripheral nervous system* consists of neurons that branch into the muscles from the spinal cord. It carries messages to and from the central nervous system to control voluntary muscle activity. Within this system, the *pyramidal nerve pathways* manage fine motor activities, while the *extrapyramidal pathways* govern integrated gross motor activities. The entire peripheral nervous system is composed of networks of these pathways, the cells of which are affected by some psychotropic medications to produce unwanted side effects. Its center of integration is the cerebellum; however, the cerebrum also includes pyramidal and extrapyramidal nerve tracts that connect the cortex to the spinal cord and muscles of the body.

The three sections of the brain represent different levels at which the nervous system functions. Much of the rear and base of the brain is specialized and committed to unconscious bodily functions such as the interpretation of incoming sensations, the control of movement, and the regulation of automatic life-support functions. The forebrain, particularly the frontal and temporal lobes, is less specific. Freed from the need to maintain basic bodily functions, its components interact in complex ways to produce thinking and the higher emotions. Psychotropic medications act not only on nerve pathways involved in thinking and feeling, but also on other areas of the brain. To the extent that such drugs can reach their desired sites of action without negatively affecting other brain functions, they can serve as successful agents for intervention with clients.

Properties of Nerve Cells

As components in all systems do, neurons exist in the context of a local environment. The structure of that environment is maintained by the glial cells; neighboring organisms include adjacent neurons and cells, such as muscle or gland cells, affected along pathways. Each neuron receives input from the environment, then responds toward some externally directed activity. The present discussion will be limited to activities within and among nerve cells that impact human thought and emotion.

The *cell body,* or central area of the neuron, is its metabolic center (see Figure 2). Made up of lipid (fatty) material, the *cell membrane* separates the contents of the cell from the fluid enveloping it. Molecules or ions pass through this membrane to enter or leave the cell, but not at random. Special "channels" must be opened for this to occur, and this process is governed by chemical activities within the cell. Each cell includes one single, long limb extension called an *axon,* through which the cell body sends signals to neighboring cells. The cell also features numerous short extensions, called *dendrites,* which receive signals sent by other neurons. In the complex maze of the central nervous system, axon terminals are always found close to the dendrites of other cells. However, axons and dendrites do not actually touch each other. The minute amount of space separating them is known as the *synaptic cleft.* Each cell may have access to 1000 to 10,000 synapses. The synapse comprises the presynaptic terminal, the cleft, and the postsynaptic membrane. A *presynaptic terminal* is an axon nerve cell ending containing neurotransmitters that extend to the synapse; a *postsynaptic membrane* is a membrane of the cell body, or dendrite, on which receptor sites are located.

The transmission of signals through the nervous system involves all these cell structures. The process begins when a cell generates a *nerve impulse,* or a momentary change in the electrical conductivity of the neural membrane. Neurons maintain a negative electrical charge when at rest; an impulse gives the neuron a temporary positive charge. These impulses are generated at various speeds, sometimes as rapidly as 200 per second. The transmission of an impulse to a receiving cell is facilitated by a chemical neurotransmitter released by the axon into the synapse, which attaches to special receiving areas, or *receptors,* in the dendrite of the neighboring cell. In turn, the receiving cell, having been acted upon, incorporates this impulse as environmental

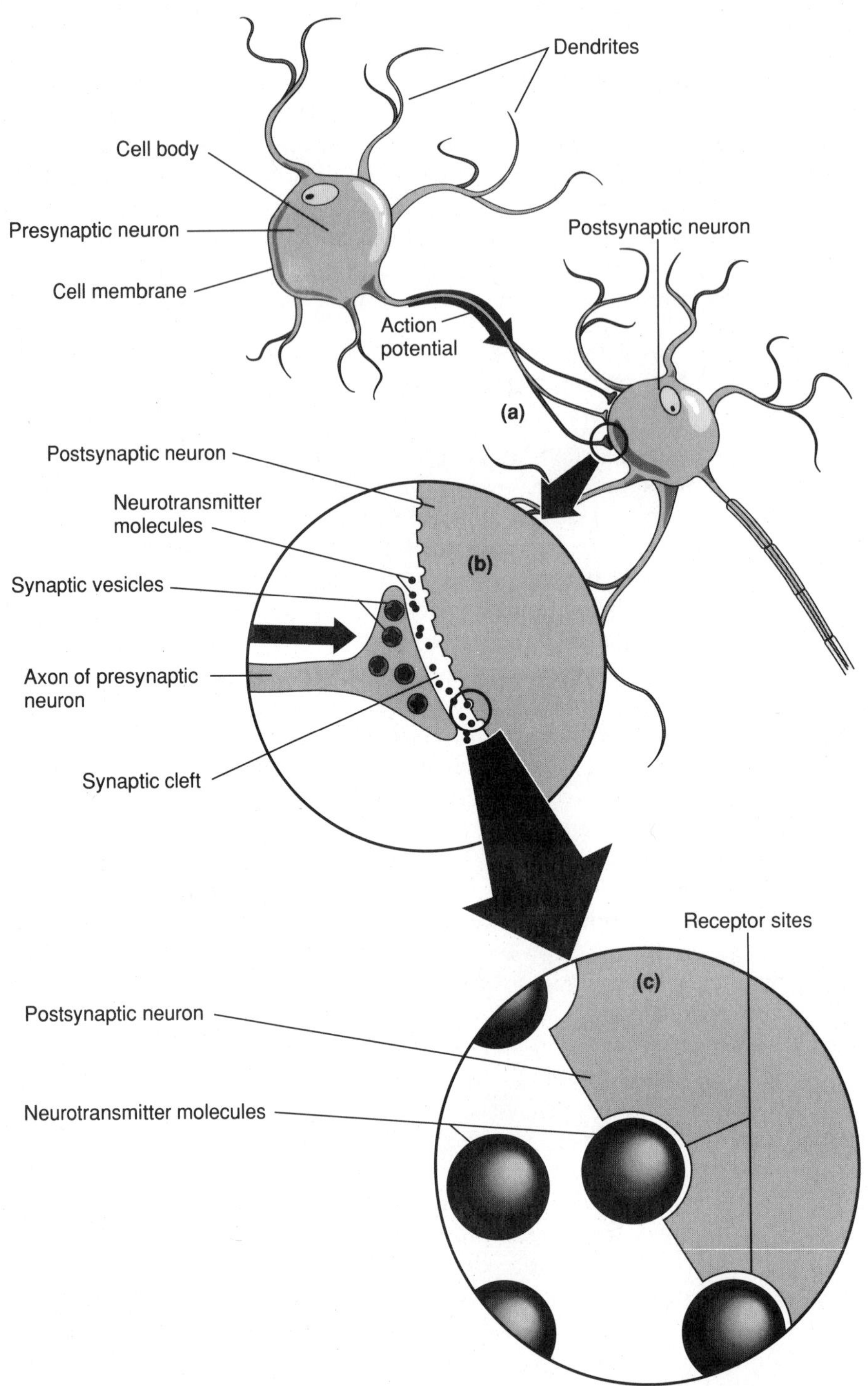

FIGURE 2
Nerve cell structure.

information and determines through its own chemical makeup how to respond. Generally, information is passed from cell to cell along a pathway. The process of signal transmission is no less complex when a social worker lifts a coffee cup than when she or he attends a client during a lengthy assessment interview. The latter activity simply requires the use of more neuron pathways.

Here we offer a more detailed description of these processes so you can understand their implications for psychotropic drug action. The axon terminals include small areas known as *synaptic vesicles,* which contain the molecules of a neurotransmitter produced in the cell body. Activities in the vesicles of the sending cell are *presynaptic* because they precede activities in the synapse. The receiving area of the synapse, on the dendrite of the nearby cell body, is called the *postsynaptic membrane.* Both pre- and postsynaptic membranes appear relatively thick and dark compared to the rest of the cell membrane because they contain the proteins that are the building blocks of some neurotransmitters. *Autoreceptors* are those receptors on presynaptic neurons that regulate the release of neurotransmitters. Though each cell probably releases only one type of transmitter at its presynaptic axon terminal, each has receptors to match many different transmitters.

The release of a transmitter into the synaptic cleft occurs through a temporary fusion of synaptic vesicles following a rupture in the presynaptic axon membrane. The process by which a neurotransmitter crosses the synaptic cleft and attaches to a receptor in the postsynaptic membrane is called *binding,* which activates chemical changes in the postsynaptic membrane. These changes can either encourage (excite) or discourage (inhibit) the production of nerve impulses, depending on the chemical composition of the receiving cell. The neurotransmitter does not itself pass through the receiving cell; rather, those impulses it prompts travel through the cell. After transmission is complete, the neurotransmitter either is discarded as waste by the glial cells or re-enters the presynaptic terminal for storage and use at another time (the process of *reuptake*).

At a given time, a nerve cell may receive a barrage of both excitatory and inhibiting impulses from many sources. Single cells continuously act on or respond to their environment. For instance, in reading this chapter, you have focused on the content before you, but perhaps you have also been listening to music, thinking about certain clients, shifting your posture every few minutes, or smelling dinner cooking. These simple, effortless activities require the exchange of signals among millions of nerve cells along pathways, with each cell doing its part to sustain millions of pathways throughout the nervous system.

NEUROTRANSMITTERS

Drugs work by modifying natural events in the synapses along pathways in certain areas of the brain. Medication affects these events, and subsequently brain function, in the following ways:

1. Altering presynaptic activity to prompt neurotransmitter release
2. Altering postsynaptic activity to affect receptor binding
3. Interfering with normal reuptake processes
4. Altering the manufacture of receptors

An *agonist* binds to a receptor and stimulates the same intrinsic cellular activity as the neurotransmitter, thereby increasing its effect. An *antagonist* binds to a receptor but fails to stimulate intrinsic cellular activity, thereby decreasing the effect of the neurotransmitter.

Though more than 40 chemical neurotransmitters have been discovered, the intended benefits of psychotropic drugs are generally attributed to only five: acetylcholine, norepinephrine, dopamine, serotonin, and gamma aminobutyric acid (GABA). Norepinephrine and dopamine are classified as *catecholamines* because they have certain structural similarities. The catecholamines, along with serotonin, are further categorized as *monoamines* because their chemical structure includes a single amine (an organic substance that is the building block for the amino acids). These transmitters are present in groups of neurons primarily located in the brain stem but also associated with more diffuse pathways in the central nervous system. They extend in pathways from the brain stem to other regions of the brain. Acetylcholine, norepinephrine, dopamine, serotonin, and GABA together account for transmissions at less than half of the brain's synapses. GABA, the most prevalent of these substances, is found in 25–40% of the brain's synapses. Dopamine is used by only 15% of the nerve terminals in those areas where it is most highly concentrated. Acetylcholine is found in 5–10% of neuron terminals in the brain. Only 5% of neurons process norepinephrine where it is concentrated, and serotonin is found in less than 1% of central nervous system terminals. However, all these substances are crucial in regions of the nervous system associated with emotional behavior.

The study of neurotransmitters and the effects of drugs on them represents a major field of neuroscience. Current knowledge about transmitter processes has been derived primarily from observations of activities within the peripheral nervous system. Establishing that similar mechanisms exist in the central nervous system is a far more difficult and somewhat speculative challenge. In fact, the specific actions of psychotropic drugs on neurotransmitter activity is in some cases still very uncertain.

Here are fuller descriptions of the major transmitters known or believed to be agents in psychotropic drug treatment.

Acetylcholine

The first neurotransmitter to be identified, almost 65 years ago, acetylcholine is most highly concentrated in the brain stem but is also present elsewhere. It is released by all neurons that control the activities of the skeletal and smooth muscles, including the heart beat. It is also released by autonomic nerve cells in the parasympathetic system that control some glandular functions. Acetylcholine is critical to the transmission of messages between the brain and spinal cord.

Norepinephrine

This transmitter, located in the sympathetic nerves of the peripheral and central nervous systems, is secreted by the adrenal glands in response to stress or arousal. Not widely distributed throughout the nervous system, it functions in two major *tracts,* or bundles of nerves with the same origin, termination, and function. First, norepinephrine influences affective behavior by connecting the brain stem with axons in the hypothalamus and limbic system. The second tract, which extends from the brain stem to the cerebral cortex and *hippocampus* (a part of the temporal lobe essential in memory regulation), influences alertness. Norepinephrine tracts also extend toward the spinal cord, where they regulate anxiety and tension.

Dopamine

Dopamine is present in three nerve tracts that have different functions. One tract extends from the brain stem to portions of the limbic system, which influences emotional behavior, and the cerebral cortex, which impacts cognition. Dopamine abnormalities in the limbic system are implicated in schizophrenia. A second dopamine pathway extends from the brain stem to the basal ganglia area of the forebrain, where motor activity is regulated. A lack of sufficient dopamine here causes physical tension, rigidity, and movement difficulties (the parkinsonian side effects of antipsychotic drugs). In its third tract, dopamine helps regulate the endocrine system, directing the hypothalamus to manufacture hormones eventually released into the bloodstream.

Serotonin

The tracts of this neurotransmitter originate in the midbrain and extend into all brain regions, particularly in the hypothalamus. Serotonin is also present in blood platelets and the lining of the digestive tract. It affects regions in the brain that facilitate sensory processes, muscular activity, and thinking. Strategically positioned in the midbrain, serotonin coordinates complex sensory and motor patterns during a variety of behavioral states. Serotonin is also a factor in regulating states of consciousness, mood, depression, and anxiety; it affects basic bodily functions such as appetite, sleep, and sexual behavior. Some hypothesize that it contributes to affective disorders, states of high aggression, and schizophrenia.

Gamma Aminobutyric Acid (GABA)

GABA, an amino acid, is present throughout the central nervous system. Most neurons possess GABA receptors. This transmitter inhibits virtually all neurons; that is, it inhibits the firing of impulses from cells on which it acts and thus plays an essential role in controlling neuron excitability. Almost every cerebral function is likely to be influenced by drugs that act on GABA. These functions include the regulation of locomotor activity, cardiovascular reflexes, pituitary function, and anxiety. Certain anti-anxiety medications enhance GABA's effectiveness. Alcohol and sedatives such as barbiturates also act on GABA.

How the Body Handles a Drug

The way in which the human body responds to the presence of a drug is called pharmacokinetics. Knowledge of pharmacokinetics can help social workers understand why some clients respond differently to the same medication than others and why, when a client stops taking medication, its effects can continue. The four bodily processes important to understanding pharmacokinetics are absorption, distribution, metabolism, and excretion.

Absorption

Absorption is the process by which a drug enters the bloodstream, most commonly by the passive diffusion of the drug into the bowel wall. Factors relevant to efficient absorption include the chemical makeup of the drug and the other materials used in its production, as well as the activity of liver enzymes, which break down the drug. With oral medication, this efficiency depends on its strength of concentration, its ability to dissolve into fatty tissue (of which intestinal cell membranes are composed), and the spontaneous movement of a given person's intestines. Taking a drug on an empty stomach favors rapid absorption because the presence of other substances promotes competition for digestive enzymes and slows the process. Though most psychotropic drugs are prescribed orally, in tablets or capsules, some are administered intramuscularly. Medications injected into muscles enter the bloodstream more quickly than oral medications because they bypass the digestive process. Intravenous administration of drugs is the quickest, most direct route for absorption; however, it is rarely prescribed, because it is impractical and includes the highest risk of adverse effects. Other routes of drug administration, such as the skin, lungs, and rectum, are not used to administer psychotropic drugs yet.

Distribution

Distribution is the process by which the drug, having entered the bloodstream, travels to its desired site of action. Once in the bloodstream, the drug can take one of two routes. It can either dissolve in the blood plasma for transport to the site of action or become attached to plasma proteins. The process of attachment to plasma proteins, or binding, is problematic because it prohibits the drug from advancing to its site in the brain. After binding, the drug breaks down or is metabolized, and its intended effects diminished. Though protein binding rates vary among drugs and even individuals, most psychotropic drugs are fairly high in protein binding capacity (up to 95% in some cases). Only the unbound portion of the drug can cross into the brain. Because average rates are already so high, small variations in the binding of a drug make a significant difference in its effectiveness.

The *blood-brain barrier* refers to characteristics of capillaries in the brain, through which a drug must pass to enter neuron sites. Because these capillaries are tightly compressed, this barrier is relatively difficult for a substance to cross. Medications and other substances must be *lipid-soluble* to pass through brain capillaries because their cell membranes are lipid, or fatty. In other areas of the body, capillaries are not so tightly bound, so that water-soluble substances can leak between them into the surrounding tissue. Generally speaking, efficient absorption into the fatty intestinal wall implies that a drug will enter the brain as well.

A drug can enter the brain directly, through the circulatory system, or indirectly, through the cerebrospinal fluid after diffusing there from the bloodstream. Access of a drug to the brain depends in part on the blood flow at the intended site, with a higher volume of blood increasing the likelihood of entry. Access also depends on the drug's relative affinity for the receptors in that area of the brain. Distribution into the brain is facilitated by the large mass of blood vessels that feed it. Nevertheless, the amount of the drug that passes through the blood/brain barrier is usually small compared to the amount that remains in other areas of the body. Physicians take these facts into account when selecting drugs and dosages.

Metabolism

Metabolism is the process, generally carried out by enzymes in the liver, by which the body breaks down the chemical structure of a drug into derivatives that can be eliminated from the body. The drug's molecules are altered from lipid-soluble substances into water-soluble salts. High water-solubility prevents the drug's continued recirculation through the body because it can be efficiently absorbed into the body's water and excreted. *First-pass metabolism* refers to the extensive initial breakdown of the drug within the liver. This process significantly reduces the amount of drug available to proceed toward its site of action. *Bioavailability* refers to the amount of a drug that leaves the liver without being metabolized. It is important to note that the products of metabolism, known as *metabolites,* may be themselves pharmacologically active. That is, even though they represent a chemical breakdown of the drug, they may maintain a set of therapeutic effects on thought or mood similar to that of the original drug. The metabolites of most medications are well known, so their effects are taken into account by physicians making decisions about prescriptions. However, metabolism can be differently affected by disease and interactions among drugs. Also, the efficiency of metabolism, as well as kidney function, declines with age.

Excretion

Excretion is the process by which drugs are eliminated from the body, primarily by the kidneys. *Elimination* refers to all processes, including metabolism and excretion, that lower the concentration of a drug in the body. The speed of this process is proportional to the concentration of the drug in the body; that is, elimination proceeds more slowly as less medication remains within the consumer's system. *Blood level* refers to the measure of a drug's presence in the plasma at a given time; *steady state* refers to the point at which a consistent level of a medication is present in the bloodstream; and the *peak (plasma) level* of a drug refers to the time after ingestion at which it reaches its highest concentration in the bloodstream. This peak varies, depending on the type of drug and the amount ingested. Because elimination continues the entire time a drug is in the bloodstream, relative drug-elimination rates determine whether blood levels are increasing or decreasing. That is, the amount ingested and in circulation corresponds to the amount eliminated. *Clearance* is the amount of a drug excreted over a given amount of time. Excretion is carried out through the urine or bile, although sweat, feces, saliva, tears, and even milk in lactating women can serve this function.

An important concept for understanding the frequency with which a client must take a prescribed medication is that of *half-life,* or the time required for a drug to fall to 50% of its peak level. The half-life is determined by metabolism and excretion, after absorption and distribution are complete. To clarify a frequent point of confusion, a drug is not completely eliminated, as might be assumed, after two half-lives have passed. In fact, each successive half-life requires the same amount of time as the previous one but accounts for the elimination of only 50% of the remaining medication. For example, the antidepressant trazodone has a half-life of 5 hours; thus, 50% of the peak level of a single dose of trazodone is eliminated in 5 hours. However, only 75% is cleared in 10 hours, or 2 half-lives (50% of the remaining 50% equals 25%); 87.5% is eliminated in 15 hours, or 3 half-lives (50% of 25%, or 12.5%); 93.75% in 20 hours, or 4 half-lives; and approximately 97% in 25 hours, or 5 half-lives. Knowledge of a drug's half-life is essential to determine the dosage that must be taken to maintain a steady state within the circulation. If a client takes a drug too frequently, his or her blood level will eventually rise to a point of toxicity. Similarly, taking a drug less frequently than is therapeutically advisable would limit or perhaps even eliminate its effectiveness.

In determining a psychotropic drug treatment, physicians try to insure that a steady concentration of medication in the consumer's bloodstream will be delivered to the site of action to produce the desired therapeutic effect. When a drug's half-life is known, the prescribing physician can tell the consumer which frequency of dosage will achieve a steady state; that is, the physician provides a schedule so that the amount entering the system will offset the amount leaving it. Logically, medications with longer half-lives should be taken less often than those with shorter ones. Of course, taking any medication more frequently than indicated by its half-life would be dangerous, leading to a buildup of the substance in the system and toxic effects. Many antipsychotic medications and antidepressants can be taken once per day. Mood-stabilizing medications, on the other hand, are generally taken several times per day because of their shorter half-life. Most oral medications are taken at least once per day, but injectable medications can be consumed as seldom as once per month because they are stored and released slowly by muscle tissue.

The Effects of a Drug on the Body

Pharmacodynamics is the study of the effects of a drug on the body. Social workers can use their knowledge of pharmacodynamics to respond to the client's and family's needs to learn about medications, including understanding differential drug response and the reasons for all the drug's effects, positive and negative. Pharmacodynamics offers several helpful concepts to the social worker, including the therapeutic index, dose response, lag time, and side effects. Because drugs interact with body tissues, individual consumer characteristics account for differences in what the drug can do. In general, drug action is influenced by a consumer's age (efficiency of metabolism), weight (rate of absorption), gender (hormonal differences), and any organ problems or diseases that interfere with the body's efficiency.

The *therapeutic index* of a drug is the ratio of the lowest average concentration needed to produce a desired effect and the lowest average concentration that produces toxic effects. In *toxicity*, the amount of an active drug in the body exceeds the amount required for efficacy, putting the consumer at risk for serious negative side effects. A high therapeutic index implies that a drug is relatively safe, as opposed to a drug with a low therapeutic index. That is, a person will not likely overdose if he or she accidentally takes more than is prescribed.

The *potency* of a drug is its relative strength in grams, milligrams, or micrograms required to achieve a desired effect. The *median effective dose* (ED_{50}) is the dose that causes a therapeutic effect in 50% of clients. However, a drug's effectiveness cannot be measured merely by its potency. Two different antipsychotic drugs, for example, may be administered in very different dosages. One milligram of haloperidol is the equivalent of ten milligrams of thiothixene, a similar drug. Though haloperidol is the more potent of the two, their effectiveness may be the same, and they may be equally safe when given in comparable therapeutic amounts. However, differences in potency do relate to certain types of side effects (see Chapter 4).

The *dose response* is the measure of therapeutic effect as a function of increasing dose. Many drugs demonstrate an enhanced therapeutic effect when given in greater amounts, but only up to a point: They may become ineffective or harmful once that peak dosage level is passed. When plotted on a curve, dose responses can be compared with each other. Again, this information does not necessarily help the prescribing physician determine which medication is preferable, because two medicines may have different therapeutic and side effect profiles.

Lag time is the time a medication takes to affect the targeted behavior. Lag time in part depends on the delay caused by the natural distribution of the drug, but in some cases it may reflect an adaptive response in the central nervous system. That is, the drug may reach the site of action, but the natural activity of neurons may change in reaction to it so that the desired nerve cell activity is temporarily thwarted. Some anti-anxiety medications demonstrate an almost immediate therapeutic effect after consumption, while antidepressants may take two weeks or more to produce a desired effect. Though factors involved in lag time are not well understood, the time intervals are predictable. One theory holds that the presynaptic nerve fires rapidly in the presence of a neuroleptic drug. Eventually, though, the presynaptic neuron can no longer build up a charge. When the neuron fatigues, the efficacy of the drug can be observed. This phenomenon has clinical implications; that is, it will do the physician no good to increase dosage to obtain a quicker response. To impact the symptoms of mental illness, one often has to wait.

Tolerance refers to the body's reduced responsiveness to a drug because the sensitivity of receptors changes over time. Although tolerance may be observed with the benzodiazepines and, rarely, with heterocyclic antidepressant drugs, tolerance does not affect the therapeutic effects of most psychotropic drugs. However, certain unwanted side effects of medications may diminish over time, making tolerance positive for some clients.

Side effects refer to any physical effects of a drug that are unintentional and unrelated to its desired therapeutic effect. Though side effects are generally considered negative, the client may perceive some as either neutral or positive, such as weight loss or increased energy with some antidepressant medications. These generally occur because a drug acts on multiple sites in the nervous system, though only one site is targeted for the positive effect. Negative side effects can have serious short- and long-term consequences for the consumer or relatively harmless but uncomfortable or inconvenient effects, such as sedation. Significant side effects may be themselves treated by the physician, sometimes with other medications. The social worker's important role in this process will be discussed in later chapters.

Four Classes of Psychotropic Medication

We are mainly concerned with psychotropic medications that belong to one of four categories: antipsychotic, antidepressant, mood-stabilizing, and anti-anxiety. The drugs in a particular category are used to treat the same mental illnesses and psychiatric symptoms, and tend to take similar actions, with important exceptions. The following sections detail how each type of drug acts on the body and how the body handles each.

Antipsychotic Medications

It is a widely accepted notion, but still hypothetical, that persons with schizophrenia have a relatively high concentration of the neurotransmitter dopamine, or a high sensitivity at its receptor sites, in pathways extending into the cortex and limbic system. Firmer evidence exists that antipsychotic drugs are dopamine antagonists and that stimulating dopamine activity induces psychotic symptoms (Wilson & Claussen, 1993). Almost all the antipsychotic medications act by blocking dopamine receptors. The medications differ primarily in their potential side effects and their potency as indicated by the number of milligrams in equivalent doses. Because the drugs act on postsynaptic receptors, they are classified as dopamine antagonists. The antipsychotic drugs block dopamine transmission by binding to dopamine receptors. Previously believing that there was one type of dopamine receptor in the brain, scientists have now identified five subtypes, grouped into two classes, one of which produces therapeutic effects and the other which produces adverse effects when affected by psychotropic drugs. The therapeutic actions of the antipsychotic medications result from their blocking one of these types of receptors. The reduction of dopamine activity in persons with schizophrenia is accompanied by a reduction in many of the *positive symptoms,* which feature an excess or bizarre distortion of normal functions (such as delusions and hallucinations). However, for reasons that are not clear, antipsychotic medications are not as effective in reducing delusional thinking or *negative symptoms,* which feature a loss or reduction of normal functions (withdrawal, poverty of speech and thought, lack of motivation).

Though the antipsychotic medications act on all dopamine sites in the brain, only one of these is the site of symptom-producing nerve cell activity. The other pathways extend from the midbrain to the basal ganglia and occupy areas of the brain that govern motor activity through the peripheral nervous system. A reduction in dopamine in these other areas causes negative side effects. Clients may experience muscle spasms, tremors, or stiffness because normal amounts of the transmitter are needed there to facilitate muscle activity. Symptoms of parkinsonism and tardive dyskinesia have their source in these areas.

Several new types of antipsychotic medication, all from the same chemical family, have been introduced into the American market and seem to act differently than previous drugs. Clozapine, the best known of these, does not carry the risk of side effects for the muscular system. Though its action is not well understood, it may selectively act on only those dopamine receptors that produce psychotic symptoms. However, its sites of action were once hypothesized as limited to the limbic forebrain and the frontal cortex, though recent evidence suggests otherwise. Clozapine also blocks receptors for serotonin, which raises the possibility that this neurotransmitter may affect psychotic symptoms in some people. The Food and Drug Administration mandates that physicians prescribe this drug only if the client does not respond to typical antipsychotic drugs, because of its unusual side effect profile (see Chapter 4).

After oral administration, the peak effects of most antipsychotic medication are achieved within 2 to 4 hours. There is a significant first-pass effect in the liver, in which much of the chemical substance is metabolized before it enters the circulatory system. However, the metabolites also act as dopamine antagonists and thus have therapeutic effect. The drugs are highly protein bound: Fully 85–90% remains in the bloodstream. The drugs have a high therapeutic index, making it difficult to overdose accidentally to the point of toxicity. Depending on the specific drug, there is a range in half-life from 10 to 40 hours. Because any point in this range is considered lengthy, the antipsychotic drugs can be taken once per day to maintain a steady state.

Antidepressant Medications

There is much uncertainty about how the antidepressant medications specifically work. Until the early 1980s, it was believed that certain depressions resulted from a deficiency of norepinephrine or serotonin in the limbic area of the brain. The antidepressants developed in the 1950s and 1960s, still in wide use, were thought to work by increasing the prevalence of norepinephrine and serotonin in the nervous system. However, the newer antidepressants are known to act differently. Further, it is suspected that the antidepressants have additional effects on presynaptic and postsynaptic receptors and perhaps other neurotransmitter systems.

Three types of antidepressants, each with different actions, include the MAO inhibitors, the "heterocyclics," and the serotonin-reuptake inhibitors, or "atypical" antidepressants. Despite uncertainties about their actions, some general characteristics of the drugs can be described. They must all be taken for several weeks before the client experiences beneficial effects, because their actions are initially resisted by cells at the sites of action. They have a low therapeutic index, that is, the amounts required for therapeutic effect and overdose do not differ greatly. This is a particular problem because the drugs are often prescribed for clients with self-destructive tendencies. Overdose can often be achieved with a 10-day supply of the heterocyclic drugs.

The MAO inhibitors were among the first antidepressants. While still effective for some clients, they are not frequently prescribed because of rather extensive dietary restrictions needed to prevent serious side effects. These drugs act by inhibiting certain enzymes within cells that metabolize, or break down, norepinephrine and serotonin, so that levels of those transmitters in the central nervous system increase. The MAO inhibitors are effective with some clients who do not respond to the other antidepressant medications, and they appear to have anti-anxiety effects as well.

So named because of their chemical structure, the heterocyclic drugs (many of which have been called "tricyclics") were the most commonly prescribed antidepressants in the 1980s. They are believed to work by blocking the reuptake of norepinephrine and serotonin. Their metabolites are also active antidepressants. The drugs are highly effective, accounting for their long popularity. As a result of actions in other areas of the autonomic and central nervous systems, many heterocyclic drugs produce discomforting side effects. Fortunately, tolerance does develop to some of the side effects, but not to the therapeutic effect. These medications are lipid-soluble and have a high rate of binding to plasma proteins. With a half-life of approximately 24 hours, they can be taken once per day.

A number of new antidepressants that target only serotonin add to the uncertainty about how antidepressant drugs act on relevant neurotransmitters. The actions of these new drugs may include stimulating certain neurotransmitter building blocks in the cell body in ways that are not well understood. More potent than the heterocyclics, these "atypical" drugs have a long half-life. One of their major attractions is that they have fewer adverse side effects than the other antidepressant groups. They also offer less potential for an overdose.

Mood-Stabilizing Drugs

Since its introduction in the United States as an antimanic drug in 1969, lithium carbonate has been the primary drug treatment for bipolar disorder. The lightest of the solid elements, lithium circulates through the body as a small ion with a positive electrical charge. It is not clear how lithium achieves its therapeutic effect, but numerous theories have been considered. One hypothesis is based on lithium's high rate of passage through cell membrane ion channels, which impedes the activity of the naturally occurring impulses that contribute to mania and consequently stabilizes electrolyte imbalances in the cell membrane. Another hypothesis differentiates the antidepressant and antimanic effects of the drug. The antidepressant effect of lithium may result from its reducing the sensitivity of postsynaptic receptors for serotonin, thus increasing the amount of that transmitter in the nervous system. Its antimanic effect may relate to reduced sensitivity in dopamine receptors and an inhibition of cellular enzymes that produce dopamine. Though highly effective, lithium does not take effect for several weeks after initiation. It is sometimes given, at least temporarily, with an antipsychotic drug to stabilize a manic individual.

Lithium circulates freely through the body completely unbound to plasma proteins, unlike antipsychotic and antidepressant drugs. Distributed in the extracellular fluid, it enters body tissues at varying rates. Peak blood levels are reached in 2 hours (4 hours for time-release forms), and there is complete absorption within 8 hours of administration. The half-life of lithium is 24 hours on *maintenance doses,* defined as the minimum dosages required to maintain a steady therapeutic effect. It must be taken two or three times daily, except in its time-release form. Lithium is not metabolized in the liver into derivative compounds. The kidneys excrete 95% of the drug. At steady states, which occur in 5–8 days, an equilibrium is reached in that plasma lithium reflects levels of lithium in the entire body, and thus the drug can be efficiently monitored by measuring levels in the blood. Lithium is excreted by the kidneys in the first few hours after peak levels. Because lithium has a relatively low therapeutic index, adverse reactions (such as muscle tremor and kidney damage) can occur at blood levels only slightly higher than a client's therapeutic level.

Certain antiseizure medications also act as effective mood stabilizers. Like lithium, their mechanisms of action are not clear. One theory holds that they control a "kindling" process in limbic system neuron tracts that contributes to manic states. It is speculated that in mania, a repetitive application of low-grade electrical or chemical stimuli is set in motion, which eventually produces a manic episode. The drug carbamazepine, also a potent blocker of norepinephrine reuptake, inhibits such repetitive firing of sodium impulses, which can potentiate a manic episode, by binding to them when they are inactive. It may also inhibit enzymes in the central nervous system that break down GABA. The GABA neurotransmitter may have antimanic properties and thus its increased prevalence in the nervous system may enhance mood stability. Valproic acid, another atypical antimanic medication, also has presynaptic and postsynaptic GABA receptor effects. By blocking the convulsive effects of GABA antagonists, it increases levels of GABA. While effective, these medications are generally not prescribed unless lithium is first ruled out, since they can have more serious side effects.

Anti-Anxiety Medications

Though several types of anti-anxiety medication are currently available, the most frequently prescribed are the benzodiazepines. The name comes from their chemical structure: a benzene ring is fused to a diazepine ring. These drugs have frequently been referred to as "minor tranquilizers." Speculated to have evolved as fear regulators, natural benzodiazepine chemicals may exist in the brain, potentiated by the GABA neurotransmitter. As described earlier, GABA is a major inhibitory neurotransmitter in the brain. The benzodiazepine medications achieve their therapeutic effect by causing the GABA neurotransmitter to bind more completely with its receptor sites. GABA receptors in various regions of the brain thus regulate the anti-anxiety (or anxiolytic), as well as the sedative and anticonvulsant, effects of the benzodiazepines. While it is not clear how they specifically act as anti-anxiety agents, benzodiazepines act on the central nervous system by binding to specific sites on GABA receptors. This enhances GABA activity and results in a blockage of stimulation in areas of the brain associated with emotion. The drugs also raise one's seizure threshold. The locations of both antiseizure and sedative activity are the cortex and limbic areas, where receptors are known to decrease anxiety. As a general rule, the benzodiazepines are anxiolytic in lower doses and sedating in higher doses.

Benzodiazepines are usually taken orally. Quickly absorbed in the gastrointestinal tract, they act rapidly—in many cases, within 30 minutes.

Because they have a high therapeutic index, the benzodiazepines do not present a risk for overdose. The numerous company brands of these medications vary a great deal in their particular characteristics. But peak levels are generally reached in 1–3 hours, and most benzodiazepines form active metabolites. They bind to plasma proteins, with the quality of distribution corresponding to their lipid solubility. Their half-lives vary widely.

An important characteristic of the benzodiazepines is that they are physically addictive at some dosages with continuous use. Long-term use (more than two weeks) can cause production of the body's natural benzodiazepine compounds to shut down. Thus, if the drug is abruptly withdrawn, no natural production will occur for a given time. Clients must be taken off these medications gradually to prevent the effects of physical withdrawal, which can persist for several months, and in some cases up to one year. For these reasons, the benzodiazepines are generally designed for comparatively short-term use, even though physicians sometimes prescribe them for periods up to several years.

There are several other, smaller classes of medications used to control anxiety. These include the beta-blockers, so named because they compete with norepinephrine at certain receptor sites in the brain and peripheral nervous system that regulate cardiac and muscular functions. These medications effectively treat anticipatory anxiety; that is, they lower anxiety by reducing its symptoms of rapid heartbeat, muscle tension, and dry mouth. Because the client does not experience these physiological indicators, his or her subjective experience of anxiety is diminished. Another type of anti-anxiety medication, buspirone, is a partial agonist of serotonin receptors. Although its impact on anxiety is not yet well understood, serotonin is believed to be anxiolytic in the hippocamus and limbic areas. To be effective, this medication must be taken regularly, like the antidepressant and mood-stabilizing drugs but unlike the benzodiazepines. It is quickly absorbed but has a short half-life. Because buspirone is not potentially addictive, clients who have taken benzodiazepines for an extended time will often be gradually changed over to buspirone. Finally, the antihistamines are occasionally used as anti-anxiety agents. These drugs block histamine receptors associated with anxiety and agitation. Rapidly absorbed, they maintain a therapeutic effect for at least 24 hours. The antihistamines tend to sedate, however, and work effectively as anti-anxiety agents for only a few months. Though not addictive, they do not treat anxiety as effectively as the benzodiazepines.

Summary

Psychotropic medications produce changes in a client's emotions, thoughts, and behaviors by altering existing processes in the central and peripheral nervous systems. Though the details of how these systems work still lie beyond the full comprehension of scientists, enough is known about the structure of the brain and its neurons that reasonable hypotheses exist to account for the actions of medications. Because these actions are not specific enough—that is, they affect more than their targeted sites in the brain—adverse effects are common. The social worker must be able to assess and monitor all medication effects as they impact the client's overall physical, mental, and emotional well-being. A physician may prescribe medications as a primary or secondary method of intervention, but in either case, drugs do not represent the entire problem-solving process in the treatment of mental illness. The social worker must be prepared to use other interventions to enhance a client's social functioning fully. A basic knowledge of pharmacokinetics and pharmocodynamics does, however, equip the social worker to understand well the effects of drugs on clients, to explain such effects to clients and their families, and to make wise decisions about interventions from a biopsychosocial systems perspective.

CHAPTER 4

Specific Medications for Specific Disorders

Having examined the structure of the body's nervous system, the characteristics of neurotransmitters, and the actions of psychotropic drugs within the body, we now turn more specifically to the range of drugs used in the treatment of mental disorders. In this chapter we outline the specific disorders the four classes of medications are intended to treat and the symptoms they most significantly impact. Particular attention is given to side effects and the roles of the social worker in helping to manage them. We emphasize again that the social worker is in an ideal situation to mediate among the physician, the client, and his or her significant others toward monitoring both positive and negative effects of medications.

The primary sources used in this chapter include the American Psychiatric Association (1994), Arana and Hyman (1991), Campbell (1981), Devane (1990), Gelenberg et al. (1990), Kaplan and Sadock (1993), and Pirodsky and Cohen (1992). Additional sources are cited within the chapter.

Side Effects

As monitors, client educators, and possibly the first line of intervention if problems develop, social workers have first-hand involvement with side effects. As defined in the last chapter, side effects are the physical, psychological, or social effects of a medication that are unintentional and unrelated to its desired therapeutic effect. Clients may experience side effects as pleasant, such as the mildly sedative effect of some anti-anxiety drugs, but even these may present health and safety concerns. Because all medications act on areas of the nervous system, side effects are most readily recognized in their physical form. However, such effects may also be psychological, insofar as they affect the consumer's sense of self, and social, insofar as they impact how he or she is viewed by others. Still, the physical side effects are frequently of immediate concern to the physician and social worker because of their potentially negative impact on physical well-being. All three types of side effects, however, are equally important to monitor over the long run.

Physical Side Effects: Definitions of Terms

1. Anticholinergic effects (ACE). Dry mouth, blurred vision, constipation, and urinary hesitancy. These side effects result from the suppressive action of some antipsychotic and antidepressant medications on the pyramidal nerve pathways (those parts of the peripheral nervous system that govern fine motor activities). Specifically, the drugs block cholinergic receptor subtypes, which is the source of the name of these effects.

2. Extrapyramidal symptoms (EPS). Akathisia, the dystonias, parkinsonian symptoms, and tardive dyskinesia. These effects are related to the actions of drugs on extrapyramidal nerve pathways via central basal ganglia pathways and occur most commonly with the antipsychotic medications. *Akathisia* refers to an internal state of restlessness, or the perceived need to be in constant motion, which is accompanied by muscle discomfort. *Dystonia* refers to the uncoordinated and involuntary twisting movements produced by sustained muscle spasms. *Parkinsonian effects* include the reduction in range of one's facial and arm movements, muscle rigidity and tremor, shuffling gait, drooling, and difficulty either starting or stopping movements.

In *tardive dyskinesia,* the word *tardive* is defined as "appearing late," and *dyskinesia* refers to a distortion of voluntary movements. In contrast to dystonia, this condition refers to coordinated but involuntary rhythmic movements in facial muscles, including spasms of the eyelids, repeated puckering of the mouth, licking or smacking movements, and lip tremors. The tongue may curl or push on the cheek. This disorder can also affect the body's extremities and trunk region.

3. Neuroleptic malignant syndrome. Hyperthermia (high fever), muscle rigidity, fluctuating levels of consciousness, and instability in the autonomic nervous system. A rare (0.1% of consumers) but potentially fatal (15–25% of those afflicted) toxic complication of antipsychotic drug treatment, this syndrome generally occurs within two weeks after the initiation of treatment.

4. Orthostatic hypotension. A drop in blood pressure that occurs when rising from a lying or sitting position to a standing one, accompanied by dizziness, lightheadedness, weakness, and an unsteady gait. Though transient, this effect may cause one to fall and thus is of particular concern with physically frail persons.

5. Sedation. Drowsiness.

6. Sexual dysfunction. Changes in sexual desire, including problems with erection, ejaculation, and impotence in men, and orgasmic dysfunction in women. These symptoms all relate to disruption in the normal functioning of the autonomic nervous system.

7. Tachycardia. An increase in heart rate resulting from side effects of antidepressant medications acting on the autonomic nervous system. It is a serious concern for consumers with cardiac problems.

Physical Side Effects: Factors in Their Production

Many tables in this chapter outline the physical side effects of psychotropic medications. However, factors besides the chemical makeup of a drug also determine the side effects a consumer will likely experience. One obvious factor is dosage. Generally speaking, the higher the dosage, the greater the likelihood of adverse reactions. The following five characteristics of clients also impact the occurrence of adverse effects (Dewan & Koss, 1989). (See Chapter 5 for a more detailed discussion.)

1. Age. One's rate of metabolism slows down during later life. For this reason, elderly consumers are particularly susceptible to such adverse effects as sedation, weight gain, and parkinsonian symptoms. Orthostatic hypotension (lowered blood pressure), though not more common among the elderly, is potentially more serious given their relative frailty and proneness to injury in the case of a fall, for example. However, young people are more at risk for dystonias, or muscle spasms, indicating that there is not a simple correlation between age and all adverse effects.

2. Gender. Women are at higher risk for tardive dyskinesia, parkinsonian symptoms, and akathisia than men. Women with bipolar disorder are at higher risk for experiencing a manic reaction to antidepressant medication than are men. On the other hand, men are at higher risk for dystonia than women. These differences are apparently due to hormonal characteristics, but there is a need to study more fully how gender influences the positive and negative effects of medication.

3. Diagnosis. People with organic brain damage and affective disorders demonstrate a greater propensity for tardive dyskinesia and neuroleptic malignant syndrome than people with other diagnoses. Those with medical illnesses have an increased risk for neuroleptic malignant syndrome with antipsychotic medication, and delirium with the antidepressants. Furthermore, depressed persons seem to be at a higher risk for orthostatic hypotension than other diagnostic groups, for reasons not yet clear.

4. Personality. There is some indication that consumers with an action-orientation and a high need to control their environment tend to react paradoxically to sedating medications, becoming agitated and confused rather than calmed.

5. Ethnicity. Though race and ethnicity are not frequently differentiated in research on drug effectiveness, they are occasionally relevant factors in consumer response. Asian clients improve on lower doses of antipsychotic medications than Europeans or Americans do, but they also experience EPS at lower doses than comparison groups. They may also metabolize anti-anxiety medications at a slower rate and experience toxicity more often. Asian and Hispanic clients also respond more quickly to, and have more side effects from, cyclic antidepressant medications than other groups. African Americans seem to respond more rapidly than Caucasians to cyclic anti-depressant medications.

Psychological Side Effects

Psychological side effects occur when the act of taking medication affects the client's self-concept negatively. No less important than physical side effects, psychological effects probably account for an equal number of cases in which clients discontinue medications (Sclar, 1991). The range of effects follows.

The ongoing use of any type of medication brings up several concerns about dependency for clients. For instance, they must accept at some level that they, at least temporarily, depend on a chemical agent to function socially at a desired level. Clients must also acknowledge that previous coping skills have proven insufficient to manage certain thought or mood problems. Though clients may be relieved to have a means to regain a desired mental status, their sense of psychological efficacy may nevertheless be diminished.

It is true that many people with serious mental illness will need to take medication for the rest of their lives. Still, social workers may be insensitive to how this idea affects the client's sense of identity as a self-determining agent. They need to help the client come to terms with the need to take medication, to gradually integrate this fact into his or her sense of self. This phase of adaptation and integration is one of six outlined by Dawson, Blum, and Bartolucci (1983). During this phase, the client needs support in adjusting to a new self-image and the ways that others view him or her. It may take years before the client can accept the need to rely on medications; indeed, this may never happen. In the roles of consultant/collaborator and educator, the social worker must work with clients, family members, and perhaps others in the client's social environment to help them understand the normal ambivalence generated by this identity issue.

One negative outcome of reliance on medication occurs when clients come to feel that only medication can help them function adequately, that they are powerless to generate changes in other ways. Assuming a helplessness with professionals and peers, clients may fail to invest in other interventions. Many of the case examples below reflect clients' complex reactions to learning that they need medications to function acceptably in society. As validator, the social worker must ensure that these clients maintain an awareness of their strengths and other resources that will help promote healthy social functioning.

Some clients also develop a dependence on the physician or other providers, including the social worker. Clients may become unassertive with caregivers—that is, not disclose the full details of medication effects and life events—if they fear that doing so may disrupt any predictable patterns of social functioning established with these persons. It is certainly undesirable for clients to withhold information about medication or any other intervention issues from professionals who need to understand their reactions to these strategies. However, if social workers develop a relationship of trust with clients in accordance with the partnership model of practice, this situation is more likely to be avoided than if they do not.

Another psychological side effect is clients' anger at having to take medication. Their anger may center on the idea that they have a disorder requiring medication, that treatment providers are promoting the point of view that the clients are "ill," and that others in their social system, including family and friends, are stigmatizing them. These feelings may also represent a grief reaction. To accept that their situations can be dealt with constructively, clients may first need to work through negative feelings (Heyduk, 1991). On the other hand, clients may simply disagree that they have an illness, and never accept that there is a need to take medication. Again, the social worker can best address this issue through his or her relationship with the client, as well as collateral work with the client's significant others. Appropriate roles include that of the consultant/collaborator, who acknowledges the normalcy of the client's point of view. Drug education is another major component of this process.

Social Side Effects

Social side effects refer to the interpersonal and organizational barriers clients face daily as they proceed as identified consumers of psychotropic medications. Dawson et al. (1983) have outlined aspects of the "sick role." In receiving the diagnosis of a mental disorder and accepting treatments for it, including medication, an individual acknowledges that he or she has a condition that requires the help of experts. Regarding social norms, the client may be temporarily excused from certain responsibilities if he or she agrees to participate actively in treatment for the illness. Of course, some clients may refuse to take medications, because they do not want to acknowledge a sickness or accept that role's stigmas. They may not agree that they have a problem, may not agree with the details of its assessment, or may not believe that it is serious enough to require certain treatments, including medication. However, if clients who are mentally ill reject the sick role and fail to maintain work, family, and other social responsibilities, they will be labeled as irresponsible. They may, for example, lose a job rather than be given temporary leave if they fail to manage ordinary work responsibilities.

Of course, acknowledging a mental illness does foster a social stigma. For example, the law requires that one list medications and illnesses on job applications, but many employers may be reluctant to hire persons with mental disorders, despite the legal implications of the Americans with Disabilities Act. Further, because of the chronic nature of some disorders, the person's genuine growth may go unacknowledged by those around him or her, who may assume that more serious problems will soon follow. The social side effects of taking medication are very serious and may be addressed by the social worker in the roles of advocate (in the case of job discrimination, for example), monitor, and educator.

ANTIPSYCHOTIC MEDICATIONS

Mental disorders that feature symptoms of psychosis, which this class of medications targets, are generally characterized by the client's being out of touch with reality. That is, these are disorders of thought that greatly impair one's reality testing, or ability to evaluate the outside world objectively. The individual with psychosis is at least temporarily unable to evaluate the accuracy of his or her perceptions and thoughts, making incorrect inferences about the outside world even in the face of contrary evidence. With respect to the Diagnostic and Statistical Manual of Mental Disorders (DSM-IV), disorders featuring psychosis include the schizophrenias, delusional disorders, other psychotic disorders, schizoaffective disorder, schizophreniform disorder, bipolar disorder, major depressions that include psychotic symptoms, and some organic mental disorders. People with schizotypal personality disorder, not technically a psychotic disorder, may also be treated with antipsychotic medications. Though other types of emotional trauma may include transient psychotic symptoms, these are not classified as psychotic disorders if they are secondary to some other stress related to social functioning.

Symptoms of Psychotic Disorders

Though psychotic disorders are primarily disorders of thought, they can include mood elements as well. Listed below are common symptoms of psychosis, which all stem from the underlying thought disorder the medications are intended to treat. Examples are in italics. Not all persons with psychosis exhibit all these symptoms, and some of these are not specific to psychotic disorders. Because the DSM-IV organizes diagnoses around clusters of symptoms, a diagnosis is rarely made on the basis of one psychotic symptom in the absence of other features.

1. **DELUSION.** A false belief firmly maintained though contradicted by social reality. Types of delusions include the following:
   a. **Persecutory delusion.** The belief that certain people or forces are attempting to bring one harm.
   Spirits follow John to and from school each day to make sure that he is too distracted to perform his course work. John does not see the spirits but is certain that they are nearby.
   b. **Thought broadcasting.** The belief that one's thoughts are overheard by others.

Sarah is anxious with her parents because she knows that they can hear her thinking about sex at the dinner table.

c. **Thought insertion.** The belief that others are putting thoughts into one's head.
Paul cannot sleep at night because corporate executives from a neighboring state are negotiating with him about adopting his business ideas. They relay information about their plans directly into his mind.

d. **Thought withdrawal.** The belief that others are taking thoughts out of one's head.
Paul also believes that other businessmen are stealing his ideas, which he does not write down but keeps in memory.

e. **Delusions of being controlled.** Experiencing thoughts, feelings, or actions as not being one's own but imposed by an external force.
Brenda feels that her deceased mother is controlling her actions and causing her to commit sinful acts, such as stealing money from her friends.

f. **Delusions of reference.** Experiencing actual events as having a special significance, usually negative.
Leon, who lives in a violent neighborhood, believes that every crime committed there is a manifestation of his evil nature.

g. **Somatic delusion.** A delusion in which the main content pertains to the functioning of one's body.
For three years Gail has continually believed that she is pregnant by a young man she admires in the neighborhood, even though they have never met.

h. **Grandiosity.** An exaggerated sense of one's power, knowledge, or identity. Grandiosity may be religious in nature.
Dave believes that it is his responsibility to mediate in the great war being waged here on earth between God and Satan.

2. **HALLUCINATIONS.** The sensory perception of an external object when no such object is present.

a. **Auditory.** Hearing voices or sounds that are not in fact present.
Susan hears the voice of her father, who lives hundreds of miles away, asking for her support as he deals with his difficult job.

b. **Visual.** Seeing objects or images that are not present.
John is afraid to attend his socialization group because there is always an alien seated across the room from him who makes him afraid.

c. **Tactile.** Feeling an object that is not present.
Robert feels a rubbing against his leg. He believes a woman who wants to become sexually involved with him is doing it. He also wakes up many nights with the sensation that someone is smothering him.

d. **Somatic.** Feeling an unreal experience within the body.
Kathy continually feels the sensation of blood streaming down the back of her throat.

e. **Olfactory.** A false sense of smell.
Mary reports that she smells rotting food all the time.

f. **Hypersensitivity (to sight, sound and smell).** This is not a true hallucination, but borders on such because the person's perceptual capacities are altered to a significant degree.
Holly, when becoming psychotic, reports that the colors of nature are blinding in their brightness, and objects are surrounded by misty, colorful halos.

3. **DISTURBANCES IN THE FORM OF THOUGHT.** Loose associations, or thinking processes that become illogical, confused, and bizarre. Normal associations are the threads that guide logical thinking, but in psychosis these threads can lose their contiguity.
Kevin cannot carry on any conversation for long, because his thoughts always get sidetracked onto tangents influenced by his preoccupation with colors. Thus, mention of a fire engine makes him think of and speak about roses, cherries, cardinals, etc.

4. **DISTURBANCES IN AFFECT.** Disturbances in the experience and presentation of mood.
   a. **Flat affect.** Constriction of emotional expression or the feelings that accompany thoughts. Also, an incongruity between affect and thought; a shallowness in response to ideas and events.
   Cynthia sits with her relatives at family gatherings and demonstrates no visible emotional reactions to their behaviors, giving the impression that she is lost in her own world. Regardless of the topic, she does not respond emotionally when old friends or neighbors talk with her.
   b. **Inappropriate affect.** Inconsistent or exaggerated mood; a lack of ability to modulate one's mood according to one's thoughts.
   Cheryl tends to giggle uncontrollably when in groups of people, regardless of the nature of the interactions.

5. **WEAKENED EGO BOUNDARIES (THE BOUNDARY, OR SENSE OF DISTINCTIVENESS, BETWEEN THE SELF AND THE EXTERNAL WORLD).** Losing the ability to distinguish between what comes from within and what comes from without. In boundary loss, perceptions take on an unfamiliar or unreal quality.
Ray believes that his moods control the weather. When it rains, it is because he is in a depressed mood. Sunny days are the direct result of his optimism.

The following are nonpsychotic symptoms commonly seen in persons with psychotic disorders.

6. **AMBIVALENCE.** The desire to do a certain thing accompanied by an equally strong desire not to do that same thing. Many persons with schizophrenia, for example, have great difficulty making or sustaining commitments to carry out even minor intervention plans.
Scott cannot commit himself to attending his job-training program every day. He wants to work, and has some confidence in his abilities, but at the same

time he is overwhelmed with anxiety and self-doubt. As a result, he has not shown up at his training site several days per week.

7. **VOLITION.** Sustained deliberation giving way to whimsy in decision making, and goal-oriented behavior disintegrating into contradictory wishes and ill-sustained ideas.
   Shirley cannot sustain a focus on personal goals. By turns, she wants to be a hairdresser, a housewife, a model, a foreign-language teacher, and an interior decorator. These goals change at least weekly, and she is unqualified for any of them.

8. **AGITATION.** A state of tension in which anxiety is manifested by hyperactivity and general perturbation.
   Because of his chronic state of emotional discomfort, and feeling threatened by what most people would consider ordinary demands of daily living, Howard tends to become easily upset. When frustrated at his inability to perform simple tasks or carry out normal conversations, he lashes out verbally at those around him, blaming them for his failures. Through this process, he is in fact venting his emotional stresses.

9. **SOCIAL ISOLATION.** The disinclination or fear of making contact with other members of social groups, which may relate to the symptoms of psychosis.
   Sandy has learned during the course of her schizophrenia that she experiences fewer hallucinations and feels calmer when alone, away from the stimulation she experiences in the presence of others. She now spends most of the day in her bedroom, reading novels. Her parents try hard to engage her in family and social activities, but Sandy resists, paradoxically to preserve a sense of well-being.

10. **POVERTY OF SPEECH CONTENT.** Speech that contains little information because of vagueness or obscure word choices.
    Brian speaks in short phrases and answers questions in one or two words. His friends are not always sure what he is saying, but as they spend more time with him they better understand the meanings of his odd choice of words and terse phrasings. Surprisingly, Brian perceives himself as talkative. He is an example of a schizophrenic person whose mental life is active but who cannot communicate ideas adequately because of a poor social orientation. His odd choice of words is related to a detachment from social life and the abstract messages people typically use to convey ideas.

11. **MANIA.** A state in which one's mood is extremely elevated, expansive, or irritable. Though this will be discussed more fully in a later section of the chapter, we note it here because manic episodes can feature psychotic symptoms, most frequently delusions of grandiosity.

Besides these symptoms, people with chronic psychotic disorders sometimes neglect hygiene and personal appearance. When they exist, these behaviors generally indicate a preoccupation with mental processes at the expense of social and self-care concerns. By no means do all persons with serious mental disorders behave this way, but when they do, it indicates not a willful disregard for self-care, but rather an impairment in their ability to focus their thoughts on the normal activities of daily living.

Specific Medications

There are many drugs currently available for treating psychotic disorders (see Table 1). Though all effectively reduce or eliminate the symptoms just described, not all are suitable in every case. Clients respond to them differently because of variations in body chemistry, metabolism, and other personal characteristics. Interestingly, for reasons that are not clear, antipsychotic medications generally succeed more at treating hallucinations than delusions. Further, they tend to control the positive symptoms of psychosis (bizarre thinking and behavior) more so than the negative symptoms (apathy,

TABLE 1
Commonly Prescribed Antipsychotic Medications

Drug	Trade Name	Preparation*	Usual Daily Dosage
Acetophenazine	Tindal	T	60–120 mg
Chlorpromazine	Thorazine	T,C,S,P	300–800 mg
Chlorprothixene	Taractan	T,S,P	50–400 mg
Clozapine	Clozaril	T	400–600 mg
Fluphenazine	Prolixin	T,P	1–20 mg
Haloperidol	Haldol	T,S,P	6–20 mg
Loxapine	Loxitane	C,S,P	60–100 mg
Mesoridazine	Serentil	T,S,P	75–300 mg
Molindone	Moban	T,S	50–100 mg
Perphenazine	Trilafon	T,S,P	8–40 mg
Risperidone	Risperdal	T	4–6 mg
Thioridazine	Mellaril	C,S,P	200–700 mg
Thiothixene	Navane	C,S,P	6–30 mg
Trifluoperazine	Stelazine	T	6–20 mg
Triflupromazine	Vesprin	P	100–150 mg

*T = Tablets, C = Capsules, S = Solutions, P = Parenteral (injectable)
Source: McCandless-Glimcher et al. (1986).

withdrawal, and poverty of thought). Most work by blocking dopamine receptors in the brain.

Two of the medications, *clozapine* and *risperidone,* are considered to be part of a new wave of antipsychotics, partly because they have fewer motor side effects than other antipsychotic drugs. The reasons for fewer side effects are not yet clear. It is hypothesized that clozapine may act primarily, but not exclusively, on those dopamine receptors associated with psychotic symptoms (Wilson & Claussen, 1993); clozapine may also block acetylcholine receptors. Furthermore, both drugs may block serotonin receptors. Physicians, clients, and families in the early 1990s greeted clozapine with much enthusiasm because it was found to be effective with about 30% of clients who had not responded to traditional antipsychotic drugs.

The half-lives of all the antipsychotic drugs are relatively long (10 to 20 hours), so that in many cases they can be taken once each day. As with all medications, choices made about specific drugs by physicians are based on the consumer's history of response (if any) to a medication; the relative risk/benefit profile with respect to therapeutic and adverse effects, which is based on the consumer's characteristics (age, gender, diagnosis, personality, race); and the physician's own preferences, acquired from his or her history of success with certain types of medication.

All the medications have side effects. Though some are more serious and lasting than others, all cause the consumer discomfort; therefore, it is important to evaluate them throughout the treatment period. Table 2 summarizes the adverse effects of the antipsychotic medications, with the effects falling into four categories. As defined earlier, sedation refers to the relative degree of drowsiness caused by the drug. The anticholinergic effects (ACE) include dry mouth, constipation, blurred vision, and urinary retention. Hypotensive effects involve the lowering of blood pressure. Extrapyramidal symptoms (EPS) include muscle spasms, stiffness, tremor, reduced movement in the facial muscles, and restlessness. These factors vary predictably between low- and high-potency medications. As discussed in the last chapter, high-potency medications are those prescribed in lower milligram dosages (such as haloperidol), while low-potency drugs are given in high milligram amounts (such as chlorpromazine). The potency is unrelated, however, to effectiveness. Though clozapine has fewer extrapyramidal effects than the other medications and is not yet associated with tardive dyskinesia, it carries the potential for a unique set of adverse effects, including hypersalivation, nasal stuffiness, and agranulocytosis (a depletion of the white blood cells). The first two do not present a health hazard, but the small risk of the last is very serious and can be fatal if not monitored. For this reason, people who use clozapine are required to receive weekly blood tests as a preventive measure. If the blood condition begins to develop, the medication must be discontinued immediately.

Two other types of potentially serious side effects of antipsychotic drugs include tardive dyskinesia and neuroleptic malignant syndrome. Defined earlier in this chapter, these are summarized in Table 3 along with other

TABLE 2
Adverse Effects of Antipsychotic Medications

Drug	Typical Adverse Effects
Chlorpromazine Chlorprothixene Clozapine Thioridazine	Significant levels of sedation, blurred vision, constipation, urinary impairment, dry skin, weight gain, gastrointestinal discomfort, and lowering of blood pressure (lightheadedness)
Acetophenazine Haloperidol Perphenazine Thiothixene	Moderate levels of muscle spasms (in tongue, face, neck, and back); restlessness and anxiety
Fluphenazine Molindone Trifluoperazine	Moderate levels of sedation; greater possibility of spasms (in tongue, face, neck, and back); restlessness and anxiety
Loxapine Mesoridazine	Moderate levels of sedation, blurred vision, constipation, urinary impairment, dry skin, weight gain, gastrointestinal discomfort, and lowering of blood pressure (lightheadedness). Greater possibility of spasms (as described above), restlessness, and anxiety
Risperidone	Moderate levels of sedation, blurred vision, constipation, urinary impairment, dry skin, weight gain, and gastrointestinal discomfort
Triflupromazine	Significant levels of sedation; moderate levels of blurred vision, constipation, urinary impairment, dry skin, weight gain, and gastrointestinal discomfort; high possibility of lowered blood pressure; moderate levels of spasms, restlessness

types of side effects and information about their treatment. Neuroleptic malignant syndrome, though rare, is the most severe because it represents an immediate life-threatening reaction to a medication. Symptoms evolve over a period of 1 to 3 days, with the untreated course of the syndrome unfolding over two weeks. Clients with these symptoms must immediately stop taking the medication and receive emergency medical treatment. Tardive dyskinesia, also extremely serious, can be a long-term side effect of the neuroleptic medications. Though there is some controversy regarding its prevalence, its incidence increases by about 4% per year after 5 years of antipsychotic medication treatment (Jeste & Caligiun, 1993). Tardive dyskinesia tends to occur later in treatment and strike older people, and people with mood disorders.

TABLE 3
Types of Side Effects of Antipsychotic Medications

Reaction	Features	Treatment
Acute Dystonia	Spasms of tongue, face, neck, back; miniseizures	Antiparkinsonian drug
Akathisia	Restlessness with anxiety or agitation	Reduce dose, change drug, propranolol, benzodiazepines, antiparkinsonian drug
Anticholinergic Effects	Blurred vision, confusion, constipation, dry skin, delayed urination, sweating, gastrointestinal discomfort, sexual dysfunction, tachycardia, weight gain	No medical treatment; specific symptoms may be alleviated with diet, exercise, use of fluids
Malignant Syndrome	Catatonia, stupor, fever, unstable pulse and blood pressure	Stop medication
Parkinsonism	Motor slowing, retarded facial movement, rigidity, gait disturbance, resting tremor	Antiparkinsonian drug
Tardive Dyskinesia	Involuntary rhythmic movement in mouth and face, spastic movements in limbs	No treatment; gradual remission is possible

Its symptoms become worse when consumers take reduced doses of the responsible medication; however, the potential for permanent damage will continue with higher doses of medication, even though the observable symptoms may remit. The prognosis is variable, but anticholinergic drugs apparently worsen the condition. Finally, the more acute dystonias occur early on and strike younger people, males, and people with mood disorders. Anticholinergic (also known as antiparkinsonian) drugs may ameliorate the condition.

Although the antipsychotic medications produce common unpleasant side effects, other medications, listed in Table 4, can minimize the extrapyramidal effects. Most of these are classified as *antiparkinsonian medications* because the symptoms they treat resemble those of Parkinson's disease. However, antianxiety medications, antihistamine medications, and betablockers may occasionally be prescribed as side effect medications. Unfortunately, many of these drugs have their own side effects. For instance, the

TABLE 4
Medications for the Treatment of Extrapyramidal Symptoms

Drug	Trade Name	Preparation*	Usual Daily Dosage
Amantadine	Symmetrel	T,P	100–300 mg
Benztropine	Cogentin, Tremin	T	0.5–8 mg
Biperiden	Akineton	T,P	2–20 mg
Clonazepam	Klonipin	T	2 mg
Clonidine	Catapres	T	0.3 mg
Diphenhydramine	Benadryl	T,P	25–200 mg
Ethoprozapine	Parisidol	T	50–600 mg
Lorazepam	Ativan	T	3 mg
Orphenadrine	Norflex	T	50–300 mg
Procyclidine	Kemadrin	T	5–20 mg
Propranolol	Inderal	T	60–120 mg
Trihexiphenidyl	Artane, Trihexane, Trihex-5	T,P	2–20 mg

*T = Tablet, P = Parenteral (injectable)

antiparkinsonian medications produce anticholinergic effects (dry mouth, blurred vision, constipation, urinary retention). In many cases, clients adjust at least partially to these additional negative effects or may find them more tolerable than those produced by the antipsychotic medications. In the roles of consultant/collaborator and monitor, the social worker must continuously evaluate with the client the effects of medications and communicate these observations to the physician and the client's significant others, so as to promote a positive outcome of medication intervention.

Finally, Table 5 outlines the effects of other drug interactions with antipsychotic medications. The impact and effectiveness of any medication, psychotropic or otherwise, depends on many factors, including the concomitant use of additional substances. The role of educator is essential in making the client aware of these possible interactions. Though combining drugs is unavoidable in many circumstances, the client must be encouraged to discuss such combinations with the treatment team to evaluate potential risks fully.

Case Examples

1. Brad was a 30-year-old, single male, living alone, who had experienced schizophrenia since the age of 18. Highly delusional, he believed he was a central figure in a religious war taking place between God and Satan. He had frequent visual hallucinations, some of which represented real people in his

TABLE 5
Drug Interactions with Antipsychotic Medications

Drug	Possible Effect
Alcohol	Nervous system depression
Anesthetics	Hypotension
Antacids	Decreased absorption of antipsychotic drug
Anticholinergics	Decreased absorption of antipsychotic drug
Anticoagulants	Increased bleeding time
Antidepressants	Increased blood levels of both drugs
Antihypertensives	Hypotension
Barbiturates	Decreased blood level of antipsychotic drug, increased depressant effect
Beta-blockers	Hypotension
Caffeine	Reduced antipsychotic drug effect
Carbamazepine	Decreased blood level of antipsychotic drug
Cigarette smoking	Decreased blood level of antipsychotic drug
Diuretics	Hypotension
Estrogen	Increased blood level of antipsychotic drug
Lithium	Possible additive toxic effect
Narcotics	Decreased ability to experience pain, increased respiratory depression
Sedatives/Hypnotics	Additive depressant effects

life while others represented historical religious figures. Atypically, he had few auditory hallucinations. Despite the severity of his symptoms, Brad's level of social functioning was surprisingly strong, indicating some interpersonal skills. He managed his own apartment and finances and worked responsibly as a newspaper carrier, required to rise at 5:00 A.M. each day. He had few relationships outside his family but did make occasional efforts to cultivate friends. Unfortunately, his bizarre ideas interfered with long-term friendships. His mother was his primary support.

Without medication, Brad was a social recluse, staying in his basement apartment for weeks at a time, staring into space, and talking to himself. After entering treatment, his behavior did not improve, because he refused to take his oral medications. He did not believe that he had any problems. The social worker could not initiate any psychosocial rehabilitation activities, because Brad was unconcerned with most routine activities of daily life. However, the worker eventually engaged Brad in treatment through careful partnership building with Brad and his mother. Brad eventually saw the agency physician and agreed to take injectable fluphenazine, which the physician chose because of its effectiveness and the possibility that Brad, in his ambivalence, would not take oral medication.

Brad's symptoms improved dramatically. With the medication, his anxiety level decreased, his preoccupations with delusions abated (but did not disappear), and he more fully attended to his interpersonal needs. Eventually, at Brad's request, and after he seemed well engaged with his treatment team, his medication was changed to include the low-potency oral medication thioridazine, with trihexiphenidyl for control of side effects. The physician believed that thioridazine was both effective and relatively safe, and its sedating quality would help control Brad's anxiety and allow him to sleep. He began with a low dose, gradually increasing the dosage until it reached a point of perceived maximum effectiveness. The social worker continued educating Brad and his mother about the expected actions and side effects of these medications.

The drugs worked well until, several years later, Brad began complaining that sedation was interfering with his ability to manage his job and social activities. Reluctant to change an effective medication regimen, Brad's doctor agreed to place him on a high-potency medication, trifluoperazine, which would not be as sedating. This eliminated Brad's drowsiness but increased his extrapyramidal symptoms of hand tremor and general anxiety. In fact, he became hypomanic, indicating that the new medication was not as effective in controlling his symptoms as the former one. In the roles of consultant/collaborator and monitor, the social worker helped evaluate these effects over time. Brad reluctantly agreed to go back to thioridazine because the doctor felt that, all things considered, this would be the most effective plan. Though not happy, Brad came to accept that all medications have side effects, and the best he could do was make decisions about them based on the overall profile. Interestingly, Brad never agreed that he had a mental disorder, believing instead that the medication was prescribed merely to control his anxiety.

2. At age 23, Valerie had been extremely low-functioning since she was 16. She was completely dependent on her parents for support and material care. She was withdrawn, anxious, hostile, delusional, and continually hallucinating. Valerie tended to have grandiose thoughts, believing that she was more talented, better looking, more famous, wealthier, and more intelligent than other people. Through these fantasies and the auditory hallucinations consistent with them, she seemed to cope with her isolation. Because she had not responded to a series of psychotropic medications, the physician recommended treating her with clozapine when the drug became available in the early 1990s. A complicating factor in this plan was that she would need to be transported almost 20 miles to a pharmacy each week for the required blood tests, because home health care was unavailable for this service. Valerie, it must be emphasized, could tolerate the intrusions of very few people. It was a major accomplishment for the social worker to engage her in the intervention process, and then convince Valerie to agree to the weekly trip to the pharmacy and allow yet another professional to draw her blood. The social worker spent much time with Valerie's parents to cultivate their partnership and support in developing the relationship with Valerie. She visited Valerie frequently to demonstrate that she could be trusted and to teach Valerie how to use this medication. The social worker further acted as an advocate in arranging for the pharmacy to accept Valerie as a client. After 6 months, Valerie agreed to try the medication and travel to the pharmacy with the worker. Though not dramatically successful, the medication seemed to control the client's anxiety to a degree that she tolerated other facets of the treatment process without much reluctance. She eventually agreed to join clubhouse and job readiness programs.

3. Glenn was diagnosed with schizophrenia at age 22. He lived with his mother for the next 5 years, very socially withdrawn and without sufficient confidence or motivation to risk any interpersonal relationships. Though he had chronic schizophrenia, his thought processes were not thoroughly dominated by his auditory hallucinations and delusions. He did hear voices: one was the soothing voice of God, and the second was an unknown other who criticized and mocked Glenn, telling him that he would always be a failure. Furthermore, he had rare tactile hallucinations, sensing someone rubbing his legs at times or smothering him while in bed. Despite this, Glenn was well attuned to the real world around him and had reasonable aspirations for job success and relationships. He also had friends, including an occasional girlfriend. Other people did not perceive him to have a mental disorder, although they did feel he was odd and rather withdrawn. Glenn had insight into his schizophrenia and worked to control his symptoms psychologically as well as through medication and rehabilitation programs.

Glenn's main problem with antipsychotic medication was that he was very sensitive to its side effects. His physician initiated five types of medicine at different points in time, none of which satisfied the client. Glenn tended to feel drowsy and experienced hypotension, significant muscle stiffness, and restricted coordination. Because Glenn experienced strong anticholinergic effects, the medications for treating EPS offered only limited assistance. He was particularly troubled by dry mouth and constipation. In addition to working on Glenn's overall rehabilitation, the social worker monitored his side effects and, in the role of consultant/collaborator, encouraged Glenn to be assertive with the physician about his reactions to the drugs. Eventually Glenn and the doctor settled on a small dose of thiothixene. Though a smaller dose than might effectively control his symptoms, it was potent enough to reduce Glenn's hallucinations and anxiety level so he could work with reasonable comfort in his overall rehabilitation program.

Antidepressant Medications

A *mood* can be understood as a pervasive, sustained emotional state that colors an individual's perceptions of the world. Though there is no truly "normal" mood, a *euthymic* state implies the absence of any serious or persistent mood problems that might negatively affect social functioning. However, all people deal at times with feelings of depression. Furthermore, even a depression that occurs frequently and interferes to some degree with effectively managing daily tasks may not signify a problem requiring professional intervention. The line between a "normal" or manageable depression and a situation requiring intervention is not clear and will be defined differently by lay persons and professionals alike. Clinical depression, or that type suggesting a mental illness, goes beyond mere feelings of sadness in relation to certain conditions of living. It consists of a lowered mood often accompanied by difficulties in thinking and psychomotor changes (either excessive physical activity from tension, or slowed physical movements and reactions). Furthermore, depression can be masked by anxiety, agitation, and obsessive thinking. However manifested, clinical depression tends to persist and impair one's ability to deal with daily life and relationships.

The range of mood disorders that may be treated with antidepressant medications includes major depression (all types), dysthymia, adjustment disorder (with depressed mood, anxiety, or mixed emotional features), bipolar disorder (depressed type), bipolar II disorder, and insomnia. Antidepressant drugs may also be used to treat some phobias and anxiety disorders including panic disorder, obsessive-compulsive disorder, and generalized anxiety disorder when they accompany or mask a primary depressive disorder. This broad listing of diagnostic categories indicates the lack of a neat correlation between diagnosis and appropriate medication intervention. All disorders are manifested by symptom clusters, which may be similar among various diagnostic categories.

Symptoms of Mood Disorders

A range of symptoms characterize how mood and associated disorders are classified. Furthermore, because the intensity and duration of the symptoms of depression vary, accurately describing symptoms is important in determining appropriate interventions, including medication. The primary diagnostic categories are described here with examples of how their symptoms impact clients.

1. **Major depression.** A severely depressed mood or loss of interest in almost all normal activities, which persists for at least two weeks and represents a significant change in the person's usual quality of functioning. Associated symptoms include weight gain or loss, sleep disturbance (insomnia or hypersomnia), psychomotor changes (physical agitation or retardation), decreased energy level, feelings of worthlessness, a general sense of guilt, concentration problems, and recurring thoughts of suicide or death. Though not every person experiencing a major depression will experience all these symptoms, most will exhibit at least five of them. Episodes of major depression

may occur only once or may recur, and may occasionally include brief psychotic features or occur as the depressive component of a bipolar disorder. However, before diagnosing depression, social workers must rule out organic causes.

Adrienne is a young adult who has recently left her family's home, where she was a victim of sexual abuse for many years. Because of her ongoing trauma, she feels extremely socially isolated after leaving home and experiences frequent episodes of depression. She is unable to sleep at night, feels worthless, feels guilty about what has been done to her, and cannot concentrate on most tasks, including her work. Contemplating suicide often, she has acted on these thoughts at times with serious attempts.

2. Dysthymia. A chronic disturbance of low mood, once known as depressive neurosis, that persists most of the time for at least two years and is characterized by such symptoms as appetite disturbance, sleep disturbance, low energy levels, low self-esteem, concentration problems, and feelings of hopelessness. Though these same symptoms are found in major depression, dysthymia tends to last longer, with milder symptoms. Many people with dysthymia function with some degree of success and do not seek treatment, because they have integrated the symptoms into their personality patterns and identities. When receiving professional intervention, people with this disorder may or may not be treated with medication. Sometimes dysthymia is identified as a secondary characteristic of another mental disorder, such as an anxiety or a substance-dependence disorder.

Judy has never felt that her life has any direction. She has failed in two marriages, works adequately but without any enthusiasm in a job for which she is overqualified, and spends time with friends without feeling much attachment to them. She thinks little of herself and does not expect her lot to change. Nevertheless, she attends to her daily responsibilities in a bland, routine manner with a persistently sad resignation.

3. Adjustment disorder. A reaction to an identifiable environmental stressor that is maladaptive, but persists for no more than 6 months. While the stressor is real, one's ability to work or maintain social relationships is more impaired than usual. This disorder is characterized by a depressed mood, tearfulness, and feelings of hopelessness (with depressed mood); nervousness, worry, and jitteriness (with anxious mood); or a combination of these symptoms (with mixed emotional features).

Peter's youngest son moved out of the family home four months ago to live on his own. Though he and his wife had planned this for months, Peter felt a severe loss once the move occurred. He could not sleep and had no appetite. Though their son keeps in touch regularly, Peter has realized that he was simply not prepared emotionally for this loss. He cannot seem to resume his own work and social routine, because his son's absence is constantly on his mind. He has lost effectiveness at work and tends to isolate himself in the house. Peter wants to talk constantly about this loss to his wife and always breaks into tears when doing so.

Specific Medications

There are three general types of antidepressant medications: cyclic antidepressants, serotonin-reuptake inhibitors, and monoamine oxidase inhibitors. The established medical practice with each is to begin by prescribing a low dose and then build to a level that seems optimally therapeutic, alleviating symptoms while limiting side effects. The most widely prescribed class of medications through the 1980s, and that which contains the most types, is the *cyclic antidepressants* (see Table 6). As discussed in the previous chapter, the mechanism of action is not clear for these drugs, but they are believed to act on the neurotransmitter norepinephrine (Snyder, 1980). Unlike the antipsychotic medications, daily dosage does not vary much among these drugs and thus does not distinguish them. Only protriptyline is manufactured in a comparatively small dose, but it does not have different side effects than the others in its class, though side effects do differ between the high- and low-potency antipsychotic medications. All the cyclic medications have relatively long half-lives, so they can be prescribed in daily doses. Most produce significant anticholinergic effects, although desipramine and nortriptyline tend not to do so. These effects, detailed in the previous section, account for most of the unpleasant effects of the medications. The drugs, all of which have a demonstrated effectiveness, require 2 weeks or more to achieve therapeutic impact. However, they have an immediate sedative effect which, while troub-

TABLE 6
Cyclic Antidepressants

Drug	Trade Name	Preparation	Usual Daily Dosage	Side Effects: Sedation	ACE
Amitriptyline	Elavil, Endep	T,P	100–200 mg	High	Low
Amoxapine	Asendin	T	200–300 mg	Low	Low
Clomipramine	Anafranil	C	150–200 mg	High	High
Desipramine	Norpramin	T,C	100–200 mg	Low	Low
Doxepin	Adapin, Sinequan	C,P	100–200 mg	High	Medium
Imipramine	Tofranil	T,C,P	100–200 mg	Medium	Medium
Maprotilene	Ludiomil	C	100–150 mg	Medium	Low
Nortriptyline	Aventyl, Pamelor	C,P	75–150 mg	Low	Low
Protriptyline	Vivactil	T	15–40 mg	Low	High
Trimipramine	Surmontil	C	100–200 mg	High	Medium

*T = Tablets, C = Capsules, P = Parenteral (injectable)
Source: Based on Gelenberg, Bassuk, & Schoonover (1990) and on Kaplan & Sadock (1993).

ling to some consumers, may provide relief to a depressed person with insomnia. The ACEs also begin at the time of first administration.

Table 6 summarizes the side effects of the cyclic antidepressants. Though these effects tend to be strongest in the first few hours after a person takes the medication, many persist. The side-effect profiles of these medications vary. For example, amoxapine, desipramine, and nortriptyline are all comparatively low in both sedation and ACEs. One might assume, on this basis, that these would be prescribed more frequently than the other medications. However, the medications are not equally effective in reducing symptoms in all consumers. Therefore, a medication with positive therapeutic benefit may be prescribed even if it has a greater amount of adverse effects. Remember, too, that physicians tend to prescribe certain medications with which they have a history of success. If necessary, however, physicians will usually experiment with several medications until they find one with a high therapeutic benefit. Because the medications can be taken once daily, it is often desirable for clients to take the medication at night. Though they will be asleep when the side effects most prominently appear, the medication will remain in their systems the entire next day.

Table 7 lists possible adverse drug interactions in people taking cyclic antidepressant medications with other substances. All these effects are negative in that they either interfere with the targeted amount of medication that reaches clients' bloodstreams or else may cause clients to be unenthusiastic about taking their medications. Besides providing face-to-face education, the social worker should make sure that the client receives a written list of these interactions. The social worker should also help the client monitor certain routine practices, such as eating habits, that may interfere with the drug's effectiveness. For example, some clients experience stomach distress if they do not take their medication with meals.

Table 8 lists the newest group of antidepressant medications, including the *serotonin-reuptake inhibitors* (fluoxetine, paroxetine, sertaline, trazodone, and venlafaxine) and *bupropion* (the action of which is not clear). These are sometimes called *atypical drugs* because they differ chemically from the cyclic antidepressants and the MAO inhibitors. The serotonin-reuptake inhibitors also differ chemically from each other as well as bupropion. As more of these compounds are marketed and prescribed, they will probably cease to be considered atypical and may in fact become the most frequently prescribed of the antidepressants. Much of their appeal comes from their side-effect profiles, markedly less characterized by ACE activity than other antidepressants, making these atypical drugs more agreeable to clients. Additionally, their overdose potential is much lower than that of other antidepressant drugs. They are effective in treating symptoms of depression, although no more so than the other classes of drugs. Their potency varies somewhat, particularly that of fluoxetine and paroxetine, which are given in relatively low milligram doses.

Table 9 outlines the side effects of the serotonin-reuptake inhibitors, and though the range of these effects overlap with the other antidepressant medications already discussed, the ACEs of the newer drugs are much less

TABLE 7
Drug Interactions with Cyclic Antidepressants

Drug	Possible Effect
Alcohol	Sedation, decreased antidepressant blood level
Amphetamines	Increased antidepressant blood level
Antihistamines	Sedation, additive anticholinergic effects
Antiparkinsonians	Additive anticholinergic effects
Antipsychotics (all)	Sedation
Antipsychotics (low potency)	Hypotension, additive anticholinergic effects
Antispasmodics	Additive anticholinergic effects
Beta-blockers	Hypotension
Carbamazepine	Decreased antidepressant blood level
Cigarette smoking	Decreased antidepressant blood level
Dilantin	Decreased antidepressant blood level
Diuretics	Hypotension
Fluoxetine	Decreased antidepressant blood level
Oral contraceptives	Increased antidepressant blood level
Phenobarbitol	Decreased antidepressant blood level
Thyroid hormones	Increased antidepressant blood level
Sedatives	Increased sedation, decreased antidepressant blood level

pronounced. More common side effects include anxiety, weight loss, headache, and gastrointestinal discomfort, but many consumers tolerate these without serious complaint. The most common side effects of bupropion are headaches, restlessness, and nausea. Though agitation and irritability may also occur, this medication is not associated with hypotension, weight gain, drowsiness, and ACEs. Table 10 includes a short list of drug interactions with the atypical antidepressants, demonstrating again that using drugs in combination tends to inhibit the effect that each drug might have by itself, and may in fact produce additional unpleasant or even dangerous effects.

A third group of antidepressant drugs, the *monoamine oxidase* (MAO) inhibitors (see Table 8), were developed in the 1950s as the first specific antidepressants. Structurally different from the antidepressant medications that have followed them, they inhibit action on enzymes that metabolize norepinephrine and serotonin. Though they relieve some refractory depressions that do not respond to other drugs, the MAO inhibitors are not usually pre-

TABLE 8
Atypical Antidepressants and MAO Inhibitors

Drug (Tablets)	Trade Name	Usual Daily Dosage
	Atypical Antidepressants	
Bupropion	Wellbutrin	100–300 mg
Fluoxetine	Prozac	20–40 mg
Paroxetine	Paxil	20–50 mg
Sertraline	Zoloft	50–200 mg
Trazodone	Desyrel	150–300 mg
Venlafaxine	Effexor	150–375 mg
	MAO Inhibitors	
Isocarboxazid	Marplan	45–90 mg
Phenylzine	Nardil	10–30 mg
Tranylaypromine	Parnate	10–30 mg

scribed first, because consumers must observe extensive dietary restrictions to avoid potentially serious adverse reactions. The MAO inhibitors react with foods rich in the amino acid derivative tyramine, prompting a hypertensive condition that can be fatal. Table 9 includes a list of their predictable side effects, and Table 11 presents many of the foods to be avoided when one takes MAO inhibitors. Because a significant amount of discipline is required of the consumer to avoid all of these foods consistently, some people do not wish to take MAO inhibitors or are not good risks for taking them. The social worker must assume an unusually strong monitoring role with clients using these medications, reviewing dietary habits with the client regularly, making sure the client keeps a written record of foods to be avoided, and quickly referring the client to the physician if the client, knowingly or by accident, consumes any prohibited foods.

In addition to dietary precautions, care must be taken in combining the MAO inhibitors with other drugs. Table 10 includes a list of the drugs most commonly taken with MAO inhibitors. In the role of educator, it is important for the social worker to ensure that the consumer of MAO drugs have this information in writing.

Case Examples

1. Matt was a 35-year-old single male who lived alone and worked part-time as a high-school communications system specialist. He suffered from a recurrent endogenous major depressive disorder, that is, his depression seemed

TABLE 9
Side Effects of Serotonin-Reuptake and MAO Inhibitors

Common	Less Common
Serotonin-Reuptake Inhibitors	
Anxiety and restlessness	Diarrhea
Constipation	Dizziness
Dry mouth	Excessive Sweating
Headache	Memory impairment
Nausea and vomiting	Sexual dysfunction (impotence)
Sedation	Weight loss
MAO Inhibitors	
Constipation	Agitation
Dizziness	Blurred vision
Dry mouth	Headache
Hypotension	Hypertension
Insominia	Hypomania
Nausea	Impaired muscle coordination
Sexual difficulties	Muscle cramps
Skin reaction	
Weakness	
Weight gain	

primarily due to heredity rather than environment. Since his early adulthood, Matt had experienced occasional episodes of suicidal ideation, hopelessness, an inability to sleep or work, and social withdrawal. The disorder ran in his family. His father and two uncles had committed suicide. Matt had himself attempted suicide twice, both times seriously—these were not the ambivalent cries for help sometimes seen in depressed persons. After the second hospitalization, he was referred to the mental health agency for psychosocial and medication treatment.

With the introduction of a moderate dose of imipramine, Matt's depression was quickly stabilized. Though the drug did produce uncomfortable side effects, including dry mouth and constipation, Matt tolerated them without complaint. Challenges for the social worker included educating Matt about the ongoing role of the medication in controlling his biological depression; encouraging his adherence to it when Matt wondered, frequently, if it

TABLE 10
Drug Interactions with Atypical Antidepressants and MAO Inhibitors

Drug	Effect
Atypical Antidepressants	
Benzodiazepines	Increases effect
Buspirone	Decreases effect
Carbamazepine	Changes levels unpredictably
Cyclic Antidepressants	Increases effect
Lithium	Changes levels unpredictably
L-Tryptophan	Toxic effect
MAO Inhibitors	
Alcohol	Hypertensive crisis
Anti-asthmatic drugs	Hypertensive crisis
Antihistamines	Hypertensive crisis
Antihypertensive drugs	Hypertensive crisis
Antisthetics with epinephrine	Hypertensive crisis
Cyclic antidepressants	Nausea, confusion, anxiety, hyperthermia, hypotension
Diuretics	Hypertensive crisis
Fluoxetine	Nausea, confusion, anxiety, hyperthermia, hypotension
Sinus, cold, and hay fever medications	Hypertensive crisis
Stimulants (amphetamines, methylphenidate, etc.)	Hypertensive crisis

was necessary; and identifying the stressors that apparently put him at greater risk for a depressive episode. Because Matt's judgment was impaired when he was depressed, it was particularly important for the social worker to see that he continued to take medication as well as seek supportive counseling. Fortunately, finding an effective medication was relatively easy in Matt's case. The psychological aspects of long-term medication represented the greatest initial concern to the social worker; however, over the course of several years, Matt accepted his need for regular medication. Responsive to the interventions, Matt continued to function well interpersonally and in his job.

2. Nora's circumstances were different. A 40-year-old working homemaker with a grade-school daughter and unemployed husband, Nora suffered from a depression that seemed to stem from the chronic stresses of

TABLE 11
Foods and Drugs to Be Avoided when Taking MAO Inhibitors

Foods	Drugs
Aged cheeses	Amphetamines and other stimulants
Banana skins	Cocaine
Beer	Decongestants
Broad-bean pods	Dental anesthetics containing epinephrine
Caffeinated beverages	Fluoxetine
Canned figs	L-Dopa
Chocolate	Meperidene
Nonfresh, fermented, or preserved fish, liver, and meats	
Pickled herring, sardines, and anchovies	
Red wine	
Yeast extracts	
Yogurt and sour cream	

overwhelming domestic responsibilities and a lack of personal support. She grew up in a culture that restricted women to the roles of mother and homemaker. Further, she accepted these roles even though she felt trapped and saw few options for resolving her family problems. Though getting an outside job was a partial solution for Nora, in that she enjoyed being away from home and with other people, it added to her range of daily pressures. Nora took two antidepressant medications, doxepin and protriptyline. Though her physician had experimented with various single drugs, Nora had not responded positively to any of them, because her depression included a significant component of anxiety. Finally, a regimen was discovered that seemed to work for her.

The social worker's concern was that Nora, after experiencing even modest relief through medication, showed no interest in psychosocial interventions. Because Nora decided not to address her personal and family problems in different ways, she ran the risk of staying depressed; that is, she was not changing the source of her depression, her environment. Instead, she was becoming medication reliant. Though Nora's medications were not physically addictive, the social worker did not want to promote such reliance indefinitely. Eventually the physician, client, and social worker had a series of meetings in which they agreed to a 2-year plan for gradually decreasing, but not eliminating, her medications. The social worker educated the client about the limitations of medication for insuring a high quality of life over the long run. In the ensuing months, the social worker was able to focus Nora more directly on identifying problem-solving practices for coping with her family problems, complicated by her husband's refusal to participate in treatment. The worker acted as a validator in helping Nora come to value her own aspirations for herself and the family, rather than subjugate herself so completely to her husband and child.

3. In contrast to Nora, Patrick had an extremely difficult time with antidepressant medication because of his sensitivity to their side effects. A strong obsessive-compulsive component to Patrick's personality contributed to his almost phobic reaction to the drugs. However, his physician felt that most of his adverse reactions were genuine, and so he worked at length with Patrick to find an appropriate type and dose. Patrick experienced some side effects common with cyclic antidepressants, such as dry mouth and blurred vision, but he also experienced urinary tract problems, impotence, and heightened anxiety. Patrick presented an unfortunate example of the wide range of discomforting side effects that medications can produce. The role of the social worker in this process was to help Patrick monitor his response to the medications, communicate them to the physician, and in a collaborative mode evaluate the extent to which Patrick continued to experience significant symptoms of depression. Patrick and his physician finally settled on one of the newer antidepressants, sertraline. Not a perfect choice, because it made Patrick feel uncomfortably anxious, it allowed the social worker finally to move beyond the issue of medication and look with Patrick at how his low mood level related to his broader coping strategies.

Mood-Stabilizing Medications

Though the antidepressant medications work toward elevating a low mood into a normal range, and though this action seems synonymous with that of the "mood-stabilizing" medications, their actions are not the same. Mood-stabilizing medications, besides raising moods, are unique in that they also lower mood levels from a manic state. That is, they treat bipolar disorder, in which one or more manic episodes are usually accompanied by one or more major depressive episodes. This disorder is thought to be fundamentally different from the purely depressive disorders, with different etiologies and courses. Mood-stabilizing medications, then, work to keep the individual's mood from swinging too far in either direction. People with a bipolar, or cyclic, mood disorder do not necessarily swing from mania to depression with equal frequency; the disorder can be primarily manic, depressed, or mixed. Even so, all these manifestations of bipolar disorder tend to respond to the same medications, although they may be used in conjunction with other medications, depending on the disorder's specific characteristics.

The symptoms of major depression, already described in this chapter, characterize the depressive phase of the bipolar disorder. Here follows a description of the symptoms of mania, as well as a description of how mood-stabilizing drugs can treat all aspects of bipolar disorder.

Symptoms of Mania

According to the DSM-IV, a manic episode is a distinct period in which a person's predominant mood is elevated, expansive, or irritable to a degree that seriously impairs relationships and occupational and social functioning. These episodes come on rapidly and may persist for a few days or several months. A diagnosis of mania requires that at least three of the following symptoms be present:

1. **Unrealistically inflated self-esteem.**

Jerry, a high-school science teacher, believes that he is the most intelligent scientist in the world and is on the verge of discovering a cure for all types of cancer.

2. **Decreased need for sleep.**

Diane stays awake for 4 days during her latest manic phase, driving around town at night and trying to get her friends out of bed to organize parties with her.

3. **Pressured speech.** The compulsion to talk both constantly and rapidly.

Debbie rambles on for hours, expressing anger at all who will not spend time with her. She quickly annoys and exhausts all who encounter her, so that they have to demand that she leave them alone. She has no idea that she alienates others with this behavior, not that such awareness would change it.

4. **Flights of ideas—Racing thoughts.**

Claire cannot maintain a train of thought for more than a minute at a time. She talks about her pets, her dislike of work, her need for friends, her inability to tolerate certain neighbors, and her loneliness, all in rapid succession, guided only by her loose associations and without allowing others time to respond to her.

5. **Distractibility.** Very short attention span and a tendency to be drawn to whatever is immediately perceived in one's environments. The attention of manic people shifts in response to extraneous stimuli that most people filter out.

Maude is sexually preoccupied with the male staff in the hospital, but they can distract her from making inappropriate comments by leading her into the kitchen. She immediately becomes preoccupied with the baking activities there.

6. **Increased goal-directed activity.** The tendency to become extremely focused on whatever captures one's attention but rarely complete any complex task. This goal-directed activity is usually unrealistic.

Despite his lack of education and experience in business and his ignorance of how to even operate a computer, Bill decides to start a software company. He spends 3 days drawing up plans for such a venture, only to abandon them when he cannot enlist the interest of his friends in the scheme.

7. Involvement in pleasurable activities that offer potentially painful consequences. For example, some manic persons go on buying sprees with credit cards.

Rod goes to the local mall and spends $800 on new shirts one night, feeling that he needs a wardrobe to fit his new image as a man of high society. Several days later, when his brother learns of the activity, he forces Rod to return the clothes.

The medications discussed in this section are used to treat all three types of bipolar disorder and some types of major depression. Mood-stabilizing medications are sometimes prescribed along with antipsychotic medication for a manic type, and antidepressants for a depressed type, of bipolar disorder. They may also be prescribed for people with major depressive disorders who do not respond to antidepressants alone. With a related mood disorder, cyclothymia, an individual experiences mood swings that may be abnormally high and low but are not severe enough to indicate a bipolar disorder. Though this may be a milder form of the disorder, it is not always clear whether it can or should be treated with mood-stabilizing medications. Because it is not frequently diagnosed, cyclothymia will not be further discussed in this book.

Specific Medications

The primary medication chosen to stabilize the mood of a client with bipolar disorder is *lithium* (see Table 12), though several other medications, originally developed as anticonvulsants, have also proven effective. *Carbamazepine* or *valproic acid* may be prescribed for mania if the consumer does not respond to lithium or has a serious adverse reaction to it, or if the mood fluctuations are characterized by rapid cycling. Lithium is relatively inexpensive because it occurs naturally. With a shorter half-life than the antipsychotic and antidepressant drugs, it must be taken more than once per day (unless in time-release form) to maintain a consistent blood level. Lithium takes 2 or more weeks to establish a therapeutic effect. Table 12 indicates the drug's availability in four preparations and several dosage levels. After a consumer's manic episode recedes, lithium must still be taken as a prophylactic agent, or a guard against recurrence. Frequently, people want to terminate a medication once they feel normal again; however, stopping medication can put the individual with bipolar disorder at risk for the recurrence of a manic episode, because the mood swings are unpredictable and alternate with long periods of normal mood (Walsh, 1989). Though physicians disagree about how long lithium should be taken after recovery from a manic phase, in most cases they prescribe it well beyond the point of stabilization.

TABLE 12
Mood-Stabilizing Medications

Drug	Trade Name	Preparation*	Usual Daily Dosage
Lithium	Lithium carbonate	C,P	900–2100 mg; 8mEq (milligram equivalents per 5 ml)
	Lithonate	C	900–2100 mg
	Eskalith	C,T (includes slow release)	900–2100 mg
	Lithobid	T (slow release)	900–2100 mg
	Lithotabs, Lithane	T	900–2100 mg
	Lithium Citrate, Cibalith-S	P	8 mEq
Valproic Acid	Depakene, Depakote	C	1200–1500 mg
Carbamazepine	Tegretol	T,P	400–1600 mg

*T = Tablets, C = Capsules, P = Parenteral (injectable)

Like other drugs, lithium is only effective as long as a constant blood level of the drug is maintained. Because the amount of the drug in the client's blood is equal to that in the nervous system, lithium levels are more easily monitored than those of most other medications. People who take lithium must become accustomed to getting blood drawn regularly, although this is done most often during their first months of taking the medication, because the difference between therapeutic and toxic levels is not great; that is, monitoring lithium is particularly important. A measurement of 1.0–1.5 mEg (milligram equivalents per liter of plasma fluid) is considered therapeutic. At lower levels, the medication has no effect, and the physician may increase the dosage. Levels higher than this amount indicate toxicity, requiring at least a temporary tapering of the medicine or a lowering of the prescribed dose. When a client is asked to get a lithium blood level drawn, a physician's order is required, and the person should not take any lithium for 12 hours prior to the test. Taking it would cause a misleading elevation in the blood level at the time of the test. Physicians usually ask clients to have their blood drawn in the morning before taking that day's first dose. This way, clients will not be without a required dose for more than a few hours, and their schedule of usage will not be disrupted.

Most of the common side effects of lithium, listed in Table 13, are considered transient and benign. However, they need to be carefully monitored, particularly with the introduction of the medication or any dosage changes,

TABLE 13
Side Effects of Lithium Carbonate

Common	Less Common	Potentially Serious (Toxic)
Confusion	Acne	Diarrhea (severe)
Diarrhea	Edema (swelling)	Dizziness
Fatigue/Lethargy	Hair loss	Drowsiness (severe)
Hand tremor		Marked tremor/twitching
Increased thirst		Muscle weakness (severe)
Increased urination		Nausea/Vomiting (severe)
Muscle weakness		Slurred speech
Nausea/Vomiting		Spastic movements in limbs or facial muscles
Weight gain		

because serious symptoms may develop. Thirst and weight gain are often experienced, with the other effects slightly less common. The potentially serious side effects listed in the table may result from the client's physical reactions to a regular dose or toxic effects from a buildup of lithium in the blood. Table 14 includes a listing of symptoms associated with mild, moderate, or severe degrees of toxicity. As soon as they are reported or observed, any unpleasant side effects must be reported to a nurse or physician because determining which adverse effects are benign and which are serious is difficult. The social worker should assume that all side effects are serious and arrange for a client's full evaluation by a physician. Severe toxicity can kill a person, implying that a dangerous overdose can also occur with lithium.

Table 15 lists drug interactions between lithium and other substances. Any effect that increases the lithium blood level is potentially serious, of course, because it can produce a toxic effect. Note that antidepressants used with lithium may prompt a manic phase, which is why antidepressants should not usually be taken with lithium. However, if the client has a primarily depressed type of bipolar disorder, lithium can enhance the therapeutic effect of the antidepressant.

Table 12 includes two alternative medications used in the treatment of bipolar disorder. Initially developed as anticonvulsant medications and still used primarily for that purpose, valproic acid and carbamazepine were later discovered to be effective for treating mood disorders and are increasingly used as such. Their actions differ from the action of lithium (see Chapter 3). As is true with many drugs, the nature of their effect is hypothetical, but they may retard the kindling process in the nervous system that can set off either convulsions or manic episodes (see again Chapter 3). Like lithium, they need

TABLE 14
Signs of Lithium Toxicity

Mild/Moderate (1.5–2.0 mEq per L*)	Moderate/Severe (2.0–2.5 mEq per L*)	Severe (Over 2.5 mEq per L*)
	Gastrointestinal System	
Abdominal pain (persistent/ severe)	Anorexia	Coma
Dry mouth		Decreased urination
Nausea/Vomiting (persistent)		Kidney failure
	Neurological System	
Dizziness (severe)	Blurred vision	
Drowsiness (severe)	Confusion (severe)	
Lethargy or excitement (severe)	Convulsions	
Marked tremor or twitching	Coordination impairment	
Muscle weakness (severe)	Delirium	
Slurred speech	EEG (electroencephalogram) changes	
	Fainting	
	Hyperactive muscle reflexes	
	Spastic movements in limbs, face	
	Stupor	
	Circulatory System	
	Arrhythmia (irregular heart beat)	
	Lowered blood pressure	

*Milligram equivalents per liter
Source: Adapted from "Psychopharmacology and Electroconvulsive Therapy," by J. M. Silver, M.D., & S. C. Yudofsky. In J. A. Talbott, R. E. Hales, & S. C. Yudofsky (Eds.), *The American Psychiatric Press Textbook of Psychiatry,* 2nd Edition, p. 970. Copyright © 1994 American Psychiatric Association Press. Used with permission.

TABLE 15
Drug Interactions with Mood-Stabilizing Medications

Drug	Effect
Lithium	
Antibiotics	Increased toxicity
Antidepressants	Possible mania, tremor
Anti-inflammatory drugs	Increased toxicity
Antipsychotic drugs	Increased toxicity
Cardiovascular drugs	Possible toxicity
Diuretics	Increased excretion
Loop/Distal-tube diuretics	Increased concentration
Carbamazepine	
Benzodiazepines	Decreased effect
Cyclic antidepressants	Decreased effect
Dilantin	Unpredictable
Valproic acid	Decreased effect
Valproic Acid	
Alcohol, other depressants	Increased effect
Antidepressants	Increased effect
Aspirin	Increased anticoagulance

to be taken more than once daily to maintain a therapeutic level. Their use does not require frequent blood tests, however, because they do not share lithium's characteristic of being evenly distributed throughout the circulatory and nervous systems. One advantage of these medications over lithium is that, when effective, they begin to stabilize the consumer's mood in as few as 2 to 5 days. Because valproic acid has also been found to increase the effects of antidepressants, it is frequently used for this purpose as well. Carbamazepine does not share this effect and may in fact decrease the effectiveness of some medications. These interactions as well as others are outlined in Table 15.

Table 16 lists the side effects of these two drugs. The common side effects are predictable, generally transient, and similar to those of lithium. However, the less common side effects may be more troubling than those associated

TABLE 16
Side Effects of Other Mood-Stabilizing Medications

Common	Less Common
Carbamazepine	
Confusion, memory disturbance	Anemia
Dizziness	Cardiac conduction
Lowered white blood cell count (benign)	Double vision
Nausea	Dulling of vision
Sedation	Hepatitis
Skin rash	Impaired muscle coordination
Tremor	Lowered white blood cell count
	Speech impediment
Valproic Acid	
Hair loss	Anxiety
Nausea/Vomiting	Depression
Sedation	Hand tremor
Vomiting	Headache
	Hepatitis
	Impaired muscle coordination
	Pancreatitis

with lithium. As a general rule, lithium is the first drug chosen for treating bipolar disorder, because it has been used and tested for so long with satisfactory results.

Case Examples

1. Sharon was a single, 23-year-old college student referred for outpatient care following her hospitalization for treatment of a manic episode. She had been psychotic during her mania, characterized by sleeplessness, hyperactivity, racing thoughts, hypersexuality, paranoid delusions, and alcohol abuse. Sharon, who had never lived away from her parents, was well stabilized on lithium and thiothixene at the time of her referral. An initial trial of haloperidol had to be discontinued because, in combination with the lithium, it had produced severe muscle stiffness, particularly in her arms and neck. Sharon was seen monthly, or more often as requested, by the agency psychiatrist. The social worker always participated in these meetings to ensure collaborative continuity of care. Maintained with periodic adjustments throughout her agency involvement, the medications kept Sharon's mood stable. The thiothixene was gradually eliminated but had to be reintroduced in small doses on a few occasions when her anxiety level escalated because of environmental stress. Her bothersome side effects included weight gain and a mild tremor in one hand.

Sharon's mood disorder was exacerbated by environmental stresses, which required regular attention from the social worker. While outwardly successful, Sharon's father was alcoholic and physically abused his wife. Though most of the children had detached themselves from the family turmoil, Sharon remained materially and emotionally dependent on her parents. She became uncontrollably anxious whenever they left town, even for short weekend trips. With only two semesters remaining in her college curriculum, Sharon had begun to fail her classes; she later admitted that this was an effort to postpone the onset of adult responsibility. The course of her bipolar disorder was connected to these issues. As a result, the social worker met with Sharon weekly to help her develop strengths for coping with various age-appropriate responsibilities and to become less reliant on her parents. They worked on her fears, lack of confidence, poor self-image, and awkward interpersonal patterns, including her family and siblings in the process. To keep from driving the parents away, the worker did not confront them about certain family problems. Instead, the worker educated them about medications and the impact of mental illness on family systems. The worker invited the family to the agency's education and support group, which they did attend, although irregularly. The worker also validated Sharon's feelings of dependence, of which she was ashamed but which she needed to accept and work through. Because Sharon tended to be passive, the worker acted as an advocate for her regarding vocational training and clubhouse involvement.

Sharon made steady progress in her treatment, although it came slowly with setbacks. She experienced two additional manic episodes over the next 4 years. The first occurred when she secretly stopped taking her medications, prompting a regression to avoid a planned but dreaded move into an apartment. The second episode took place one year later when Sharon was beginning a new job and her parents were out of town for several weeks. This time, she needed short-term hospitalization to get stabilized. Because the course of Sharon's bipolar disorder was closely related to her self-image, family situation, and management of stress, all these factors needed to be addressed in a holistic manner that included but was not limited to her medication treatment.

2. Mark, age 20, had already experienced three hospitalizations for manic episodes characterized by hyperactivity, delusions of power and importance, excessive spending, and ventures into high-risk investment projects that inevitably failed because of his poor judgment. His episodes of depression were relatively mild. During his most recent episode, Mark responded quickly to a combination of lithium and the antipsychotic drug trifluoperazine. The medications so effectively stabilized his mood that within three months he was taking a prophylactic dose of lithium. Though Mark did not report any side effects, his social worker and physician suspected that he was trying to present himself as positively as possible and might withhold negative reactions. Thus, because the client's history suggested that he might not present his mental status and use of medications accurately, the social worker's role of monitor was very important.

Negotiating appropriate social work intervention with Mark was problematic because he believed that his problem was purely a chemical imbalance beyond his control and that exploring his style of functioning as a way to develop improved self-control was irrelevant. However, the social worker did initially help Mark secure an apartment and job-training assistance. Soon, however, Mark began to miss or cancel appointments with the social worker. He seemed to feel that his life was back on track and that he could manage life adequately without help. Though the temptation often exists for clients with bipolar disorder to ignore psychosocial interventions when they are stable, the social worker was uncomfortable with what he perceived as a lack of capacity to exercise sound judgment, which might prompt another manic episode. Paradoxically, Mark tended to be most at risk for mania when his social, financial, and vocational problems stabilized. He did remain free of symptoms for a year on his small dose of lithium; however, his mania escalated again while he was absent from the treatment process. The social worker, who had formed a partnership with Mark's father, learned from him that the client was developing symptoms of mania, but by this time Mark had given up his apartment and was traveling out of state.

3. Todd had a more subtle manic disorder, in that he never exhibited dramatic manic episodes; in fact, he had been diagnosed for several years with dysthymic depression and treated with a moderate dose of nortriptylene. He tended to mask his depression in an effort to conceal, perhaps even to himself, his situational problems. His social worker and physician were aware that Todd had experienced serious losses in the past few years, including the bankruptcy of his small business and the moving away of his adult son, and were aware of his isolation from previous sources of support, including his church. Despite being articulate and superficially personable, Todd felt alone and unhappy.

One winter, Todd made a videotape for his son in which he described his reasons for wanting to die. After he sent the tape to his son, he drove halfway across the country to a mountain range and hiked aimlessly into the woods. Notified of possible trouble by Todd's son, the police located Todd's car and found Todd asleep under a tree and unprotected from the cold weather. They transported him to a psychiatric hospital, where he was diagnosed for the first time as having a bipolar II disorder, which features depression. The manic episode, potentiated by Todd's biological predisposition, was prompted by his growing sense of helplessness. Because mood-stabilizing medications sometimes make antidepressant medications work better for depressed people, Todd's agency physician did not question the value of adding carbamazepine to his regimen and thus complied with the recommendations of the hospital staff. Todd responded positively and recovered quickly from his hypomanic state. Discharged within a week from the hospital, he resumed working with his agency social worker and physician, this time more productively. The social worker assumed the roles of consultant/ collaborator and monitor in evaluating Todd's response to the new regimen.

ANTI-ANXIETY MEDICATIONS

Anxiety is difficult to isolate as a symptom of emotional distress because in its various forms it occurs in the daily lives of all people. A normal, functional emotion built into human physiology, anxiety helps people anticipate threats that may become real. It differs from fear in that the threat is unrealistic or unknown. Anxiety prompts an individual to react before a problem becomes unmanageable or traumatic. However, in its more severe, unfocused, and chronic forms, anxiety may hinder normal functioning.

Symptoms of Anxiety

Anxiety has both psychological and physical components. In terms of its psychological effects, anxiety becomes problematic for an individual when it (1) creates a sense of powerlessness to resolve a problem, (2) suggests an impending danger that is in fact unrealistic, (3) produces an exhausting state of alertness, as if the person were facing an emergency when none exists, (4) produces a level of self-absorption that interferes with effective problem solving, and (5) creates doubt about the nature of reality when a perceived threat is processed. The physical manifestations of anxiety include increased heart rate, disturbed breathing, trembling, sweating, and motor tension. The DSM-IV outlines three aspects of anxiety—apprehension, uneasiness, and tension—that stem from a person's anticipation of internal or external danger. Dysfunctional anxiety is phobic when it is focused on some object, situation, or activity; and free-floating when it persists without any particular object. Manifested as panic, anxiety appears in bursts of unexpected and overwhelming tension. Anxiety disorders are common in all phases of a person's life and appear as a secondary characteristic of many other disorders.

In fact, almost all mental disorders include some symptoms of anxiety. However, the major types of anxiety disorders that may be treated in part with anti-anxiety medications include generalized anxiety disorder, panic disorder, agoraphobia and other phobic conditions, obsessive-compulsive disorder, posttraumatic stress disorder, acute stress disorder, somatization disorder, adjustment disorders featuring anxiety, separation anxiety, overanxious disorder, and insomnia. Some, but not all types, of anti-anxiety medications may also be used in the temporary treatment of substance withdrawal, including that of alcohol.

Rather than describe all the specific symptoms of anxiety, as we did for the other major disorders, we will simply list and characterize the most common anxiety disorders. Anxiety symptoms tend to occur together rather than in isolation, even through a severe and long-lasting case. Because the various diagnostic conditions overlap quite a bit, we here highlight the most distinguishable symptoms of anxiety within the DSM-IV diagnostic categories:

1. **Motor tension.** Trembling, twitching, feeling shaky, muscle tensions, muscle aches and soreness, restlessness, easy fatiguability

2. **Autonomic nervous system hyperactivity.** Shortness of breath, the feeling of being smothered, accelerated heart rate, sweating or feeling cold, clammy hands, dry mouth, dizziness, lightheadedness, abdominal distress (including nausea and diarrhea), hot flashes or chills, frequent urination, difficulty swallowing, the sensation of a lump in the throat

3. **Hypervigilance.** Feeling edgy or keyed up, an exaggerated startle response, difficulty concentrating or feeling that the mind is going blank, trouble falling asleep or staying asleep, irritability

Examples of the common anxiety disorders follow. In making a diagnostic assessment, clinicians must determine that the associated symptoms are not due to any organic factors that would imply different or additional interventions.

1. **Panic disorder.**

Virtually housebound because of her fear of experiencing panic attacks when outdoors, Geneva cannot go out to shop, drive anywhere in her car, or even take short walks because, when outside, she feels certain she will die. Her heart races, her limbs tremble, she cannot breathe, and she feels as if she is going to have a heart attack or pass out. She has been subject to these terrifying experiences since living alone after her husband's death. The only time she feels safe is in bed. She can go out in the company of others, but only because she feels that she will be assisted if any physical problems develop.

2. **Agoraphobia.**

Though Curt does not want to go outside, this is only a problem during the daytime. He feels that everyone is looking at him and perceiving him as an inadequate human being. Rather than face this embarrassment day after day, Curt organizes his life around his fear of being in open public places. He works a night shift, does all of his shopping at night when few others are out, has no social life, and spends most weekends at the home of his extended family, where he feels safe, in a city 40 miles away. Curt never feels panic, but he is sufficiently distressed by anxiety that his life is ruled by fears of being in public.

3. Social phobia.

A reasonably effective grade-school teacher, Heather cannot tolerate attending the weekly teacher meetings. Because she feels she has less talent than others on the staff, she fears that she will embarrass herself in these meetings, where all are expected to contribute to discussions about faculty policies. Heather has no similar anxieties elsewhere in her life. Still, the thought of these meetings fills her with intense fear and makes her restless, nauseous, irritable, unable to concentrate on her work, and unable to sleep during the preceding nights. As she develops many excuses for missing the sessions, her performance evaluations suffer because the sessions are required as part of her job.

4. Specific phobia.

Mark, also a schoolteacher, is terrified of cats, for reasons he cannot understand. Normally this does not interfere with his ability to function, but whenever he encounters a stray cat on the playground, for example, he actually has to flee in terror. Though most people find this amusing, it is genuinely distressing to Mark, who has to remove himself from social and other work situations whenever he sees a cat or suspects that one is nearby.

5. Obsessive-compulsive disorder. Obsessions are persistent thoughts or impulses; compulsions are repetitive behaviors. Both are characteristics that some people develop to prevent anxiety from entering their conscious lives.

Tracy attempts to control her persistent, free-floating anxiety with compulsive activity rituals. Each morning she performs a precise routine in getting dressed and groomed, including brushing her teeth and hair with the same number of strokes. She cleans her house in the same exacting way, and becomes extremely upset if anything interferes with these routines, such as phone calls or unexpected guests. Every day by noon she completes her schedule of rituals and can relax for the rest of the day.

6. Posttraumatic stress disorder.

Brian was in a car accident 6 years ago in which his father was killed, and he was seriously injured himself but recovered fully. Now, several years later, he has begun to feel increasingly anxious about traveling by car, particularly whenever he encounters an intersection resembling the one where his accident took place. Some days he feels so afraid that he will not take even short trips in the car. He has come to understand that he responds in near panic to cars resembling the one in his accident or to being in a place that resembles the scene of the accident.

7. Generalized anxiety disorder.

Having experienced much interpersonal and family trauma in her life, Roberta has developed a personality characterized by excessive worry about routine life events. She worries about her health, her family's health, her future, her finances, her personal safety when out in public, being alone, and some less routine matters, such as the condition of the ozone layer and her personal astrology. Not focused on any realistic issues that might generate anxiety, she instead projects her continuous free-floating anxiety on whatever happens to confront her at a particular time. Roberta can admit that her concerns are irrational but nevertheless cannot seem to change her outlook.

Specific Medications

Three types of medication are used to treat anxiety disorders: *benzodiazepines, beta-blockers,* and the *atypical medication buspirone.* The *benzodiazepines* comprise the largest class of anti-anxiety medications and have been the most frequently prescribed since their introduction in the late 1950s. Table 17 lists these drugs with their brand names and usual daily dosages. While the dosage range and half-lives of these drugs vary, they act similarly by enhancing the effectiveness of natural GABA, which inhibits neurons, in the central nervous system (see Chapter 3). The drugs all take effect relatively rapidly, un-

TABLE 17
Benzodiazepine Medications

Drug	Trade Name	Preparation*	Usual Daily Dosage
Alprazolam	Xanax	T	0.5–6 mg
Chlordiazepoxide	Librium	T,C,P	15–100 mg
Clonazepam	Klonipin	T	0.5–10 mg
Clorazepate	Tranxene	T,C	7.5–60 mg
Diazepam	Valium	T,C,S,P	2–60 mg
Estazolam	ProSom	T	1–2 mg
Flurazepam	Dalmane	T	15–30 mg
Halazepam	Paxipam	T	60–160 mg
Lorazepam	Ativan	T,P	2–6 mg
Midazolam	Versed	P	7.5–45 mg
Oxazepam	Serax	T,C	30–120 mg
Prazepam	Centrax	T,C	20–60 mg
Quazepam	Doral	T	7.5–30 mg
Temazepam	Restoril	T	15–30 mg
Triazolam	Halcion	T	0.125–0.25 mg

*T = Tablets, C = Capsules, S = Solution, P = Parenteral (injectable)

like the other medications discussed thus far. The consumer may begin to experience relief from anxiety between 30 minutes and 2 hours after taking the drugs. Their short half-life means that, unless taken on an as-needed basis to control anxiety, the medication must be taken two or three times per day to maintain a therapeutic blood level.

Table 18 summarizes the side effects of the benzodiazepine medications, which tend to be mild and transient. Dizziness, drowsiness, and impaired muscle coordination are those most frequently reported. Sometimes clients

TABLE 18
Side Effects of Anti-Anxiety Medications

Common	Less Common
Benzodiazepines	
Confusion	Allergic skin reaction
Dizziness	Blurred vision
Drowsiness	Depression
Headache	Dry mouth
Impaired muscle coordination	Nausea/Vomiting
Irritability/Restlessness	Sexual impairment
Memory impairment	Weakness
Beta-Blockers	
Hypotension	Abdominal pain/diarrhea
Sedation	Depression (mild)
Slowed heart rate	Dizziness
	Insomnia
	Nausea/Vomiting
	Sexual impairment
Buspirone	
Dizziness	Insomnia
Headache	Nervousness
Nausea	Skin rash
	Sweating

experience gastrointestinal distress as well as irritability and memory problems. However, these side effects tend to abate after several weeks. Other, less common side effects include vision impairment and decreased sexual drive. Depending on the duration of and the level of discomfort experienced from these effects, the client may be advised to try another medication. The benzodiazepines also may become physically addicting over time. Because there is no clear rule of thumb about when a person will develop a risk of dependence, and though many clients use the drug safely for years, clinicians should always consider addiction a possibility and use it as a rationale not to prescribe the drugs for an extended time. Also, to prevent a withdrawal reaction, they should taper clients off the medication when it is being discontinued and advise clients not to take themselves off these medications abruptly. Table 19 lists the withdrawal symptoms, generally defined as the experience of a rebound effect, with the most common being anxiety, restlessness, headache, muscular pains, and diarrhea, and the most serious, seizures. All can be avoided by proper precautions when adjusting or terminating the benzodiazepines.

Table 20 lists substances with which the benzodiazepines interact to produce a differential drug response. Several substances, including all foods, decrease the rate of gastrointestinal absorption, so that the drug takes effect most quickly when taken on an empty stomach. Even so, rate of absorption does not affect the drug's effectiveness. Some medications increase the blood level of the drug, enhancing its anti-anxiety action but also its side effects. Anticonvulsant medication decreases its blood level, while the final group of drugs listed depresses a consumer's central nervous system. Thus, for example, drinking alcohol will result in a feeling of intoxication or sedation beyond what the drinking would produce by itself.

TABLE 19
Benzodiazepine Withdrawal Symptoms

Transient	True Withdrawal
Agitation	Delirium
Anxiety	Depression
Blurred vision	Enhanced sensory perceptions
Diarrhea	Hypothermia
Dizziness	Nausea
Headache	Paranoia
Insomnia	Seizures
Muscle aches	Tinnitis
	Tremors

Table 21 lists the other anti-anxiety medications. The *beta-blockers* do not impact the central nervous system but target the autonomic nervous system to reduce the physiological manifestations of anxiety, including increased heart rate and sweating. When clients do not experience symptoms, they do not perceive that they are anxious. These medications were originally developed for lowering blood pressure in people with hypertension. The several types of these medications come in four preparations. Though their dosages are greater than those of the benzodiazepines, their strength does not necessarily differ. An advantage of these medications is that they are not addicting. Even so, they are prescribed less often than the benzodiazepines because while they act quickly, they also do not last long. Their side effects, as listed in Table 19, tend to be minimal, and primarily include sedation, hypotension, and dizziness. These medications are generally not prescribed for people with cardiac problems or asthma.

The final type of anti-anxiety medication is *buspirone* (see Table 21). A newer option for the treatment of anxiety, it is intended to have a similar effect to the benzodiazepines. However, because it is a weak partial agonist of one type of serotonin receptor, it exhibits a fundamentally different action. Buspirone is similar to the benzodiazepines and beta-blockers in that it has a short half-life and must be taken three times daily to maintain a therapeutic level. However, it does not act quickly, becoming effective 2 to 4 weeks after

TABLE 20
Drug Interactions with Benzodiazepines

Drug	Effect
Alcohol and other sedatives	Increased nervous system depression
Antacids	Decreased absorption efficiency
Antibiotics	Increased blood levels
Anticonvulsants	Decreased blood levels
Antihistamines	Increased nervous system depression
Barbiturates	Increased nervous system depression
Cimetidine	Increased blood levels
Cyclic antidepressants	Increased nervous system depression
Disulfram	Increased blood levels
Estrogen	Increased blood levels
Fluoxetine	Increased blood levels
Isoniazid	Increased blood levels
Tagamet	Increased blood levels

TABLE 21
Other Anti-Anxiety Medications

Drug	Trade Name	Preparation*	Usual Daily Dose
		Beta-Blockers	
Atenolol	Tenormin	T,P	50–100 mg
Metoprolol	Lopressor	T,P	150–300 mg
Nadolol	Corgard	T	80–240 mg
Propranolol	Inderal	T,C,S,P	240–420 mg
		Buspirone	
Buspirone	Burspar	T	15–30 mg

*T = Tablets, C = Capsules, S = Solution, P = Parenteral (injectable)

initiation. Its major advantages are that it is not sedating and carries no risk of physical addiction. Its side effects, the most common of which are headache, nausea, and dizziness, are listed in Table 18 (on p. 99).

Case Examples

1. Lynne was an unemployed 43-year-old divorced white female with two adult children and a history of labile moods and dependent relationships. Several months after divorcing her husband of 20 years, she entered counseling with a psychiatrist for help with anxiety and panic attacks. She was having great difficulty living on her own and coped with stress by withdrawing to her bedroom in states of high anxiety. Lynne was hospitalized for several weeks after becoming suicidal. Her doctor initiated treatment with both antidepressant and anti-anxiety medications, but soon after discharge she was tapered to a moderate dose of the benzodiazepine alprazolam. This became Lynne's standard medication regimen, which persisted through her transfer to a mental health facility.

Lynne received psychosocial intervention from a social worker and medication from a physician. After several years of intervention in which she reached many of her psychosocial goals, including a successful employment experience, her physician and worker became concerned that she was psychologically dependent on the medication. Though the drug served a therapeutic purpose, Lynne discounted the need to make further adjustments in her coping strategies and relationships with family, friends, and employers. Fearing a return of anxiety attacks, Lynne initially resisted the suggestion to change medication but eventually agreed to a gradual 1-year plan to transfer from the benzodiazepine to the nonaddictive drug buspirone. The social worker, who met with Lynne much more frequently than the physician did, assumed a crucial monitoring and consultant/collaborator role through this process. Every month or two, the physician decreased the alprazolam by 0.25 milligrams daily and increased the other drug. She also increased her visits with the client. If Lynn experienced high anxiety, she could call her social worker between their biweekly visits. These instances usually came about because of Lynne's ambivalence about the change in medications rather than her primary emotional disorder. The social worker was careful to validate rather than discount Lynne's reactions to the change so that she would not feel a need to either hide or exaggerate them. The transition proceeded smoothly. Eighteen months later, the client was functioning well with a modest dose of buspirone. She did not report any bothersome side effects from the medication.

2. Don's treatment had a different outcome. Like Lynne, he had a history of extreme anxiety in all interpersonal situations. His symptoms were more debilitating, however, in that every situation in which he needed to be assertive made him panic. For example, he could not bring himself to approach his son's football coach about helping out during the team's practices. His marriage and job were both in jeopardy because he could not negotiate any conflicts with others. Clearly in need of medication to get through his life, Don took a high dose of diazepam. He also sought psychosocial support for developing personal strengths and assertiveness. However, Don frequently took his entire daily dose of medication in the morning, and extra medication later in the day, calling his social worker or doctor to request additional drugs toward the end of each month. Furthermore, he occasionally missed his appointments with the social worker. The social worker soon saw that Don was not participating fully in the treatment program. Though appropriate to his care, the drugs were never intended to provide a long-term solution to his problems. The social worker and physician needed to address his fears of confronting his problems through psychosocial means. The social worker and physician carefully collaborated on the details of a strategy to set a limit with Don, asserting that he could not see the physician unless he kept his biweekly sessions with the social worker. Don tested these limits for several months by continuing to miss some sessions while requesting extra medication. Finally, when confronted again by the social worker, he decided to leave the agency. As expected, he did so passively, by ignoring his appointments and the social worker's calls. However, the agency staff did not deny Don his medication, but rather gave him a final month's supply to prevent withdrawal symptoms and give him ample time to seek services from another agency.

3. Vanessa, a divorced 35-year-old woman living with her sister, had milder, or less apparent, anxiety than these other clients did. Though she appeared cocky, confident, and assured, this outward demeanor masked a strong sense of inferiority and discomfort around others. She experienced chronic unemployment because, whenever she felt threatened by her employers, Vanessa acted out her anxiety with inappropriate, aggressive outbursts and later resigned in embarrassment. Assuming that she was more capable and functional than she really was, some mental health workers suspected that she was requesting medications unnecessarily. She received a moderate dose of the benzodiazepine clorazepate for several years, but at the same time she was expected to work on her interpersonal problems with a social worker. However, she did not develop a sense of trust in any professional helpers for many years because of her intense wariness of others, tending to alienate many social workers who suspected erroneously that she had a primary personality disorder. Her feelings of anxiety had to be validated so she would not feel so compelled to maintain her defenses. Once she found an accepting social worker and focused on her own distress rather than her aggressiveness, she could make strides in her personal growth and eventually be weaned off the medication. Vanessa is an example of the client who masks very real anxieties and requires a great deal of careful assessment and patience from a social worker who can tolerate an antagonistic defensive style. Clearly, one does not always demonstrate the classic outward signs of anxiety when experiencing serious symptoms.

Summary

This chapter has consisted of discussions of four major classes of medication; the symptoms they treat; the types of medication within those classes; and their effects, positive and negative, on clients who use them as part of their intervention strategies. In the next chapter we turn to special issues with psychotropic medication as they apply to specific populations of clients.

CHAPTER 5

INTERVENTION CONCERNS WITH SPECIAL POPULATIONS

A major strength of the social work profession is its appreciation of human diversity—the understanding that all persons are unique and that members of different genders, age groups, and racial and ethnic populations tend to experience some biological as well as social differences. This appreciation of diversity impacts psychopharmacology as much as every other aspect of social work intervention. In the previous two chapters, we outlined the actions and impact of psychotropic medications, as well as what they implied for the social worker's six roles. However, besides those general actions, distinct reactions to some medications occur in some special populations. Because few other professions are educated about issues of diversity, social workers have a particularly important responsibility to understand these differences and communicate their implications to the client, physician, and others involved in client care. However, there is not universal agreement about these specific effects; much remains to be learned about how different populations react to psychotropic drugs. In this chapter, we will focus on the following groups: women, the elderly, children and adolescents, members of several racial and ethnic populations, and people diagnosed with both mental illness and substance abuse.

GENDER DIFFERENCES

General Considerations

More likely than men to take prescription medications, women consume 70% of all psychotropic drugs. They are more likely than men to report the medications they used in the past year. They also report greater psychotropic drug use between the ages of 45 and 64 than in other age groups (Robbins & Clayton, 1989). Of course, the reason men tend not to report all their own medication use may be a "psychological Calvinism," or a reluctance to admit use even when drugs are helpful. Even so, it is ironic that women have been traditionally underrepresented in pharmacological research (Rodin & Ickovics, 1990). This lack of data presents serious limitations in understanding the effectiveness and risks of medication for women. Further comparative gender research is essential because of known physiologic differences between men and women in hormone levels, brain structure, and body mass composition. For instance, researchers have established that reproductive hormones impact both the absorption and metabolism of drugs. Gender differences may significantly affect a given drug's therapeutic efficacy, side effects, and interactions with other drugs. For example, one comparative study found that women were more frequently diagnosed with depressive disorders and received more drug prescriptions for their treatment, but men responded more positively to antidepressant medications and also experienced more adverse effects (Rodin & Ickovics, 1990). The psychological and social side effects of drug use, discussed in Chapter 4, suggest another important area for study: why women are prescribed a disproportionate amount of drugs. As researchers, social workers, might productively monitor their own caseloads for trends in medication use and response along gender lines.

Several studies have reported neurotransmitter differences between the sexes. These differences include rates of serotonin-binding capacity, which is greater even in adolescent girls than in adolescent boys (Biegon & Gruener, 1992). One study concludes that a serotonin-response difference causes women to react to stress with greater physiological affect, and to respond therapeutically to different doses of some anti-anxiety medications than men (Blanchard, Yudko, Rodgers, & Blanchard, 1993). Researchers have also studied serotonin's role in producing affective disorders related to the menstrual cycle (Veeninga, Westenberg, & Weusten, 1990). Though the practical applications of these differences are not great in most cases, they provide evidence of gender-specific medication effects that the social worker should note.

Most research about medication's effects on women focuses on pregnancy. The physician and social worker must consider four general issues when deciding which medications, of all types, to give a pregnant woman:

1. The risks and benefits of taking medication with regard to the mother's overall mental status
2. The effects of medication on the fetus
3. The long-term physical effects on the newborn (some of which may not become apparent for years)
4. The effects on the mother and newborn together if a current mental disorder is inadequately treated (Janicak, Davis, Preskorn, & Ayd, 1993).

In general, it is considered best to prescribe no medications for a pregnant woman, particularly during the first trimester, when the fetus faces its highest risk of damage. The blood-brain barrier, as well as the blood-placenta barrier, is the layer of fatty tissue that serves as a boundary between the circulatory system and those other organs, and which medication must penetrate to produce an effect within those sites. Medications cross the blood-placenta barrier as well as the blood-brain barrier, and thus become part of the fetus's bloodstream. Additionally, physicians should avoid prescribing medications during breast-feeding, because most drugs pass through the milk, directly affecting the newborn. Professionals may also discourage breast-feeding in many cases. Though abstinence from drugs is always the physically safest strategy for the fetus or baby, it cannot always be implemented, because the physician and social worker must carefully weigh all four of the above considerations in prescription and medication management. However, studies about the possible adverse effects of medication on fetuses are not extensive. Avoidance of medication is based largely on the possibility of adverse effects rather than their inevitability. Nevertheless, the social worker as educator must fully inform the expectant mother and her significant others about special risks in pregnancy.

By implication, the intensity of interventions other than psychotropic medication should increase during pregnancy to offset any precautionary drug measures taken by the physician. These interventions include supportive counseling, client and family education, assistance with mental status monitoring, and encouragement of client participation in psychosocial rehabilitation programs. They also allow the physician and social worker to monitor the client's physical and mental status more closely. The social worker may need to link up with community agencies that provide prenatal services.

Classes of Medication

When the risks of not taking medication, including unmanageable symptoms and self-care limitations, are more serious than those of using it, professionals must follow several principles. For psychotic disorders, it may be safer to use the high-potency medications (such as haloperidol and trifluoperazine), which have fewer negative effects on the fetus, such as sedation, hypotension, gastrointestinal slowing, and tachycardia. The social worker can expect these medications to be discontinued several weeks before delivery so that the newborn will not experience problems related to side effects. Unless she has chosen to breast-feed, the client should resume psychotropic medication immediately after delivery, particularly because there is always the possibility of postpartum psychosis. The social worker should thus be prepared to advocate medication. Furthermore, the physician may avoid or minimize antiparkinsonian drug treatment, because this presents a further risk to the newborn. The nursing baby may experience infant extrapyramidal effects if his or her mother consumes these medications.

Antidepressant medications are also best avoided during pregnancy. Some antidepressants, such as nortriptyline and desipramine, have been studied in this regard more extensively than others. Because they have not demonstrated adverse effects, they are considered relatively safe. Looking for alternatives to medications during pregnancy, the physician may consider electroconvulsive therapy, now used more frequently than before to treat depression in all populations. Taking a newly pregnant mother off medications must be done gradually so as not to cause withdrawal in either the mother or the fetus. The social worker may need to increase his or her educational and family support roles through this process so that the client and her family understand the rationale for these changes and can actively help maintain a safe environment. Again, because postpartum depression may occur at any time up to 6 months after delivery, it may be necessary to begin antidepressant therapy at any time following delivery, at which point such therapy is safe.

Mood-stabilizing medications are more risky than those in other classes for the pregnant client. Lithium use may cause fetal heart problems, specifically the development of the large vessels of the heart. Carbamazepine has been associated with various developmental delays and cranial defects in newborns. Though these studies are inconclusive, the possibility of serious negative effects makes the use of mood-stabilizing medications an extremely delicate problem. When they are used, the fetus needs to be monitored with sonography to detect any adverse changes. Thus, the social worker may need to assume some responsibility for planning and advocacy so that such procedures occur promptly and regularly. Furthermore, because a pregnant woman's blood volume increases and its levels become more unstable, lithium becomes more difficult to monitor during pregnancy. Here again, the social worker's roles need to expand to provide alternative services and to help the client monitor effects for the physician and treatment team.

The effects of anti-anxiety medications in pregnancy are also largely untested. There is evidence that lorazepam accumulates less in fetal tissue than some other similar medications (Janicak et al., 1993). Diphenhydramine, on the other hand, should not be prescribed, because it may cause withdrawal complications for the newborn. Because this medication is available without prescription, the social worker must ensure that the client is aware of pregnancy risks even with these types of drugs. For instance, "neonatal withdrawal syndrome" can occur with anti-anxiety medications.

Psychotropic medication may adversely affect the sexual functioning of both men and women. Symptoms may include a decrease in sex drive for both, an impaired ability to ejaculate or maintain erections for men, and an inhibition for orgasm for women. Because many clients are uncomfortable discussing these issues with professionals, part of the social worker's task in the partnership model of practice is to create an environment where these concerns, if present, can be shared. The social worker must also determine if raising the possibility of these side effects, which are not inevitable, is worth the risk of increasing the client's anxiety. If the client is not sexually active while using medications, some of these effects may not be problematic; however, they will still impact a client's sense of self. Of course, adverse effects present a major problem to clients who wish to be sexually active. Physicians can make medication adjustments that may alleviate these side effects. In any case, the social worker must explore this area of the client's life as well as others to provide a relevant assessment in the event that psychotropic medications will be used.

Older Adults

General Considerations

Many of the normal physiological changes that come with aging are relevant to decisions about any medication prescription. These include changes in these five areas:

1. Rate of gastrointestinal activity. With the aging, the rate of gastrointestinal tract activity slows, and while this slows medication absorption, the process ultimately remains as thorough as in earlier life. Medications will not, however, take effect as quickly in most cases.

2. Body mass and weight. Older adults have less total body water, less lean body mass, and more body fat (particularly women). As a result, the distribution efficiency of water-soluble drugs is reduced, while that of fat-soluble drugs is increased. The plasma concentrations of water-soluble drugs such as lithium thus increase; conversely, concentrations of fat-soluble drugs decrease. A lower body weight implies that the physician may determine dosage levels on a "milligram by weight" basis rather than strict milligram dosages, though this occurs in some other cases as well, such as for some people who weigh more than average. Furthermore, in older people, the number of drugs that remain unbound increases.

3. Metabolism. Both therapeutic responses and side effects may occur at blood levels lower than expected. As the metabolism slows, the half-lives of all psychotropic medications increase, with the half-life of some medications doubling or tripling. Physicians will thus usually prescribe less medication for the same therapeutic effect. The social worker must also be aware that toxic amounts of medication may build more quickly in an older client's bloodstream. Toxicity (see Chapter 4) also becomes problematic because of decreased rates of renal clearance (up to 50% less by age 70). Clearance is also less efficient in older men because prostate enlargement causes greater urinary retention.

4. Cardiovascular efficiency. The aging process impacts cardiovascular system functioning, as cardiac output and blood perfusion into other organs diminishes. Kidney function is therefore slowed and liver function compromised.

5. Sensitivity of certain nervous system receptors. Certain neurotransmitters in the brain become more sensitive in older people, another reason why the same amount of medication may have a greater effect. Studies have been done regarding age-related changes in serotonin availability (McEntee & Crook, 1991). A decrease in serotonin levels in older adults is associated with enhanced memory, and thus serotonin-antagonist medications may actually help some elderly people with memory problems.

Social workers need to assess continuously the extent to which psychiatric symptoms in the elderly result from psychological problems, medical illnesses, using multiple medications, or all of these. Both the starting and maintenance doses of all psychotropic medications prescribed for the elderly are usually one-third to one-half the prescribed dose for young adults because of metabolic changes but also as a precaution against the dangers of polypharmacy, or the prescription of more than one medication to treat the same or various physical or mental disorders (Wise & Tierney, 1992; Greenwald, Kremen, & Aupperle, 1992). These dangers include the frequently overlooked problems related to misuse of over-the-counter drugs by elderly persons and alcohol abuse among many older adults (Butler, Lewis, & Sunderland, 1991). In the role of consultant/collaborator, the social worker must continuously update the physician about the client's physical status and changes in other medications.

Classes of Medication

Psychotic disorders among the elderly population, excluding organic disorders, are no more or less prevalent than at any point during life (Butler et al., 1991). Though drug treatment strategies for the elderly resemble those used for the general population, physicians may implement them differently. Because elderly clients are already at risk for falls owing to hypotension, the low-potency medications must be used with extreme caution. Unfortunately, the high-potency medications produce uncomfortable extrapyramidal effects. With their increased sensitivity to the anticholinergic effects of any drug, the elderly may experience a "central anticholinergic syndrome," characterized by problems with short-term memory, confusion, and, occasionally, visual hallucinations. The effects of this syndrome resemble those of Alzheimer's disease. Currently under study, new drug treatments for these symptoms may become available in the next few years.

The elderly also experience an increased risk of tardive dyskinesia. Though the overall prevalence of tardive dyskinesia for persons using antipsychotic medication is about 24% (Jeste & Caligiuri, 1993), the risk increases with age. The onset of the disorder may be related to a cumulative effect of medications over time as well as their interactions with normal physiological changes in parts of the brain. With this movement disorder, older adults also demonstrate fewer instances of spontaneous remission. As with other risks, careful monitoring is essential; the social worker must report any evidence of tardive dyskinesia's onset to the physician and help determine appropriate interventions.

Because of their need to cope with medical disorders, physical pain, increased overall drug use, social isolation, and cumulative bereavement issues, elderly people are more predisposed to depression than younger individuals. Late-onset depression is frequently characterized by higher levels of cognitive impairment, insomnia, agitation, and mortality rates. Suicide rates are in fact highest among the older adult population (Butler et al., 1991). Unfortunately, because of their multiple health issues, these clients often receive too much or too little medication. The social worker's challenge is to assess levels of depression and sort out the various physical and emotional issues contributing to it. It is a mistake to assume that it is normal for older adults to feel depressed or that they can tolerate it any better than younger people.

The typical side effects of the cyclic antidepressants include sedation, hypotension, anticholinergic effects, and cardiac effects. Trazodone has been associated with priapism, or persistent penile erection, in men. Again, the risk of falling is most often noted for older adults. The anticholinergic effects of constipation and urinary retention can go unrecognized until they cause significant problems for the elderly patient. However, MAO inhibitors, so difficult to manage in younger populations, present certain advantages for the elderly. They do not produce anticholinergic effects and, in fact, may counteract the production of natural but potentially harmful increases in monoamine oxidase in the aging brain. Of course, the risks of hypotension and dietary reactions remain. In short, the MAO drug class may be more suitable for the elderly than some younger populations.

The newer serotonin-reuptake inhibitors do not appear to pose any special risk for elderly patients. In fact, the absence of sedation, hypotension, and anticholinergic and cardiovascular effects make them particularly attractive. However, the side effects of nausea, nervousness, and insomnia trouble those already experiencing related problems. Trazodone and bupropion also pose no special risks for aging people. However, newer compounds have not been available for research as long as older drugs; thus, social workers must take reports or observations of adverse effects very seriously (Steiner & Marcopulos, 1991).

Lithium is the only psychotropic medication that is water soluble, making age-related changes in response to lithium predictable. These changes are associated with alterations in the renal system and the increased sensitivity of some nervous system receptor sites. Decreased clearance rates put elderly patients at risk for prolonged exposure to higher therapeutic and toxic blood levels. Though lithium remains the first drug usually chosen to treat manic conditions, anticonvulsant medications such as carbamazepine and valproic acid may be used as alternatives.

Common among the elderly, anxiety is manifested differently in them than in younger people. Panic disorder is relatively rare, while phobic disorders and generalized anxiety become more common. Sleep disturbances are common. Though generally safe and effective medications for the elderly, the benzodiazepines produce side effects of sedation, cognitive impairment, lack of psychomotor coordination, and falls due to hypotension, which are all serious. However, they can be minimized by using benzodiazepines with shorter half-lives and less active metabolites. Generally, the short-acting, low-potency drugs such as lorazepam, oxazepam, and temazepam are well tolerated by the elderly (Janicak et al., 1993). Sedative and cognitive effects are similarly more pronounced with the long-acting substances. Unfortunately, these drugs can be abused, with the overprescription of benzodiazepines, particularly triazolam, a major problem in nursing homes (Butler et al., 1991). The social worker should also consider nondrug interventions for anxiety, such as encouraging clients to sleep well, maintain good hygiene, avoid stimulants, reduce environmental agitations, and exercise regularly.

With the elderly population, physicians generally initiate treatment at low doses and gradually increase the dose over a period of days or weeks. Careful physicians will also prescribe as few drugs as necessary, because the elderly tend to take other medications to treat physical conditions. During this process, the social worker must help monitor the client for both therapeutic and adverse effects, enlist the client's cooperation in individualizing the drug routine (tailoring it to a client's physical characteristics and circumstances) as much as possible, and ensure adherence by offering clear oral and written explanations of pharmacotherapy and its risks.

Children and Adolescents

General Considerations

The use of psychotropic drugs in children and adolescents has often produced controversy. Most issues pertain to either the appropriateness of medication (rationale for use, alternatives, toxicity) or inadequacies in clinical management (Cordoba, Wilson, & Orten, 1983; Gadow, 1991; Dulcan, 1992; Greenhill & Setterberg, 1993; Sylvester, 1993). The symptoms for which psychotropic drugs are prescribed can be generally categorized as either behavioral inadequacies or behavioral excesses. Besides the disorders already discussed in this book, children and adolescents receive psychotropic medications for other disorders, including attention deficit hyperactivity disorder, pervasive developmental disorder, Tourette's syndrome, and sleep disorders. With this population, two special concerns arise: the child's often reluctant participation and the possibility that otherwise effective medications may harm physical development.

The psychopharmacological assessment and management of children and adolescents is more complicated than that of adults. This is due to

1. The need for comprehensive family involvement
2. Developmental differences among clients
3. The diagnostic ambiguity of emerging first episodes of mental illness
4. Ethical issues in decision making and the rights of minors.

Social workers should view the absence of active interest by parents or caregivers as a major treatment concern. When one adds developmental issues (such as the adolescent's need to separate from the family) to the complications of prescribing medications, drug management requires a strong alliance between social worker and family to ensure collaboration. Because of fears of peer ridicule and a reluctance to participate in therapies that label clients as "ill," noncompliance with most interventions is a general problem in child and adolescent health care. The physician will therefore usually start low, aiming for the lowest possible effective dose. Monitoring and laboratory follow-up may need to be more frequent than with other populations.

School-age children, who metabolize and clear psychotropic drugs rapidly, are more sensitive to their therapeutic effects. Typically, they can tolerate a higher ratio of milligrams to body weight. Young female clients seem to achieve higher blood levels than young male clients, and they experience more side effects from the same weight-adjusted dose. The most commonly prescribed psychotropic drugs for children and adolescents, ranked from least to most troublesome with respect to side effects, are as follows: stimulants (not discussed in this book), cyclic antidepressants, and antipsychotic medications. Other drugs, such as beta-blockers, lithium, carbamazepine, and the atypical antidepressants, are more difficult to evaluate because of the relatively short time they have been available for research.

Classes of Medication

With antipsychotic medications, children and adolescents experience sedation more often than adults do. However, they may complain less about these effects, so the physician and social worker must monitor this effect closely. Long-term adverse effects of these drugs may include interference with the client's natural psychosocial stages, for example, stunted physical growth. Also, the increased risk of tardive dyskinesia with ongoing use of medications requires close monitoring. The reduced risk of movement reactions (i.e., dystonia, akathisia, parkinsonianism) among young persons using antipsychotic medications is offset by greater anticholinergic side effects. Extrapyramidal symptoms, including dystonic reactions and parkinsonianism, appear to be more prevalent among teenagers, especially males, than all other age groups. High-potency antipsychotic medications probably interfere less with learning than low-potency types, and the lower anticholinergic activity of the high-potency medications minimizes the risk of delirium, which can occur in young populations.

During the 1980s, an outpouring of research on mood disorders in children and adolescents resulted in the widespread use of antidepressants with this group. Besides uncomplicated depression, common syndromes these drugs are used to treat include hyperactivity (when stimulants are not effective), separation anxiety, refusal to attend school, and obsessive-compulsive behaviors. Several difficulties arise in the use of antidepressants with adolescents. First, hormonal changes make measuring true effectiveness very difficult. High levels of sex hormones modulate the developing neurotransmitter systems in ways that diminish antidepressant efficacy. Second, nonpharmacological aspects of treatment are more difficult to control in this population than in others. Finally, as adolescents confront identity stressors, peer relationships, and independence issues, they may be tempted to misuse medication in an attempt to take control of their lives. Early enthusiasm about antidepressant medication treatment has waned somewhat; amazingly, most studies indicate that antidepressant drug treatment is often no more effective than a placebo; that is, there is no clear evidence of its effectiveness. In fact, the placebo effect in children is so profound in research on antidepressant drugs that the social worker and physician must always be cautious about attributing signs of clinical improvement to the biological effect of a medication.

Side effects common among younger people but uncommon among adults include cardiovascular toxicity (arrhythmia) and neurological symptoms (possibility of seizure). The cyclic antidepressants produce dry mouth, nausea, constipation, dizziness, blurred vision, drowsiness, appetite changes, headaches, fatigue, and sleep disturbances including insomnia and nightmares. The adverse effects of the cyclic antidepressants are the same as those in older populations, except that the medications are more likely to increase blood pressure in younger people. Although a common cardiovascular effect is mild tachycardia, serious hypotension is rare.

Use of the serotonin-reuptake inhibitors with adolescents may be preferable because of their relatively well-tolerated side-effect profiles and their reduced potential for intentional overdose. The latter advantage is highly significant because suicide is the second leading cause of adolescent death. These atypical antidepressants appear relatively safe for children, although they may experience the same side effects as older persons. These side effects can sometimes be minimized by "halving" adult doses for children (splitting tablets in two and taking one of the halves as a full dose). Finally, some evidence suggests that adolescents may have a higher risk of a manic episode while on cyclic or atypical antidepressant drugs. Abrupt withdrawal of antidepressants may cause children to develop gastrointestinal complaints and fatigue, which may be confused with continuing depression. Because of their higher elimination rates, children may be more vulnerable than adults to adverse effects of abrupt withdrawal.

Because children rapidly clear lithium, the physician may prescribe higher doses than adults to achieve therapeutic effect. Children may experience the same side effects that adults do, but they seem to tolerate long-term treatment well. However, carbamazepine must be used with special caution because it can precipitate agitation and manic symptoms in children. The most serious concerns in children and adolescents are the long-term consequences of lithium accumulation in bone tissue and lithium's effect on thyroid and renal function. Lithium appears to be somewhat better tolerated overall than the antipsychotic medications.

Relatively few studies of drug therapy for anxiety disorders in children and adolescents exist. Antihistamines are commonly used to treat anxiety and insomnia in children as an alternative to the benzodiazepines. A lowered seizure threshold, the potential for delirium, and worsening of tic disorders are serious but less common side effects of these anti-anxiety medications. Clomipramine has been established as the treatment of choice for children with obsessive-compulsive disorder and does not pose a serious threat of side effects.

With children, there is an additional concern related to iatrogenic effects, or new developmental problems the child acquires as a result of taking medications. Concerns have been raised in the literature (Gadow, 1991) that children may

1. Attribute adjustment problems to factors beyond their control and become less responsive to behavioral interventions
2. Fail to acquire adaptive behaviors because their symptoms are suppressed and caregivers thus do not recognize the need to teach coping strategies
3. Come to regard medication as the primary or only effective way to cope with adjustment difficulties
4. Become more likely to abuse psychoactive substances

Though these effects can occur within any age group, children and adolescents have not yet formed overall coping and adaptation styles.

Racial and Ethnic Differences

While research is only beginning to focus on comparative issues in this area, some evidence exists that differences do exist in the actions of psychotropic medications among members of certain racial groups. Findings must be considered tentative, however, as perceived differences in mental disorders and treatment response in racial and ethnic groups may occur because of differences in treatment-seeking behavior, representation in research samples, presentation of symptoms, and the accuracy of diagnosis (Adebimpe, 1994). Cultural differences exist in the ways individuals cope with stress and express emotion. Such differences also exist in the ways ethnic groups conceptualize and treat mental problems (Frank, 1974; Torrey, 1986). Lantz (1987), for example, describes the work of an African-American "ghetto healer" in a large midwestern city who successfully treats neighborhood clients for "soul loss."

Enzymatic and metabolic differences among some racial groups account for some variable responses to drugs. These differences may have genetic and/or environmental causes. Additional psychosocial factors that influence psychotropic drug metabolism and response among ethnic groups include

1. Diet and nutritional factors (influence on metabolic activity)
2. Differences in consumption of cigarettes, caffeine, alcohol, herbs, and other psychoactive substances (influence on drug metabolism or response)
3. Sleep or activity and rest patterns (effect on other physiological events)
4. Environmental exposure to toxins or pollutants
5. Differences in exposure to psychological stress (Jacobsen, 1994)

A major perspective that the social work profession can bring to ethnic understanding is what health and illness mean within a culture (Raffoul & Haney, 1989). In addition to a client's physical characteristics, psychological and social factors must be taken into account when one decides what medications to prescribe. The social worker's person-in-environment perspective places him or her in a sound position for assessing clients in this holistic manner, to evaluate the context of drug use by examining the social and cultural aspects of mental illness. Social workers can coordinate the necessary interdisciplinary approach in overall intervention, such as educating both clients and professionals, sharing expectations among clients and their significant others, organizing the activities of all participating professionals, and enforcing an affirming emotional tone between workers, clients, and families (Garrity & Lawson, 1989).

Following these general principles, some differences have been noted between African Americans and Caucasians regarding mental distress. African Americans demonstrate a higher risk of depressive disorders resulting from medical illness, a higher prevalence of phobic disorders, higher rates of adjustment disorders with mixed emotional features, and episodes of delirium from drug interactions (Baker, 1994). The reasons for these differences are not known. In fact, the comparative prevalence of most psychiatric disorders among African Americans is largely unknown, perhaps because African Americans are less inclined to self-disclosure than Caucasians (Adebimpe, 1994).

Glazer, Morgenstern, and Doucette (1994) show in a study of 398 outpatients at risk for tardive dyskinesia that the syndrome occurred 1.83 times more often in African Americans than in Caucasians, a significant difference. This study also points to differences in symptom presentation and treatment by racial group. Nonwhites were more likely to be diagnosed with schizophrenia and to receive higher doses of medication (principally because they more frequently received high-potency injectible medications) but less likely to receive lithium, anti-anxiety, and antidepressant medications. In another comparative study of 263 cocaine addicts, Ziedonis, Rayford, Bryant, and Rounsaville (1994) identify other racial differences between Caucasians and African Americans in the types of problems presented to mental health professionals. Caucasian respondents had higher lifetime rates of major depression and suicide attempts. The African Americans had lower lifetime rates of affective disorders, primarily due to differences in rates of dysthymia and major depression, but they also demonstrated "hyperthymia," or a state of overactivity not quite manic in severity. Ziedonis, et al. have also found racial differences in phobia rates and speculate that the impact of racism in society may increase the vulnerability of African Americans to phobias. The authors finally note that among the Caucasian cocaine addicts they studied, the rate of alcoholism was twice as high as in the African-American group, but that in both groups the men had five times as many alcohol disorders as the women did.

Regarding other ethnic groups, Lawson (1986) reviews the literature for differences in psychiatric disorders among Caucasian, African-American,

Hispanic, and Asian populations. He notes that African Americans are more likely to experience hallucinations, delusions, somatic symptoms, and anger toward others than Caucasians, who demonstrate more mania, depression, and guilt. The tendency of African Americans with schizophrenia to demonstrate more of the positive symptomatology may contribute to the overdiagnosis of schizophrenia in this population. African-American clients with either schizophrenia or depressive disorders respond better than Caucasian clients to phenothiazines and cyclic antidepressant medications, and they experience more anxiety reduction with antidepressant medications. This appears to be a consequence of African-American clients having higher blood levels for a given dosage. Asian consumers require lower doses and experience more side effects (including extrapyramidal effects) for a variety of psychotropic drugs, including lithium and antipsychotic medications, and require lower dosages for effective treatment. While there are fewer studies of Hispanic populations, evidence exists that Hispanic clients require less antidepressant medication and have more side effects at lower dosages than Caucasians do. Hispanics also have certain different enzymes that affect metabolic processes, causing slower drug metabolism. There are no reports of differences among these racial groups with regard to response to lithium, although for African Americans it has a significantly longer half-life.

Asian populations tend to expect Western medications to exert effects swiftly, carry a high likelihood of severe side effects, and to be effective only for superficial manifestations of a problem (Lin & Shen, 1991). It is important for the social worker to elicit client beliefs in traditional Asian medical practices, elicit feedback about what effective treatments consist of, and involve family members in diagnosis and treatment planning. Because of smaller body size, Asian clients should be started on smaller dosages of medication (Lin, Poland, Smith, Strickland, & Mendoza, 1991). Asians metabolize antipsychotic, antidepressant, and anti-anxiety medications more slowly; thus, lower dosages can be more effective but carry the potential for greater toxicity. Lithium is cleared at a similar rate in Asian and Caucasian groups. Asian refugee groups show a high prevalence of posttraumatic stress disorder, for which MAO inhibitors have been demonstrated useful, as well as with depression and panic disorders.

Mendoza, Smith, Poland, Lin, and Strickland (1991) and Kail (1989) have also found differences among Hispanic and Caucasian groups in medication action. Hispanic clients experience more side effects with antidepressants, and their particular liver enzymes make them more susceptible to alcohol toxicity as well. The reliance of this ethnic group on traditional social supports rather than professional intervention suggests that the social worker will have problems in maintaining contact over time. More outreach activities, as is typical with case management practice, may be necessary to ensure a positive outcome with the Hispanic ethnic group. Of course, the social worker in every case needs to be aware of the diverse traditions of special populations and be prepared to tailor interventions accordingly to facilitate effective medication service.

Persons with a Dual Diagnosis of Mental Illness and Substance Abuse

In the past 10 years, attention has increasingly focused on the prevalence of substance abuse among people with mental illness and the difficulty in providing effective treatment for them. Substance abuse may occur in as much as 50% of relatively low-functioning people with long-term mental illnesses (Test, Wallisch, Allness, & Ripp, 1989). Substances most frequently cited as exacerbating psychotic or affective symptoms include alcohol, cocaine, marijuana, stimulants, and hallucinogenic drugs. Abuse is probably most common among those with depressive disorders (Ries, 1993). If inclined to take alcohol or other drugs, people with mental illness tend to use what is available in their environments rather than any particular substance.

Negative interactions of these substances with psychotropic drugs is a major concern (see Chapter 4). For instance, using certain substances can make the symptoms of schizophrenia more pronounced and cause severe decompensation (or, resurgence of psychotic symptoms), most frequently when their use encourages clients to stop taking prescription medications. One of our clients, for example, liked to drink beer. Because he knew that it might interact with his antipsychotic medications to produce a high level of sedation, he decided not to take his prescription drugs on nights when he drank beer. With manic conditions, substance abuse can further impair a client's already poor impulse control. To help themselves relax, people with bipolar disorder often use self-medicating agents. Self-medication is also sometimes seen when clients try to reduce the side effects of some neuroleptic medications. For example, stimulants may increase a client's affect and energy levels, which some medications decrease. Some studies note that nicotine reduces some of the muscular side effects of neuroleptic drugs, but it also impairs the drugs' therapeutic potency (Arana & Hyman, 1991).

Some of the psychotropic drugs themselves can be abused (Ries, 1993). We have discussed the potential for abusing the benzodiazepines, which are used to treat anxiety. However, the anticholinergic drugs can also produce a "high" when taken in larger amounts than typically prescribed. Some preliminary studies, which require further substantiation, indicate that the serotonin-reuptake inhibitors may be abused presumably because they produce desirable side effects for some people, including weight loss and increased energy (Pirodsky & Cohen, 1992).

All helping professionals who treat clients with dual diagnoses face a major problem: substance abuse makes accurate diagnosis extremely difficult, therefore hampering the development of appropriate interventions. In one controlled study, among professionals using a structured interview format, the diagnosis of mental illness was significantly less reliable in the presence of substance abuse (Corty, Lehman, & Myers, 1993). Results from 47 diagnostic assessments of dually diagnosed clients by nine skilled interviewers, each client assessed separately by two interviewers, indicated the lowest frequency of agreement with regard to clients having either mood or schizophrenic disorders, and slightly higher but still problematic with clients having anxiety disorders. A further problem for treatment providers is the great difficulty in treating either of the two disorders (mental illness and substance abuse) when they coexist. Lehman, Herron, Schwartz, & Myers (1993) randomly assigned 54 dually diagnosed clients to experimental and control treatment groups, with the former group receiving additional services for their substance abuse problem. No difference in outcome appeared after one year, leading the researchers to conclude that all clients were hard to engage in a treatment program, and that perhaps one year was not long enough to produce changes in social functioning with clients having dual disorders.

When the client has both a substance abuse problem and a mental illness, the social worker needs to be aware of the complications that arise in providing effective psychosocial interventions, of which medication is an essential part. The bottom line is that both disorders need to be treated; the social worker should *not* assume that if one of the client's disorders is brought under control, then the other can be more easily addressed or perhaps will disappear by itself. Before assessing clients, the social worker first needs to understand whether they have two truly coexisting disorders, are medicating themselves with substances for the primary disorder, or have a drug-induced psychotic state that may abate with rapid intervention. Though drug-induced psychoses are transient, tending to resolve themselves in several hours or several days, they do require intensive interventions at times and perhaps a brief regimen of psychotropic medications. If the client is self-medicating, the social worker needs to understand why. Finally, however serious the adverse effects of prescribed medications are, clients should negotiate with the physician as the most appropriate means to alleviate discomfort.

Professionals in the mental health and substance abuse fields have tended to work apart over the years, with different philosophies and areas of expertise (Mancuso & Emrey, 1991). Social workers have complained at times that substance abuse counselors are too rigid, while the latter group has felt in turn that social workers do not confront clients enough about substance abuse. Fortunately, today many agree that both approaches need to be combined and well coordinated for the client's sake. Interdisciplinary work can be fruitfully promoted in this area of intervention.

SUMMARY

Medical science, like other fields of science, is only beginning to appreciate the variability of effects that people demonstrate in response to all types of intervention. For years social workers have faced a major challenge in determining which treatments work for which clients under which circumstances. It has become clear that this same problem applies to drug treatments, which at one time were assumed to be more universal and predictable in their outcomes. Though not typically experts in chemistry, social workers offer an advanced perspective about individual and group differences in psychosocial functioning. With this professional strength and the partnership perspective, they can contribute important insights into the client's experience of taking medication in a social as well as physical sense.

PART THREE

Knowledge and Skills for Psychosocial Interventions

CHAPTER 6

Medication Education for Clients and Families

CHAPTER 7

Medication Adherence and Refusal

CHAPTER 8

Medication Monitoring and Management

CHAPTER 6

MEDICATION EDUCATION FOR CLIENTS AND FAMILIES

RATIONALE FOR MEDICATION EDUCATION

There are a number of excellent reasons, derived from logic, common sense, and research, for providing mental health clients and their families with education about psychotropic medications. These include patients' rights, the demands of clients and their families for information, and the hope of increased compliance with medication. We will look briefly at these issues individually.

Many professionals have discussed medication education in the context of patient rights (Bisbee, 1988; Whiteside, Harris, & Whiteside, 1983). With growing legal pressures to provide all health clients with full and accurate information about their diagnosis and treatment as a matter of right, a consensus has arisen that client safety and security is also a right. These rights closely relate to the notion of informed consent, the idea that to be able to make choices about treatment, the clients need complete knowledge about the benefits and risks of all available treatment options, including medication.

Similarly, one can also see medication education in terms of supply and demand. That is, the increased emphasis on such education is surely related to the growing client and family demand for current knowledge. In addition to society's orientation toward consumers, this increased demand may be related in part to the renewed emphasis on biological factors in mental illness and their relationship to medication as a major treatment strategy (Goldwyn, 1988).

Data support the perception of such high demand for information. In a recent survey, outpatients, relatives, and close friends in Philadelphia reported that acquiring knowledge about pertinent medications and side effects was of highest importance (Mueser, Bellack, Wade, Sayers, & Rosenthal, 1992). Out of 45 identified "educational needs," relatives of clients with either affective disorders or schizophrenia ranked knowledge of medication or its side effects as their number one educational need; clients diagnosed with affective disorders themselves ranked it second, while clients diagnosed with schizophrenia ranked it a still-high eighth.

In another survey of psychiatric patients, Zind (1991) documents low levels of medication knowledge in her patients, including their mismanagement of missed doses. This survey of 116 men with schizophrenia shows knowledge of medications to be very low, particularly of the interaction of drugs with alcohol and side effects. Interestingly, she cites a low correlation between patients' actual knowledge and their perceived knowledge, suggesting that often clients think they know more than they actually do.

On a single day in one state hospital, Geller (1982) personally surveyed 281 inpatients and found that 54% showed no understanding at all of their medications. They could not state the name of their medication, how often they took it, or what the intended effect was. Only 22 participants interviewed (8.4%) could correctly name those three things. MacPherson, Double, Rowlands, and Harrison (1993) have replicated Geller's study with a random sample of 100 long-term hospital patients on neuroleptics. Out of the 100 interviewed, only 8 named all their medications and only 23 named one. Many could describe the drug's color and shape, but by far most showed no understanding of therapeutic action. In fact, 73% did not know what tardive dyskinesia is.

A related survey cites the attitudes of staff and family members toward both medication education and each other (Bernheim & Switalski, 1988). Whereas 91% of the staff thought that education about medication management would help families, only 19% of the families said they had received enough information from that same staff or facility. Less than 21% of families had been invited to a treatment *or* discharge planning conference. This research again points to the gap between what professionals know is needed and what they provide.

Perhaps the most often cited rationale for providing medication education is the hope that increased knowledge and support will increase the client's adherence to the prescribed drug regimen and thus will prevent relapse or rehospitalization. While strong evidence supports the connection between noncompliance and relapse (e.g., Hogarty et al., 1991), the evidence regarding the actual impact of medication education on compliance is less certain but encouraging.

Professionals also hope that medication education helps clients and their families to participate more responsibly in the treatment process (see Chapter 1). For example, many have noted that education provides a flexible and empowering means of engaging families in the treatment or rehabilitation process and that even if they forget the actual information, the educational efforts remain worthwhile. "Ultimately responsible," for managing mental illness, clients and families must build competence and "take charge of their illness" (Duchin & Brown, 1990, p. 255; Buckwalter & Kerfoot, 1982, p. 15). To do this, they need medication education to increase their knowledge and skill. It is not clear whether such an increase should be thought of as a desired "side effect" or as the main goal of medication education. In any case, medication education is seen as promoting cooperation, strengthening coping skills, enhancing clients' acceptance of their mental illness or emotional disorder, increasing hope for change, providing emotional support, reducing the family's burden, and helping clients and families acquire new skills. All are considered as protective factors in the stress-diathesis model (see Chapter 1). As Goldman and Quinn (1983) state,

> We believe that education has multiple beneficial effects that could lead to reduced symptoms. It counteracts fears and defensiveness, contributes to patients' self-esteem and hope, suggests practical ways for patients to help themselves, encourages more effective communication with treatment personnel, and promotes healthy activities, including informed adherence to treatment recommendations. (p. 286)

According to Buckwalter and Kerfoot (1982), the main thing professionals can do to help clients live in the community is to teach them necessary self-care. For many, particularly those with a serious mental illness, medication may be the "cornerstone of community management" (McGill, Falloon, Boyd, & Wood-Siverio, 1983, p. 936); that is, clients may need knowledge of their medications to maintain independence in the community (Zind, Furlong, & Stebbins, 1992). Surprisingly, direct and full discussion of a client's own disorder and treatment is still a new idea in many respects in spite of medication education efforts that go back several decades (Hayes & Gantt, 1992).

Studies that have evaluated medication education programs offer good reason to be cautiously optimistic about its potential impact on clients' understanding of medication, compliance, symptomatology, attitudes, fears, and ability to negotiate with clinicians. Indeed, in an uncontrolled evaluation of a pharmacist-facilitated medication group, Batey and Ledbetter (1982) noted that with education intervention came not only greater knowledge and increased compliance among consumers of medication but also more requests for information, greater client involvement in treatment, and even a higher level of staff comfort with clients.

Several controlled studies conducted in the 1980s also support this positive appraisal. For example, Whiteside et al. (1983) present significant differences—in knowledge of personal medication regimens, side effects, and rationales for treatments—between the control group and those who participated in a structured patient education program that included written reinforcements for 28 medically ill psychiatric patients. Youssef (1984) randomly assigned 36 psychiatric patients a week from discharge to either a two-session group education program or no treatment. Those in the experimental group were significantly more compliant in terms of both their use of medication (using a pill count method) and their postdischarge appointment keeping. Robinson, Gilbertson, and Litwak (1986) examine the impact of three types of structured drug education strategies on 150 psychiatric patients ready for discharge. The first group received "standard" explanations and simple instructions; the second group received written instructions and a detailed information sheet; the third group received written instructions and an information sheet, but also met with a nursing student or psychology intern who consulted with each patient about her or his medication (using a structured format). Results suggest that personal and individualized instruction, paired with written materials, is superior to the usual brief, general explanations given to clients about medication regimens. However, the finding regarding the impact of providing written information on patient knowledge has not been replicated by another group of researchers (Brown, Wright, & Christenson, 1987). Furthermore, Brown et al. use a small sample size (N=30) and unvalidated measures and do not substantiate the anticipated relationship between knowledge gain and increased medication compliance, making theirs the only known outcome study of medication education with wholly negative results.

In perhaps the largest and best known clinical evaluation of a medication education program, researchers evaluated the impact of their Medication Management Module in 28 field-test sites around the country involving 160 patients with schizophrenia (Eckman, Liberman, Phipps, & Blair, 1990; Eckman & Liberman, 1990). The Medication Management Module is a highly structured and comprehensive behaviorally oriented program that includes hands-on problem-solving and communication skills training (see Chapter 8). The field-test sites included both public and private settings, inpatient and outpatient facilities; a range of professionals participated, including social workers, nurses, occupational therapists, psychologists, and psychiatrists. Results indicate the program effectively increased clients' knowledge of antipsychotic medications and their side effects, improved clients' skill in negotiating with health care providers about their medication-related concerns, and improved medication compliance as reported by both psychiatrists and caregivers.

Another controlled, large-scale investigation examines both in-home visits with the family and clinical visits with patients for individualized education and training (Kelly, Scott, & Mamon, 1990). The study used 418 male VA patients with chronic psychotic disorders. Results indicate that those clients who received individualized education at the clinic were slightly more compliant than those with only the home visit (family consultation). The researchers note, however, that for all their participants, compliance actually got worse over time, even if the experimental groups did less worse than the controls over time. Clearly, noncompliance remained a major concern for most participants in this study in spite of impressive individualized interventions. However, all those who received treatment of any kind (clinic only, home visit only, combined) demonstrated significantly fewer symptoms and relapses than controls.

In summary, medication education appears to rest on solid logical and ethical grounds, supported by encouraging empirical data. Nevertheless, a gap exists between what professionals, clients, and families all agree is needed and wanted and what is actually provided around the country. Before detailing the content of medication education programs, we will present some of the principles and structural issues underlying the implementation and evaluation of some of these programs.

Issues in Implementing and Evaluating Medication Education

Duchin and Brown (1990) state it is important to be aware of (and we add, capitalize on) two crucial characteristics of adult learners: (1) adults have life experiences, and (2) adults have a goal orientation.

The first characteristic is often made use of when facilitators rely heavily on interaction among group members as a source for learning. That is, clients and families sharing their experiences with other group members is a major mechanism of learning. Even if a great deal of content is delivered didactically, this approach is universally built into programs. Heyduk (1991) goes even further to suggest that programs must "involve patients in the teaching-learning process" and let participants guide the teacher in what they need to know (p. 32). Because life experiences, both positive and negative, tend to lead to strong feelings and beliefs, social workers must provide an atmosphere that validates and encourages sharing but also allows for the presentation of accurate and balanced information. Open discussions can help participants examine their attitudes, clarify their feelings, and dispel myths about psychotropic medications and their use (Sclafani, 1977).

"Goal orientation" means that adult learners tend to apply what they learn, so that medication education should address their individual hopes and dreams. In the health belief model, the extent to which people are motivated to reach their goals and the extent to which they see these goals as related to some recommended behavior determine what course of action people will choose (Youssef, 1984). Thus, participating in medication education or adhering to medication regimens (or any number of other strategies; see Chapters 7 and 8) will be most effective when successfully tied to clients' individual goals which clients are strongly motivated to achieve. For people with mental illness, such dreams can include staying out of the hospital, getting or keeping a meaningful job, or getting a place of their own. This seems related to Swezy and Swezy's (1976) notion that medication education should be guided by the behavioral principle known as "the law of effect," which says that learning will be enhanced if learners understand how the knowledge relates to their own lives.

People with mental illnesses, however, may have special learning problems. For example, Halford and Hayes (1991), in trying to explain differences in treatment response, conclude that mental health workers need to pay more attention to the client's level of cognitive functioning. Davidhizar and McBridge (1985), for example, list the learning problems of people with schizophrenia and note the potential challenge of impaired cognitive functioning among people with schizophrenia. Other potential learning problems they cite include difficulty with abstractions, handicapped intellectual functioning, denial of illness, feelings of dependency, the frequent need for medication adjustments, and family and financial issues. They also note, at least for people with schizophrenia, an "unusual resistance to participation" in treatment (p. 137). For people with affective disorders, Daley, Bowler, & Cahalane (1992) identify at least two special issues in psychoeducation: the high recurrence rate of the illness (50%) and the high potential for successful suicide (15%). Social workers should consider these facts not only when choosing content for medication education but when actually managing the dynamics of class interaction. At the same time, any psychoeducational effort should strive to debase myths, stereotypes, and misinformation about the limitations of the people who suffer from mental illness; it should reflect the social worker's sensitivity to real impairments of the population. The notion of targeting medication education at either professionals, clients, or families is one way of addressing the different needs of these groups. Though some argue that inclusive education is the most desirable because it can draw people together and enhance the empathy and appreciation of these groups for each other (Cubine, Bentley, Poe, & McCafferty, 1995), responsiveness to the specialized learning needs of each of the groups may lead to separate offerings or curriculums.

The principles of adult learning as well as the special needs of mental health clients and their families have led to much advice by the creators of medication education programs. For example, Harmon and Tratnack (1992) suggest a brief didactic method, using plain English, avoiding too much jargon and humor, providing frequent breaks, limiting class size to 12, and providing some incentive for participation such as a point system or a certificate. The latter strategy has been used at the Patient Learning Center at Bryce Hospital since 1977 (Bisbee, 1988). In addition, repeating information is helpful, especially when supplemented by written materials.

Duchin and Brown (1990) describe four deficits of general patient education programs, which social workers may find helpful when analyzing or creating their own programs.

1. **Assessment error.** An erroneous assumption about the educational needs of the learners. In medication education, this might come up as underestimating clients' concerns about side effects or overestimating a family's need for information on brain biochemistry. One way to overcome this error is to read up on what mental health clients and their families want to know about their medication (a review of topics is covered in the next section). Another way to know what is needed and wanted is simply to ask and observe. For example, one researcher administered his own informal survey at his 9-week family education and support group. He thus gathered information about family members' knowledge of medications and other issues related to serious mental illness (Walsh, 1987).

2. Analysis error. An oversimplification of the behavioral goals of the educational effort. This might occur in medication education, for example, when medication compliance becomes the entire goal, even though studies point to other powerful outcomes, such as engaging clients in rehabilitation or making them feel validated and competent.

3. Planning and implementation error. Using inappropriate teaching strategies or relying on ineffective teachers. In medication education, this error might include the use of long lectures and complicated homework assignments. Retaining unstimulating or condescending presenters would also be an obvious error in this category.

4. Evaluation error. An improper judgment about outcome. In medication education, this error would be evident in hasty conclusions about effectiveness of education too soon or in conclusions based solely on whether the education was enjoyable to participants.

The delivery structures of drug education programs, like other such interventions, run a wide gamut. For example, interventions can be single session, two sessions, all day, or longer. They may meet from 2 hours a month (e.g., Powell, Ekkehard, & Sinkhard, 1977) to 3 times a week (e.g., Pakes, 1979). When medication education is embedded in a larger psychoeducation program, which commonly occurs (e.g., Abramowitz & Coursey, 1989; Goldman & Quinn, 1988; Harmon & Tratnack, 1992; Hogarty et al., 1991; McGill et al., 1983), often the precise number, frequency, and/or duration of sessions devoted to medication is difficult to determine. Some clear themes emerge, however. For instance, we have already mentioned the overwhelming preference for using a structured group process that relies on both didactic presentation and group interaction. Professionals also tend to use written materials to accompany the sessions, such as trainer manuals, patient workbooks, and demonstration videos, available for purchase (Eckman et al., 1990). Ascher-Svanum and Krause (1991) use slides and worksheets built into a notebook. Youssef (1984) and a colleague put on a skit for their clients. Though most programs take place in an inpatient or outpatient setting, some call for the educator to work in the client's or the family's home (e.g., Spiegel & Wissler, 1987).

Though research tends to focus on adult drug education, the principles of and rationale for drug education apply to children and adolescents as well, even though they have unique needs. Families play a more critical role in the medication treatment of children and adolescents than they do in that of adults (see Chapter 5). Dulcan (1992) has compiled a useful information packet for parents and youth.

Excellent leadership is another key to a successful medication education program. Leaders in health education have traditionally been nurses (Harmon & Tratnack, 1992). Pharmacists have also frequently led medication education programs. However, social workers' training in group process and empowerment practice and their historical concern for aftercare and community management provides them with an excellent foundation for leadership as well. In one psychoeducational program, both a nurse and a social worker led the session on medication (Posner, Wilson, Kral, Lander, & McIlwraith, 1992). Indeed, the trend toward interdisciplinary collaboration is gaining momentum.

Interestingly, in a survey of 159 families using social work services, most thought of the psychiatrist as the most desired source of information, even though the social worker was reported to be the most available and therefore most used source of information (Thompson & Weisberg, 1990). This same study states that those family members with the most education received most of their information from psychiatrists, while those with the least education received most of their information from nurses. This seems to suggest, in terms of information exchange in psychiatric care, a sort of class structure worthy of further research.

One psychoeducational program, at the Payne Whitney Clinic in New York, has the most clearly defined interdisciplinary roles we have seen (Greenberg, Fine, Cohen, & Larson, 1988). In this program, the psychiatrist serves as coordinator and consultant to the team. The nurses teach patients about their diagnoses and treatments while the social workers meet with the patients' families for 4 to 10 sessions to help them develop the cognitive and behavioral skills they need. Occupational therapists follow a life skills curriculum that includes goal setting, social skills, and time management.

Nonetheless, professionals tend to have flexible roles. The leader's responsibilities, though few, are complex. The two key leadership roles are instructor and facilitator (Hayes & Gantt, 1992; Powell et al., 1977). *Instructors* find and choose curriculum materials, present them in an interesting way, and encourage discussion and questions. Facilitators provide support to participants and direct their interactions. In groups where clients and families are together, facilitators need to "modulate the level of affect" of families to protect clients and buffer them from "cognitive and information saturation" (O'Shea, Bicknell, & Whatley, 1991, p. 42).

The first task of facilitation, however, is recruitment. For inpatients, this may not be a problem; however, recruiting families, particularly minority families, may be a major challenge. One group of researchers found that 60–75% of families did not show up for their psychoeducational program, which suggests accumulated frustrations with or skepticism of the mental health system as possible causes (O'Shea et al., 1991). Similarly, disinterest, a lack of resolve about the importance of the education, denial of the illness, family chaos, and the treatment setting may also contribute to such lack of involvement.

Should leaders get special training to do medication education beyond their usual professional preparation and clinical experience? Of course, the leader should know much about medication and especially those topics usually included in medication education programs (see pp. 134 and 135). The leader should also embrace the partnership model of helping and feel very comfortable with empowerment practice. In any psychoeducational intervention, this includes believing that clients and families can learn and can live more productive lives. It also means being able to tolerate frequent repetitions and a slow pace. In addition to these basic leadership requirements, Anderson et al. (1986) provide a detailed description of a model training program in their work on family psychoeducation, including extensive training goals, an outline of topics, and suggested teaching methods. They also provide advice to clinicians on how to control the sessions effectively, deal with impasses, and so forth.

Even so, leaders may not need additional specialized training, which can be expensive and time consuming. One study compares the implementation of the Medication Management Module between professionals who participated in an on-site, 2-day training program offered by their own staff with those who received only mail about their program and a brief telephone consultation (Eckman & Liberman, 1990). While those that participated in the on-site training are evaluated as most competent, those without training are also judged satisfactorily competent to use the module. Most important, the study cites no differences in client outcome between the compared groups. We include this study not to discourage participation in specialized training programs but to encourage the well-prepared but reluctant professional to forge ahead even in its absence. It has been noted that embarking on any educational effort in psychiatry "is not a light undertaking . . . however, well-trained mental health professionals generally have sufficient knowledge and experience . . . and psychologists, social workers and nurses have proved as effective as expert psychiatrists" (Falloon et al., 1984, pp. 205–206).

How do professionals evaluate the impact of their interventions? Key outcome measures include medication compliance, usually measured by pill counts, and reports of the patient's family or psychiatrist. Some sophisticated studies have used blood levels. However, the measurement of medication compliance has yet to be satisfactorily tackled. For example, one researcher notes little correlation between pill counts and self-reports of compliance (Boczkowski, Zeichner, & DeSanto, 1985). Perhaps the most common outcome measure of medication education is actual knowledge of medications, usually judged by simply quizzing participants. Other outcome measures include satisfaction with health care providers, symptomatology, rehospitalization, and attitude toward treatment. Researchers should assess the impact of medication education, and all interventions, using a number of measures. Efforts should be replicated, analyzed, revised, and replicated again.

Content of Medication Education Programs

At least two comprehensive medication education programs are widely used and adapted and deserve more detailed description here. The first was developed by Falloon and his colleagues, including a social worker, Christine McGill, as part of their behavioral family therapy project (Falloon et al., 1984). In their comprehensive psychoeducational program, designed for people with schizophrenia and their families, family members and clients participate together in sessions that take place in the family home. The second educational session is devoted to medication, following a session on the nature of the illness (symptoms, cause, course). In the medication education session, which like the other sessions takes place in the family home, the leader uses a handout to guide the presentation and discussion. (This handout is available from the authors and reprinted in the appendix of Ascher-Svanum & Krause, 1991.)

After reviewing the previous session's main points and answering any questions the participants might have, the leader begins medication education by discussing the underlying rationale for medication. Using a stress-diathesis model of mental illness, medication is explained as a way of managing the chemical imbalance in the brain. A brief account of the introduction of neuroleptics into psychiatric care is given, followed by a review of the types of neuroleptics, their chemical and brand names, dosage issues, and the benefits of medication. Using clear and simple graphs, the leaders highlight the reduced symptoms and relapse rates of those patients who regularly take their prescribed medication. Throughout this presentation, they ask clients and families how this information relates to their own experience. For example, when presenting information on how individuals respond differently to various medications, the leader asks the client to describe her or his experience with such medications. When presenting information on relapse, the leader asks if the client has ever had a relapse related to cessation of medication.

The session continues with a list and discussion of common "warning signals," those symptoms that usually precede a relapse, such as increased tension or restlessness, poor concentration, and sleep difficulties. With input from both the family and the patient, the leader creates an individualized list (see Chapter 8). Then, the leader reviews a "what to do next" set of options so that patients and families know how to respond if and when warning signals do appear. Because most clients taking medication experience side effects (a major complaint), the Falloon program devotes a good bit of attention to this topic. Side effects are defined as unwanted, often quite unpleasant effects of medication. In terms of the ultimate benefit to clients, however, side effects may be a necessary evil; thus, successful side-effect management is a key to successful medication management. Common side effects, such as drowsiness, dry mouth, and muscle stiffness, are described along with brief advice on how to cope with them. The first overall strategy, for example, is to wait for a few days or even a week or two, because many side effects will wear off. Leaders give the client and the family opportunities to share how they have coped with side effects and to ask questions.

The Falloon program also includes a candid discussion of compliance issues. Reasons that people with mental illnesses stop taking their medication are outlined, including bothersome side effects, the medication serving as a reminder of the illness, and people searching for other cures (see Chapter 7).

Clients and families can then share times when clients have stopped taking their medication, exploring why they did it and what impact it had on each person. At this point, the group discusses alcohol and drugs. This program presents the idea that street drugs frequently make things worse and that very small amounts of alcohol may be acceptable, although neuroleptics may intensify its effects. Falloon, Boyd, and McGill (1984) conclude by pointing out that education is ongoing, that the professional keeps teaching and learning throughout the helping process.

Liberman and his associates have also developed an impressive medication education program, which has been in use for over a decade and more recently has undergone extensive field testing (see Eckman & Liberman, 1990; Eckman et al., 1990; Liberman, 1988a; Wittlin, 1988). Liberman's "stress-vulnerability-coping-competence" model of mental illness suggests that the use of psychotropic medication and psychosocial interventions to promote its use are protective factors that may forestall or prevent relapses in people with mental illness. His Medication Management Module (MMM) addresses four specific skills:

1. Obtaining information on the benefits of antipsychotic medication
2. Knowing correct self-administration and evaluation of medication
3. Identifying side effects
4. Negotiating medication issues with health care providers

This module is one of 10 or so modules developed by Liberman and his associates, each targeting a specific social or independent-living skill. Money management, food preparation, grooming, dating and friendship, and conversational skills are examples of others. Though designed for use with groups of mental health clients in inpatient or outpatient settings, these modules are readily adaptable. The MMM begins with a general introduction to the goals and rationale of the module. Each of the four skill areas entails learning a number of requisite behaviors. For skill number 4, for example, these behaviors include learning to greet the physician pleasantly and being able to describe side effects clearly (see Chapter 8). After viewing videotapes of people correctly demonstrating the specific skill, participants then do role-playing, receive feedback, and finally receive homework assignments.

The module also helps clients anticipate certain kinds of problems. Patients learn to handle their "resource management problems," which might include a lack of time to see the doctor or inadequate transportation to his or her office. "Outcome problems" are those disappointing or unexpected events that happen in the real world to upset even the best-laid plans. To address this problem, a leader might teach the client how to figure out what to do if the psychiatrist is called away for an emergency and thus unavailable as scheduled.

Other, numerous medication education programs may each emphasize different things or be more or less ambitious in their educational objectives.

For example, unlike most other programs, the medication content in the "Survival Skills Workshop" includes substantial information on neurotransmission and brain function (Anderson et al., 1986). It might therefore be useful at this point to summarize common topics found in a comprehensive program. You can find more information on these topics throughout this book. Depending on the client's need, social workers can present the content broadly or make it specific to certain mental or emotional disorders.

- *Rationale for medication use*—All medication education programs should contain information on why medication is used in the treatment of mental illnesses and emotional disorders. The stress-diathesis model of mental illness provides a useful framework for presenting the rationale. Information on the effectiveness of medications in relation to psychosocial treatments might be useful as well. Many clients appreciate the analogy of the person with diabetes needing to use insulin regularly.
- *Benefits of medication*—Mental health clients and their families should receive accurate information about the benefits of medication, including its proven impact on certain symptoms and on relapse rates. Symptoms that tend to be less affected should also be reviewed.
- *Types of drugs*—Depending on the audience, the curriculum might include a thorough review of one type of medication (antidepressants or neuroleptics, for example) or might review all the categories of drugs.
- *Side effects*—Side effects, major and minor, common and not so common, should be reviewed. Where relevant, discussion of tardive dyskinesia, neuroleptic malignant syndrome, and agranulocytosis should not be glossed over or diminished. Many programs spend a lot of time discussing creative or practical ways of coping with side effects.
- *Dosage and equivalents*—Information on the differences in dosage among medications helps clients understand changes in medication orders, the importance of taking correct doses, etc.
- *Forms of drugs*—The pros and cons and general rationale for using various forms (such as tablets, injectibles, and patches) of drugs should be included.
- *Absorption and predicted response*—Discussion of the impact of individual metabolism on absorption rates helps clients understand better why individuals respond differently to psychotropic medication. Some programs present several theories of drug action and teach clients appropriate expectations about a medication's effects at different phases of the illness.
- *Interactions*—Common interactions, particularly those involving alcohol and drug use, should be taught to clients and families. However, information on complex interactions is best left to individual consultation with the physician.
- *Addictiveness and withdrawal*—Sometimes, the fears of clients and families are unfounded. Nevertheless, strong cautions are usually in order, especially with certain types of tranquilizers and sedatives. There is new

knowledge about drug withdrawal with some cyclic antidepressant medications, for example.

- *Self-administration principles*—Clients and families often need simple advice on how to take or store psychotropic medications, read labels, manage missed doses, or use reminders.
- *Compliance*—Frank discussion of why people stop taking their medication is crucial to compliance. This includes clarifying the attitudes and beliefs of both the client and the family. It is important to anticipate both short- and long-term barriers to medication use, such as fears of toxicity or expectations of efficacy and fears based on cultural influences.
- *Communication/negotiation*—Though not enough programs include information on communication skills, many clients need help talking about medication to their social worker, case manager, therapist, or psychiatrist. Because clients often feel incompetent or frightened in this area, teaching such skills seems logical, perhaps necessary.
- *Emerging trends/research*—Clients and families are interested in and often heavily invested in the latest medication research: what scientists are testing and what new trends or philosophies of care have evolved.

Summary

This chapter has provided a rationale for medication education, reviewed issues related to the implementation and evaluation of medication education programs, and discussed the content of such programs. Implicit in the chapter is a call for social workers to freely embrace the role of educator. Even in the face of understandable doubts about their competence to do so, social workers in all settings can and should start or contribute to such groups or programs, either alone or, ideally, in collaboration with other providers, clients, and families.

CHAPTER 7

Medication Adherence and Refusal

The regularity with which health care clients in general do not comply, or at least do not completely adhere to their prescribed medication regimen, is widely discussed in relation to diabetes, epilepsy, hypertension, AIDS, and especially mental illness and emotional distress. Even those not taking psychotropic or other medications can appreciate noncompliance. Most people can remember those antibiotics that they did not quite finish or taking extra pain killers because they knew from experience that the dosages on the label weren't quite right for them. And for many, taking antibiotics or pain medications may not have the same underlying meaning, and certainly not the same side effects as the psychotropic medications.

This chapter will discuss the social worker's need to address adherence and refusal holistically, including an awareness of related legal and ethical issues as well as what medications mean to clients and families. Much of this chapter is devoted to helping social workers understand the many theories and models used to explain adherence and nonadherence. In addition, we present specific techniques, based on our own model of adherence, to help clients increase their adherence to medication regimens, including specific diets, as mandated for example by MAO inhibitors. We rely on the term *adherence* because the term *compliance* has lost favor in recent years from a perceived negative connotation of passivity and obedience. Furthermore, *noncompliance* implies that the client has done something wrong or is deviant, which "does not often reflect reality from the client's perspective" (Morris & Schulz, 1993, p. 603).

Numerous authors have pointed out that adherence to medications is not usually all or nothing; rather, some degree of nonadherence can be expected about 50% of the time (Buckalew & Sallis, 1968; Kane, 1984). Outright refusal of medications, most often discussed in the context of inpatient treatment of psychotic patients, is rare (1–3%), even though much has been written on the right to refuse. Nonadherence can include not filling the prescription or accepting medication at all, filling the prescription or accepting the medication but not taking it, taking only a part of it, or not following the prescribed dosage, either by not taking the proper amount of drug or by not taking it in the desired frequency. For example, Jamison and Akiskal (1983) describe full compliance with lithium as uncommon, with "intermittent compliance" probably the most common form of compliance (p. 177). Even though inadequately treated bipolar disorder can lead to a recurrence of symptoms, interpersonal chaos, substance abuse, financial crises, and personal anguish, many people with bipolar disorder are not satisfied with the physical side effects or the personal and social implications of the medication. Similarly, many people with depressive disorders stop taking their antidepressant medication after only a month, even before the full therapeutic effect is likely (Morris & Schulz, 1992). Estimates of nonadherence among people with psychotic disorders is, again, about 50% after 1 year and perhaps as high as 75% after 2 years (Weiden et al., 1994). Those with both psychiatric and substance abuse problems have an even harder time with adherence (Wolpe, Gorton, Serota, & Sanford, 1993).

Unfortunately, most physicians see nonadherence as caused simply by their clients' denial of illness (Jamison & Akiskal, 1983). Though we think the issue is more complicated than that, this stance does relate to the clinician's general response to nonadherence. One study of medical doctors has found that how physicians respond to nonadherence depends on their own level of frustration with the patient. Because these doctors saw nonadherence as a threat to their own ego, they countered by withdrawing, using authoritarian tactics, and even making medical threats. These doctors most often took full compliance with medication for granted. In the face of nonadherence, they rarely if ever altered the medication regimen, tried to determine the causes of nonadherence, or enlisted family support (Heszen-Klemens, 1987). In the social work profession, Cohen (1993) notes the stigma associated with being labeled noncompliant, which he says often occurs in the first place because care providers fail to respond adequately to the expressed needs of the client. An emergency room visit that results in a prescription and an appointment card for a clinic visit in 2 weeks, for example, is not good crisis intervention. Labeling patients as noncompliant is "blaming the victim" for professional inadequacies. Obviously, we hope social workers will avoid this response and others like it.

Two caveats may be in order here. First, accurately measuring adherence to medications has been problematic (see Chapter 6). Even defining adherence, the necessary first step toward measurement, is difficult. For example, if adherence is not a *dichotomous variable,* yes or no, then is it an *ordinal variable,* with such values as completely compliant, very compliant, not so compliant, and so on? Urine tests; pill counts; self-, collateral, and clinical reports; and even electronic tracking devices have all been criticized with respect to reliability and validity (Hays & DiMatteo, 1987; Weiden et al., 1994). These problems make testing the impact of interventions difficult and call for the use of multiple measures when possible.

Second, social workers obviously need to be as interested in general adherence to treatment and aftercare as in medication adherence. One group of researchers estimates that drop-out rates range from 33% to 50%, depending on the population (Carrion, Swann, Kellert-Cecil, & Barber, 1993). Reasons for dropout include lack of transportation, forgetting, unemployment, and substance abuse, as well as the numerous barriers created by the treatment environment.

Models for Understanding Adherence

People do not take medications of any kind in a "thoughtless vacuum" (Stimson, 1974); as such, decisions regarding medication use must be seen in their biopsychosocial and cultural context. Many have grouped the factors associated with medication adherence and nonadherence into "compliance domains" (e.g., Weiden et al., 1994) or some other model or framework (e.g., DeGeest, Abraham, Gemoets, & Evers, 1994; Jamison & Akiskal, 1983; Leventhal, Diefenbach, & Leventhal, 1992; Morris & Schulz, 1993; Waller & Altshuler, 1986). Similarly, we will organize our discussion of these factors around four dimensions: characteristics of the client, aspects of the treatment, aspects of the environment, and the actual mental illness or symptoms. First, though more than 20 years of research into over 200 variables has not produced consistent information, the following review will still help social workers appreciate the complexity of adherence and thus, we hope, design multidimensional strategies and techniques to address it.

One of the most salient criticisms of the literature on adherence is that studies of clients' adherence are usually based on "an ideal image" of the client as a "passive, obedient and unquestioning recipient of medical instructions. Divergence . . . is seen as irrational in light of medical rationality" (Stimson, 1974, p. 97). There are a lot of reasons why people do or do not do what the doctor says, some completely rational (whether appearing so or not) and some not so rational. Stimson encourages social workers to understand adherence in light of the clients' views, of their illnesses, treatments, experiences, interactions, and expectations. This more active view of the clients will necessarily mean greater focus on the "social context in which illnesses are lived and treatments used" (p. 97), an appropriate assignment for social workers. Other writers have echoed Stimson's call. For example, Conrad (1985) says social workers should reject the "doctor-centered perspective" of compliance and move toward a "patient perspective" that suggests greater emphasis on health beliefs, self-regulation, and the meaning of medication to clients.

Characteristics of the Client

As we mentioned in Chapter 6, the health belief model states that people base health care decisions on (1) their understanding of some desired outcome, (2) their motivation to seek it, and (3) how they see a recommended "treatment" (medication, behavior change) as helping them realize the desired outcome

(Youssef, 1984). Thus, people experiencing severe anxiety will more likely take their prescribed anti-anxiety medication if (1) they genuinely understand what a lack of anxiety would be like for them, (2) they are genuinely motivated to try to reduce their anxiety, and (3) they appreciate the connection between taking the medication and achieving or maintaining a reduced state of anxiety. Clearly, this model calls for medication education (see Chapter 6). A study of 100 patients with schizophrenia, for example, has found a clear relationship between clients' insight into their illness or disorder (a recognition that a problem exists and requires medical intervention) and the perceived benefits of medication and medication adherence (Lin, Spiga, & Fortsch, 1979).

However, clients receiving medications may or may not place medical outcome or clinical efficacy at the top of their list. Instead they usually evaluate and balance a range of competing physical, economic, psychological, and social outcomes (Morris & Schulz, 1993). Thus, to truly understand the client's decisions about medication, clinicians must try to ascertain what outcomes that individual values most. A recent study shows that the desired outcomes of medication use reported by psychotic clients were mostly indirect; that is, the desired outcomes did not relate directly to symptom reduction, but rather to keeping them out of the hospital or to helping them stay out of trouble (Adams & Howe, 1993). People with depression or anxiety may adhere to their medications because they simply want to "get back on track at work" or "be a better parent." On the other hand, they may opt against their use because the most compelling outcomes are to not be labeled "crazy," to remain sexually responsive, or to continue to enjoy fine red wine. These cost-benefit analyses are quite complex.

The self-regulation model suggests that "what appears to be noncompliance . . . may actually be a form of asserting control over one's disorder" (Conrad, 1985, p. 29). Self-regulation includes both the client's perception of the health threat and his or her management of coping devices and emotional processes (Leventhal et al., 1992). Not surprisingly, adherence has been found to be inversely related to perceived health (Aspler & Rothman, 1984). The healthier clients perceive themselves to be, the less likely they will adhere to a drug regimen. Conrad notes that people with epilepsy take their medication, often in spite of absolutely hating it, not just to control seizures, but to reduce their own worrying and to *insure* a sense of normality. This again demonstrates why the use of analogies, such as diabetes or hypertension, can be useful.

Clients may regulate their own medication by increasing or decreasing doses or stopping medication altogether. Some authors claim that clients do this to

1. Test whether or not their illness or symptoms are still there, or just see what will happen
2. Control perceptions of dependence, because clients may see taking medications as a threat to self-reliance

3. Manage stigma, because the very act of taking medication relays certain information to other people and at some level acknowledges the client's differentness
4. Practically manage their symptoms or side effects, or regulate the disruption of lifestyle

Reducing the dose to decrease a bothersome side effect is said to be the most common example of self-regulation of medication. Increasing the dose during times of stress is also common (Morris & Schulz, 1993; Conrad, 1985).

Thus, the meaning that medication has for clients and their interpretation of being medicated is of utmost concern to the social worker trying to understand adherence issues and, indeed, clients' entire adaptations to their illnesses. Specifically, negative subjective experiences, such as the medication making the client "feel like a zombie," "useless," or "weak," have been associated with nonadherence. Not only the severity of symptoms or side effects, but also the client's conclusions about the experience of taking medication play a key role in adherence (Awad, 1992; Hogan, Awad, & Eastwood, 1983).

Almost all research of factors associated with adherence and nonadherence has tested demographic and other variables such as age, gender, socioeconomic status, level of education, type of disorder, and how long symptoms have existed. A few studies have found significant relationships; for instance, Draine and Solomon (1994) have found that older patients with fewer symptoms and a greater array of daily activities have greater adherence. However, sensory or memory impairments, impaired dexterity, as well as complexity of drug regimens and cost concerns, may place elderly patients at risk for nonadherence. One study cites that living alone puts patients at greater risk of nonadherence (Seltzer et al., 1980) and another shows that patients with greater internal locus of control are more compliant with their lithium (Kucera-Bozarth, Beck, & Lyss, 1982). Researchers have begun to explore the role of visual memory and cognitive function as a factor in adherence to medication (Isaac, Tamblyn, & McGill-Calgary Drug Research Team, 1993). In addition, initial research has begun to uncover whether differential perceptions of clients from diverse racial or ethnic backgrounds regarding drug toxicity and addictiveness impact adherence. In general, however, no *demographic* variables seem consistently related to adherence or non-adherence (Frank, Perel, Mallinger, Thase, & Kupfer, 1992; Jamison & Akiskal, 1983).

Aspects of Treatment

A number of factors related to the actual treatment itself are associated with adherence and nonadherence, including those that relate to the medication regimen, effects and side effects, the treatment system, and professional attitudes and behaviors. For one thing, long-term maintenance medications, the kind used by most mental health clients, are associated with greater nonadherence (Diamond, 1983). Complex regimens are also associated with greater nonadherence. Thus, clients with more than one medication or with challenging dosing schedules (such as more than once a day) are at higher risk of nonadherence than others (Blackwell, 1979). Some have even speculated that physical aspects of the pill—the shape, size, color and even taste—may contribute to adherence or nonadherence (Buckalew & Sallis, 1986). In addition, the cost of medication, perceptions of affordability, and general accessibility may each play a role. It seems obvious that if out-of-pocket costs for medication exceed the clients' budgets or if they cannot physically get the medications from a clinic or pharmacy, some nonadherence will likely occur. Alternatively, Morris and Schulz (1993) note that those who receive free medication are less compliant with medications, leading to the speculation that free medications are not as valued as those that require some personal sacrifice.

Not surprisingly, the quality and timing of drug effects also play a role in compliance. The delay between commencing medications and any significant therapeutic effect may frustrate the client and weaken the perceived link between the treatment and its benefit. Similarly, when medications leave the body's system slowly, depending on half-life, a client may become discouraged (see Chapter 4). However, adherence improves when the actual effects of a drug most closely match the client's expectations for clinical improvement, which the prescribing physician may or may not share, while truly meaningful and reliable improvement in symptoms provides perhaps the greatest incentive for adherence. In an examination of imipramine adherence in a group of 53 patients with depression, over 80% of whom were described as compliant, researchers found that of all the variables studied, "effective prophylaxis," or prevention of depressive symptoms, was the one most associated with compliance (Frank et al., 1992).

On the other hand, nonadherence may be most heavily associated with negative physical side effects. While some providers and families argue that "illness-related" reasons figure most heavily in nonadherence, and especially refusal, clients themselves most often point to unwanted side effects as the most important factor. The most bothersome side effects for clients of a range of medications may not be the most frequent or the most severe side effects. For example, though thirst, excessive urination, weight gain, fatigue, dry mouth, and sleepiness are the most *common* side effects of lithium treatment (see Chapter 4), clients rated weight gain, problems in concentration, mental confusion, and slowness as the most *bothersome* (Gitlin, Cochran, & Jamison, 1989). Clients rated mental slowness, weight gain, confusion and memory problems as those side effects most likely to make them stop taking their medication. However, tremors and mental slowness are the side effects most associated with *actual* self-reported nonadherence. In this study, 80% of the respondents reported experiencing at least one side effect and 20% no side effects at all, but the average number of side effects experienced was 10.6 (sd 6.8), 3.4 of which occurred often.

For neuroleptics, akathisia (a subtle internal restlessness, agitation, and impatience) is most associated with nonadherence (VanPutten, 1974). A recent study examines the side-effect profiles of 185 shelter residents in California, who showed a range of diagnoses, symptoms, and medications. Mostly persons with schizophrenia on neuroleptics, 63% of the residents reported a mild degree of at least one side effect and 36% reported between 3 and 13 different adverse effects (Segal, Cohen, & Marder, 1992). Dry mouth/throat, restlessness, weight gain or loss, diarrhea or constipation, depression, apathy, and dizziness were the most common. Severity ratings follow a similar order except that loss of sex drive and sensitivity to the sun were rated as severe in spite of their low prevalence (below 6%).

Aspects of the larger treatment system itself may also contribute to nonadherence. For example, a system of services or a treatment plan that inadequately educates or prepares clients and families, or one that structures an unfriendly aftercare environment, may actually foster nonadherence. The attitudes and behaviors of the clinical staff, especially psychiatrists and social workers, play a crucial role in shaping medication adherence of clients. Marked ambivalence, antagonism toward medication itself, or an attitude of "oversell" on the part of providers is associated with nonadherence (Jamison & Akiskal, 1983; Weissman, 1972). Clients and families will immediately see any pessimism about the client's capacity to change or a sense of hopelessness about prognosis on the part of social workers. A study at the Affective Disorders Clinic at UCLA shows that physicians' attitudes toward medications, as reflected in their perceptions of how well the medications would work, are strongly related to adherence (Jamison, Gerner, & Goodwin, 1979).

In contrast, social workers' attitudes have received more speculation than systematic study (Bentley, Farmer, & Phillips, 1991). Interestingly, there has been a general assumption that social workers have historically opposed the use of psychotropic medication because such use focuses on physiological functioning or perceptions of misuse. Cohen's (1988) extensive literature review challenges this assumption. Other studies support his contention that social workers tend to see psychotropic medication use as a necessary and effective component of mental health treatment. For example, Berg and Wallace (1987) present 60 social workers in inpatient and outpatient mental health settings who said that use of medications with discharged clients is a positive step. Bentley et al. (1991) show that a group of social work students held quite positive views of medication, although they admit that their findings regarding social work attitudes are difficult to interpret. They see midrange attitude scores on a researcher-developed measure as possibly reflecting a "proper level" of medication acceptance in that "both extremely negative or blindly positive attitudes may be inappropriate" (p. 287). On the other hand, midrange attitude scores may represent a high degree of ambivalence related to both positive and negative personal and professional experiences.

A lack of empathy toward medication-related dilemmas of clients and families is also problematic. Indeed, acknowledging medication issues as a serious concern and allowing clients and families to express and clarify their feelings about medication is a first step for social workers or any mental health care provider (see Chapter 2). One program went even further. Morse, Simon, & Balson (1993) describe a program in which 20 physicians and nurses took placebos on the same pill schedule as their HIV patients to better understand and empathize with them. This meant taking three pills 5 times a day at 4-hour intervals and keeping a diary of reactions. Although this part of the study lasted only 1 week and involved *no* physiological changes or side effects, long-lasting changes occurred in provider attitude and empathy. The diaries revealed intense frustration with rigid schedules and stigma felt from the need to take pills in public.

The interpersonal interactions between clients and their social workers or physicians matter a great deal. Levy (1978) points out that "source attractiveness" may play a role in adherence. That is, a provider's focused attention on her or his client, as well as joking, laughing, and friendliness, may contribute to adherence. A study from the late 1960s, for example, uses observational ratings of psychiatrists to examine those characteristics of therapists that were associated with high versus low patient dropout from drug treatment. Low-dropout therapists, to no one's surprise, were more active and positive, delivering more personalized services (Howard et al., 1970).

The social worker's ability to communicate seems an obvious influence on adherence. Because clients must understand recommendations about medication to adhere to them, communication is essential to cooperation (Hays & DiMatteo, 1987). Indeed, many have noted that the responsiveness of providers and the perceived quality of the provider-client relationship play important roles in adherence (Weiden et al., 1994; Kane, 1983).

Aspects of the Social Environment

The societal and community culture of medications, the extent of family and social support, and general cues and contingencies in the environment all tend to influence adherence to psychotropic medications. Certainly, public attitudes about the use or acceptance of psychotropic medication relate to various ideas about the causes of mental illnesses and emotional distress. For example, a National Institute of Mental Health (NIMH) study conducted with members of the general public in the early 1970s found that those who believe that people with mental illness lack moral strength are twice as likely to view tranquilizer use as a sign of weakness (Manheimer et al., 1973).

Today, tremendous variability exists in society's acceptance, or lack of acceptance, of psychotropic medication use. First, people have many questions, such as, is the medication for "situational stress" or a truly long-standing "illness?" Is the medication addictive? It seems people more easily accept certain medications under certain circumstances, with certain people and certain problems. To complicate matters further, *whom* the public will accept as users of medication is subject to change. People may fully support a co-worker's daughter on risperidone for schizophrenia or a distant relative on lithium for bipolar disorder. People may completely accept a best friend on Zoloft (sertraline) for depression, but they do not want their spouses taking Prozac (fluoxetine) to increase productivity at work.

In popular culture, people often see psychotropic drugs portrayed in an intensely negative way, such as forced on people with mental illnesses. Movies such as *Mr. Jones, Nuts, The Dream Team,* and *Crazy People* are just a few recent examples. In addition, newspapers headline horror stories about acts allegedly committed by people because they use Prozac (fluoxetine), and best-selling books warn of continued psychiatric and psychopharmacological expansionism (e.g., Breggin, 1987; Szasz, 1994; see also Chapter 9). However, countervailing influences also exist. Recent polls suggest a growing understanding of the biological basis of many mental illnesses and its treatment (Clements, 1993). Many contemporary dramas, such as *Prince of Tides* and *Awakenings,* suggest compassionate, reasoned, and appropriate use of psychotropic drugs. In either case, "social myth can dominate the interpretive process" of mental health clients and families (Lefenthal, et al., 1992, p. 152). Therefore, social workers must appreciate this larger societal context of psychotropic medication use, including their own vulnerability to popular culture's manipulation and influence.

Families can also exert positive or negative influences on medication adherence. If the family agrees with the prescribing physician, understands the rationale underlying medication use or somehow "believes in" it, and supports and perhaps even offers concrete help in achieving adherence or monitoring the effects of the medication, the family obviously has a positive influence. However, if the family presents undue pressure or competing beliefs, such as "All she needs to do is pull herself up by her bootstraps" or "If she would just turn it over to Jesus, everything would be OK," then the outcome is likely to be less positive. Interactions with friends, co-workers, and others can similarly affect decisions about medication use. Thale (1973) calls the effects of client, family, and societal attitudes toward psychotropic drugs, whether seen as "disgraceful weakness" or "intelligent use of science," the "sociodynamics of medication" (p. 32).

Aspects of the Illness or Symptoms

The last dimension in this framework for understanding adherence concerns factors related to the illness itself or its symptoms such as depression, anxiety, paranoia, grandiosity, hostility, and cognitive impairment. For example, if an individual does not take his or her medication because of a delusion that the drug is part of some germ warfare plot, this symptom will clearly influence nonadherence or even refusal. Perhaps a man in a manic phase simply believes he doesn't need his medication because he is king of the hill and can overcome his illness on his own. Or perhaps a woman is too depressed to get out of bed to go to the medicine cabinet or so depressed that she believes there's really no use, that treatment of her devastating illness is futile.

Everyone who has devised an explanatory model for adherence includes illness-related factors. Most psychiatrists, though not most clients, attribute medication refusal to these factors. Denial is usually discussed in this particular context. Social workers need to remember that it is sometimes difficult to determine if denial of the mental or emotional disorder, its implications, or the need for treatment, is an actual symptom of the disorder, or that denial which all human beings experience to protect themselves. Unfortunately, by heavily emphasizing client symptoms or "illness" as a cause of nonadherence, a logic of forcing medication against the client's will is set up, all in the name of her or his best interest.

A restatement may be useful here. To more holistically address various forms of nonadherence, as well as more effectively help with medication monitoring, social workers should draw from the wealth of knowledge that exists about factors that influence adherence, especially the complex physical, social, psychological, and emotional responses to medication.

Legal and Ethical Issues in Adherence and Refusal

Even though overt refusal of medication is said to be rare, a well-developed body of literature on the topic exists. Social workers should become familiar with this literature for at least two reasons. First, experience shows that social workers who work in either inpatient or outpatient settings will likely encounter medication adherence issues regularly, depending on the characteristics of the clients in their caseloads and how many they see. Second, the themes that emerge from the literature on refusal offer insight into the range of clients' rights issues in relation to medication monitoring and adherence.

As Lefley (1993) states, "The question of involuntary treatment embodies some of the most basic philosophical, clinical, and political issues in any society. . . . These issues are framed within the meaning of mental illness and any given time in history" (p. 7). Unfortunately, Lefley (1993) takes the position that most people who view mental illness as a strictly biological illness accept forced medication as a necessary evil, whereas those who see it mainly as a psychological phenomenon oppose forced medication. Following this logic, however one could argue that those with cancer or Down's syndrome or epilepsy should have restricted rights to make health care decisions simply because of the physiological and genetic natures of their illnesses. On the other hand, Lefley (1993) correctly identifies some of the important conflicts that emerge from this debate:

- The rights of the individual versus the rights of the group
- Civil liberties versus survival needs of people
- The rights of the disabled versus the rights of caregivers
- The obligation of society to protect its citizens

Perhaps the two biggest questions that relate to the right-to-refuse issue are

1. What is in the "best interest" of the client?
2. Who decides?

We believe that social workers should advocate the client's right to refuse medication (Bentley, 1993). The sole exception to this principle is a true emergency, such as when clients are physically harming themselves or others. Others have appropriately described a true emergency as when the patient is "presently violent" and the state's interest is "grave and immediate" (Weiner, 1985, p. 346) or when there is a "substantial likelihood of extreme violence, personal injury or self-destruction" (Judge Tauro, quoted in Ford, 1980, p. 337). One of the issues that social workers must confront is that some define "emergency" much more broadly, even to the point where *any* refusal or even reluctance on the part of the patient that conflicts with either the professional's or the family's judgment is grounds for forced medication. For example, Eisenberg, Hilliard, and Gutheil (1981) advocate including in the definition of emergency not only all potentially life-threatening behaviors but also any behavior that *could* be seen as "seriously health-threatening, either acutely or subacutely" (p. 98). Arguments to limit the client's right to refuse medication assume that people with mental illness, especially those who refuse medication, also have impaired judgment and that they need and truly want outside intervention (Rosenson, 1993). However, only one recent study seems to support this view. In it, 17 of 24 inpatients who refused medication report that overriding their refusal of medications might have been appropriate (Schwartz, Vingiano, & Perez, 1988).

A published debate between a social worker and a physician highlights the intensity of emotions around this topic. Remler, a physician, argues that restricting the right to refuse medication is a reasonably pragmatic approach for patients with such disorders as schizophrenia, brain damage, and mental retardation because they "simply can not be allowed to determine their behavior. . . . They do not want their behavior changed. . . . They must be coerced" (Remler & Cohen, 1992, p. 304). Cohen, a social worker, argues that Remler "transforms disturbed and disturbing men and women from moral agents into brain-disordered organisms" (p. 306). We also believe that automatically equating mental disability or, for that matter, involuntary hospitalization, with incompetence leads to a global indictment of the population that is destructive and stigmatizing (Bentley, 1991; Roth, Meisel, & Lidz, 1977). Presuming competence is an important check and balance in any due process procedure in that it helps to establish the extent and direction of proof, much as presuming innocence does in criminal cases. Surprisingly, in a recent study, 20% of clinical social workers equated involuntary commitment with incompetence (Wilk, 1994).

Indeed, evidence simply does not support the argument that people who refuse psychotropic medications are irrational, paranoid, assaultive, and dangerous (Zito, Routt, Mitchell, & Roering, 1985; VanPutten, Crumpton, &

Yale, 1976). Fears that refusals would result in longer hospital stays, violence, and chaos have largely been proven invalid (Brooks, 1987; Cole, 1982; Rodenhauser, Schwenker, & Khamis, 1987). While some still argue that increased rights to refuse medication have resulted in greater costs, staff injuries, and client belligerence (Ciccone, Tokoli, Gift, & Clements, 1993), the actual evidence suggests that is not the case. Sheline and Beattie (1992), in examining the impact of a California Supreme Court case, find that over two-thirds of involuntarily committed patients in their study still consent to treatment without incident. Those on no medication at all and the small percentage who did refuse were actually in the hospital the *least* amount of time.

The two preeminent value positions of the profession, self-determination and respecting the dignity and uniqueness of individuals, seem to call for the more client-centered response. An authority on social work ethics, Reamer (1987) says that "of course" clients who either refuse or withdraw consent to treatment should be considered legally and mentally capable. "The fact that clients may be taking psychotropic medication or may be disabled to some degree by mental illness does not in itself provide grounds for denying them the right to refuse or withdraw consent" (p. 427). Wilk's study (1994) of clinical social workers has found that though social workers generally support a range of client's rights issues, they show the least support for the right to refuse treatment. Only 30% supported a client's right to refuse medication, while 57% opposed it. Wilk concludes that her study has encouraging results *except* for this "disturbing minority who disagree with or appear to be indifferent to [clients'] hard earned rights" (p. 173). Interestingly, she notes that women in their 40s with 14–15 years of experience who have received their MSW in the 1970s were the most supportive of client rights. Men in their 40s with 12 years of experience who had received their MSW in the early 1970s were the least supportive of client rights.

Cohen calls involuntary drugging harmful to clients, "inhumane and unjustifiable" because it subverts the "ethical mandate" of social workers (Remler & Cohen, 1992, p. 307). Similarly, Bentley (1993) argues that if social workers are serious about respecting the dignity and uniqueness of individuals, they must also advocate strongly for the fair due-process procedures now required by law in the case of refusal. This advocacy recognizes that "forced drugging of a patient absent a determination that a person is not capable of rationally deciding what is good for himself" cannot exist (Davis v. Hubbard, 1980, p. 936). Social workers must also advocate for *real* procedural safeguards, ones that honor either what clients say they want or, in cases where substituted judgment is called for, ones that honor what the client *would* have articulated if she or he were competent. Thus, the expressed preference of the client should be the center of all deliberations. Otherwise, so-called procedural safeguards merely give the client the right to a second opinion (Stone, 1981).

Note that this position differs from that in which the provider or family can ultimately determine "the best interest" of the client. As indicated earlier, deciding on the client's best interest is a complicated task, influenced by issues of power and paternalism. For example, should best interest be legally determined or clinically determined? Lawyers and psychiatrists have fought about that question for years. Should family caregivers decide? Brown (1985) points out that the more providers or others can portray themselves as acting in the client's best interest, the more they can expand their power base. Others argue that it is the families who "really care" about the patients and that civil libertarians and advocates are often overly concerned with autonomy issues (Rosenson & Kasten, 1991). Social workers too must avoid any professional arrogance that they *really* know what "best interest" is, given their historical commitment to client rights or their holistic perspective. This attitude flies in the face of the partnership model of practice with clients' families, and other providers.

Social workers can look to the courts to provide a number of other "causes of action" that have provided a legal and ethical basis for allowing clients to refuse their medication. These include the right to privacy, prohibitions against battery, and freedom of religion. In any case, expanding clients' rights in treatment refusal has not led them to "rotting with their rights on" (Appelbaum & Gutheil, 1979) but instead helped reduce inappropriate administration of drugs and has reduced dosages (Brooks, 1987).

Parish (1993) summarizes the arguments of clients, their families, the mental health system, and society regarding involuntary interventions including medication. From the client's perspective, involuntary treatment may alleviate suffering, pain, and embarrassment; enhance recovery; or quicken "liberty". However, it may also cause a loss of self-determination and liberty and an abridgement of civil rights. It often means living with uncomfortable side effects. From the family's perspective, forced medication may mean improved perceptions of their own personal safety, but it can also cause considerable dissension in the family. From the perspective of the system and society, forced medication may be efficient and seemingly allows them to "do the right thing" but is clearly a form of social control unlike any other permitted by society.

Interventions to Assist in Medication Adherence

Based on the model of adherence presented in this chapter, this section focuses on specific strategies and techniques the social worker can use to deal constructively with refusal and to help clients increase their adherence to their medication regimens. Assuming mutual engagement in a working relationship, intervention begins with ascertaining a client's individual reasons for nonadherence. Our model suggests, for example, assessment of the client's "health beliefs" and expectations about medication, including any ethnic or cultural influences. It suggests ascertaining the real desired outcomes for clients and their ability to make connections between taking medication and achieving those outcomes. Social workers must also assess whether the medication is accessible, affordable, and sufficiently simple to take, and if family and friends support its use or merely tolerate it. Finally, social workers must take stock of their own attitudes and behaviors, and the attitudes of those around them, to consider their influence on a client's adherence. Thus, one of the most obvious and useful strategies for such intervention is reflective discussion with the clients and their families to clarify assumptions and build knowledge to help in other interventions. In Chapter 8, we discuss many appropriate strategies, such as monitoring, coping with side effects, problem solving, decision making, negotiation, and advocacy. Medication education also serves as a major intervention for medication nonadherence (see Chapter 6). In this chapter, we present a number of useful cognitive and behavioral techniques associated with increased adherence. Though the distinction between an "educational" strategy and a "cognitive" or "behavioral" one may not be clear, the latter two usually focus on precise behaviors that present either barriers or cues to adherence, as opposed to the former's more global effort to increase knowledge and change attitudes.

Behavioral strategies involve the systematic application of the principles of social learning and operant or respondent conditioning to problems with medication compliance (Bentley et al., 1990; Dunbar, Marshall, & Hovell, 1979). Positive reinforcement suggests that if taking medication is rewarded, it will likely increase in the future. To help clients and their families design such interventions social workers can draw on many potential reinforcers, including consumables (food, drink, cigarettes), leisure activities (sports, gardening, hobbies), possessions (perfume, combs, books), activities (movies, special events, shopping), and manipulative rewards (money, tokens). Social reinforcement (that is, providing pats on the back, side hugs, congratulations, verbal praise, and smiles) is thought to be the most powerful action taken to increase adherence. With the permission of the client, of course, families, peers, co-workers, roommates, or other people significant to clients can be trained to provide reinforcement for medication use.

Providing reminders, prompts, or cues is another useful and well-substantiated way to increase adherence if clients forget to take their medications. These prompts might include a note on the refrigerator door or on the bathroom mirror or a phone call from a family member or friend. Tailoring the medication means finding a way to fit the administration of the drug, or for that matter the prompt itself, to some idiosyncrasy or ritual of the client. Bentley et al. (1990) offers "Harry," who learns to take his medication at 7:30 right before his favorite TV show, *Wheel of Fortune.* A Post-a-note reminder stuck to the remote control summarizes the main reasons he takes his medication (helps him to stay calm and to sleep).

Contracting is a more formal and often written agreement that specifies the contingencies for both adherence and nonadherence. Though familiar to most social workers, contracting often occurs implicitly rather than explicitly in everyday practice. With specific "if–then" statements, delineation of participants' roles, and planned reinforcements, contracting is also extremely common to those who rely on behavioral techniques in other professions or areas of interventions. Bentley et al. (1990) presents "Tammy," whose social worker helps to create a sophisticated contract in partnership with the family. Tammy takes her medication for a number of points each day (the points decrease the more she has to be reminded), which she can later exchange for back-up reinforcers, such as talking to a friend on the phone and renting a video. At the same time, her parents are learning about giving simple, matter-of-fact prompts (as opposed to nagging or unhelpful ones), such as "If you take your medication now, you will get 8 points."

Though *cognitive strategies* are commonly used to increase medication compliance with people who have medical problems (DiMatteo & DiNicola, 1982; Turk, Salovey, & Litt, 1986), their use is not as well documented with mental health clients. The presumption is that such disturbed thinking or judgment contraindicates their use. Nevertheless, it seems reasonable that self-instruction, guided imagery, relaxation, reframing and thought-stopping could help in a number of circumstances. For example, a social worker could lead the client in an exercise of guided imagery to help a former drug abuser on antidepressants imagine resisting offers of cocaine and reframing their thoughts of rejection and loneliness into stories of survival and hope. They could then learn how to recreate the imagery and practice the reframing at home.

Clearly, our suggested intervention in cases of refusal rests on the principles of partnership and self-determination. In certain cases of involuntary treatment, such as rare cases of unmanageable psychosis, the intervention should be "strictly time-limited, gentle, respectful and as non-intrusive as possible" (Parrish, 1993, p. 20). Though an apparent contradiction in terms, this nevertheless seems a goal worthy of pursuit. Fighting about medication is likely to be counterproductive; rather than forced treatment, social workers need an appreciation and empathy toward the client's choice and collaboration, negotiation, problem solving, and planning (Diamond, 1983). One psychiatrist writes, "I respected each patient's right to refuse while insistently keeping alive the possibility that they may decide to accept [it]" (Geller, 1982, p. 113). Problem solving and planning helps clients and families look at their options and prepare for possible crises. This process may involve increasing the psychosocial supports given, reviewing warning signs and planning for early intervention, or discussing advance directives or other substituted judgment agreements. Bernheim and Lehman (1985) suggest that clients and families create a long-term timetable for ultimate compliance with treatment, of which medication adherence may only be a part. For example, clients and families could set yearly goals as follows: year 1 as achieving medication compliance, year 2 as self-administration and monitoring, year 3 as attending day treatment, year 4 as attending a support group, and so on. Furthermore, Carpenter and Heinricks (1983) specifically suggest that marked reduction of medication use should be part of any intervention program. Alternative strategies include "targeted" or "intermittent" use in which clients receive medication only when faced with impending signs of relapse or a return of symptoms.

Achieving adherence and dealing productively with refusal over the long term calls for using a number of combined strategies such as self-monitoring, education, and cognitive, behavioral, and other psychosocial strategies in the context of a caring relationship. Social workers also need to review their own delivery of service and organizational structure for ways to create a climate conducive to accepting diversity in client choices and supporting adherence to a well-planned and supported treatment regimen. For instance, making appropriate training available to staff or revising policies and procedures can help create this climate. Though some note that social workers must sometimes accept that all of those efforts don't work, this is not permission to give up, but a call for patience and persistence.

CHAPTER 8

Medication Monitoring and Management

Monitoring both medication and the progress of treatment and general rehabilitation is crucial to reducing client symptoms and enhancing psychosocial functioning. This chapter specifically deals with how social workers can help clients and families monitor and manage their medication in everyday life. *Monitoring* and *managing* include helping clients and families keep track of the medication's physical, psychological, and social effects, cope with bothersome side effects, solve problems, make decisions, and negotiate with providers about medication-related issues. For the social worker, monitoring also means acting as an advocate on behalf of clients and their families. Of course, any discussion, with either clients or families, of the rationale, dosage, side effects, and impact of medications offers social workers an opportunity to clarify attitudes about *any* aspect of treatment and to address these concerns. Even with full medication adherence, clients and families still need education and support as they learn how to manage the illness or disorder.

As stressed in the chapter on medication adherence, "sophisticated and optimal treatment also entails careful attention to those psychosocial variables that may affect the ultimate outcome of the drug treatment regimen" (Docherty, 1986, p. 118). Docherty (1986) notes that monitoring drug response should also include monitoring the stress and activity levels of the client with an eye toward avoiding overstimulation. The social worker must first identify expected changes, then compare them to what actually occurred. Thus, the role of the social worker in monitoring and managing medication is varied and complex and, like all roles in psychopharmacology, is meant to be carried out in the context of a partnership model of practice. Luckily, there is now good evidence that mental health clients and their families can and do participate in monitoring and managing medications. For example, families usually understand the prodromal phase of their or their loved one's illnesses. McCandless-Glimcher et al. (1986) summarize the results of a number of studies showing that, by far, most psychiatric patients and their families can and do recall changes in thoughts, feelings, or behavior prior to the onset or recurrence of symptoms. In one study, 98% of the clients with psychosis knew when their symptoms were getting worse (McCandless-Glimcher et al., 1986). In another study, 70% of clients diagnosed with schizophrenia knew when they were getting sick again and 90% could tell when they were getting better (Herz, 1984). More than two-thirds of families and half of clients recognized signs of relapse over a week ahead of the actual relapse. This means that ample time often exists for social workers and others to help make decisions about what next steps can and should be taken. Furthermore, this ability to recognize an impending relapse has been associated with reduced hospitalizations among people with serious mental illness. For example, in a study of 38 clients with schizophrenia, only 8% of those judged to have "early insight" relapsed, versus 50% of those without this early recognition (Heinrichs, Cohen, & Carpenter, 1985). Such early insight will most likely be as helpful to those with less serious mental illness or emotional distress and can help social workers design useful interventions for clients and families.

The legal and ethical issues in compliance and refusal will also arise in discussions about monitoring. That is, similar questions emerge in this arena, such as Who makes decisions about treatment planning and implementation? What is the "best interest" of the client? How can the rights of the individual on medication be balanced with the responsibility of families, providers, and society? Because ethical conflict is intrinsic to monitoring and all aspects of social work, translating the lofty values of the profession into strategies for action will always be a challenge.

One ethical issue that arises in monitoring medication is *subtle* coercion. If good evidence exists to encourage clients to use medication, where do social workers draw the line between coercion and encouragement? In spite of a partnership model of practice, which emphasizes equal power between social worker and client, vestiges of major power differentials persist. Because many agencies still strongly support these differentials, social workers and clients should watch for them, especially how they influence the client's perceptions of decision-making freedom. For example, Cohen (1988) believes there can be no distinction between coercion and encouragement; therefore, social workers should simply not be in the business of recommending psychotropic drugs. However, we believe that even though the line is difficult to draw, social workers should not abandon the task of trying to find the right place to draw it.

Ethical issues and conflicts also emerge in the daily management of interdisciplinary relationships (see Chapters 2 and 9). For example, though we believe that social workers should actively assist in the medication-related dilemmas of clients and their families, we recognize that the ultimate legal responsibility for choosing and adjusting the types of medication used, prescribing the actual dosages, and watching for the therapeutic effects, physical side effects, and drug interactions lies with the prescribing physician. In addition, nurses and pharmacists each have a long and distinguished professional history related to distributing and explaining medications, which should be respected. These roles underscore the desirability of interdisciplinary collaboration.

Client Self-Monitoring of Medication

By far, most clients will change their behavior or engage in some kind of self-treatment in response to recognized signs of relapse and side effects. Kabat-Zinn et al. (1992) present the self-regulation strategies of people diagnosed with anxiety disorders, including meditation, relaxation, and other techniques to reduce anxiety, often with good success. Booker et al. (1984) examine the "self-healing" or compensatory practices of 40 inpatients in response to their own depression, stimulus overload, or perceptual problems. Contrary to the myth that people with mental illness always withdraw in response to such symptoms, these researchers have found a high amount of problem-solving efforts.

Self-monitoring involves two things: the client noting the occurrence of some behavior and then systematically recording it (Kopp, 1988). Clients who monitor their own use of medication must track (1) the taking of medication, (2) symptoms, and (3) side effects. Admittedly, clients and social workers can find distinguishing between symptoms and physical side effects challenging. Client self-monitoring not only helps social workers collect information on which to base daily treatment decisions, but also helps clients develop some level of self-awareness and increases their involvement and sense of power in the treatment process (Kopp, 1988; Lukoff, Liberman, & Nuechterlein, 1986). Even clients who do not begin with much understanding of their illness or distress can develop it in the context of a caring therapeutic relationship (Heinricks et al., 1985). One program even used self-management as a major focus of an inpatient treatment effort. So they could become better prepared for self-medication after discharge, clients on a psychiatric unit obtained their own medication from the nurses' station (Coudreat-Quinn, Emmons, & McMorrow, 1992). The mandatory education program, like many of those discussed in Chapter 6, included identifying and managing side effects and learning how to obtain more information on specific drugs.

Perhaps the most common concrete strategy for self-monitoring of medications is using a checklist of symptoms, either an existing one or an idiosyncratic one developed from the known experiences of the client. Identifying the "warning signs" of relapse and common side effects is almost always part of comprehensive psychoeducational programs for mental health clients and their families (see Chapter 6). Though an existing checklist may have dozens of items with rather general categories, such as "trouble sleeping," "avoiding activities," and "confusion" (see Table 1), social workers can help clients and families create more precise and individualized measures, and perhaps less overwhelming ones, such as "How many days last week did you wake up before 6:30 A.M.?" or "How much did you avoid contact with the members at Sunrise House today? A lot, A good bit, Some, Not much." Falloon et al. (1984) used the latter strategy in their 2-year, behavioral family management study in which participants identified two "warning signals"

TABLE 1
Symptom Checklist

____ Nervousness, tenseness
____ Trouble sleeping (too much, too little)
____ More than usual fatigue, no energy
____ Depression
____ Difficulty thinking or concentrating
____ Less active than usual
____ Unable to get going (get up, go)
____ Irritability
____ Difficulty doing work
____ Avoiding activities with others
____ Moodiness
____ Trouble eating (too much, too little)
____ Confusion
____ Hear voices
____ Recurrent thoughts
____ People are talking/laughing at you
____ Others tell you that you are strange
____ Get special messages (from the TV, radio)
____ Lapses in memory
____ Think someone is trying to hurt you
____ Getting harassed by others
____ Nightmares
____ Religious concerns
____ Headaches
____ Think you have special powers
____ Things look funny
____ Think everyone can hear your thoughts
____ Trouble talking so people can understand
____ Feel like you are losing control of your thoughts
____ Something is controlling or putting thoughts in your head
____ Feel like hurting self
____ Speech problems
____ Sexual concerns
____ You see things that others don't
____ Heart pounding
____ Feel like you are really not here
____ Feel pressure in your head
____ Feel something terrible or strange is happening to your body
____ More active than usual
____ Legal problems or trouble with the police
____ Can't stop doing something over and over
____ Having trouble getting along with other people
____ Feel being controlled by a device (computer, electrodes)
____ Feel like hurting others
____ Everyone around you seems dead

Based on McCandless-Glimcher et al., 1986.

from the client's previous relapse, which were then rated monthly on a severity scale between 1 and 7.

Two more examples may help to demonstrate this approach. A social worker helps "Bob" create a graph to monitor the side effects of his antidepressant medication as well as his depressive symptoms. On it, Bob learns to keep track of his level of hopelessness, the number of hours he sleeps, dry mouth, and sexual dysfunction. The social worker also helps "Joan," a 62-year-old woman with a psychotic disorder and a history of numerous relapses and currently taking fluphenazine and benztropine, create a simple checklist of her unique "warning signals," on which she can write "yes" or "no," depending on whether or not she experiences the symptoms on a given day. Items include "Voices are using profanity," "Voices are getting louder," "Can sit through all of *Jeopardy*." The sheet she fills out in the morning also has previously negotiated steps for her to take in case of problems. Obviously, as with any tool, clients and/or family members should be motivated and willing to use checklists, which should be easy to use and periodically checked for accuracy and relevancy.

In their comprehensive review of self-management interventions, Ivanoff and Stern (1992) report that individuals use a wide array of these techniques to address their physical and mental health concerns, including chronic pain, insomnia, depression, anger, anxiety, agoraphobia, and lack of assertiveness. Though self-monitoring "was the single component most often associated with positive outcome" (p. 37), they found not one study in the major social work journals that addresses the maintenance and generalization of self-monitoring skills. As such, social workers cannot assume that once clients have been taught to use self-monitoring techniques, they will do so indefinitely. The rationale for medication in general and medication monitoring in particular may need regular revisiting and reinforcement. Clients need to see that what they do impacts clinical decision making and the quality of their lives. Social workers can and should be a part of making those connections.

Concrete Steps for Coping with Side Effects

Clients cite bothersome side effects as a major reason for nonadherence. In addition, research has shown that the severity of such side effects is inversely related to the client's quality of life (Sullivan, Wells, & Leake, 1992). Thus, it is important that social workers respond to complaints and concerns about side effects in a way that supports the client's treatment goals, validates the client's experiences, and provides reasonable choices for action.

When complaints about side effects emerge, social workers should first make sure the medications are being correctly administered. However, because most side effects abate after a few days to a few weeks, physicians usually first recommend encouraging the client simply to wait a while. Social workers should recognize that this advice may sound simplistic and patronizing to clients asked to endure uncomfortable and meaning-laden physiological reactions.

The next piece of advice the prescribing physician usually gives is to reduce the dose, add another medication, or change the medication. Because management of dosages and schedules is largely an individual matter, relying on trial and error, minor or even major adjustments in medication are obviously extremely common. Direct observation by others and blood tests provide two possible sources of information about the effects of medication. However, because clients' descriptions of their experiences with the effects and side effects usually provide the most important information for these adjustments, skills to help clients talk to and negotiate with their physicians and psychiatrists will be discussed later in this chapter.

Client and family guides and manuals often provide the best sources of concrete and simple ways to live with some less serious physical side effects (e.g., Falloon, et al., 1984; Mueser & Gingerich, 1994; Yudofsky, Hales, & Ferguson, 1991). For example, advice to deal with drowsiness centers on taking the medication at or near bedtime and scheduling short naps during the day. Clients may reduce akathesia or internal restlessness as well as muscle stiffness by stretching or other physical activity. Dry mouth can be helped by sucking on sugar-free candy or sipping water; constipation by drinking 8–10 glasses of water daily, eating fresh fruits and vegetables, and using stool softeners or Metamucil, if needed. With increased weight, clients may need to change medications or just get some common-sense advice about diet and regular exercise. Orthostatic hypotension, or dizziness upon standing, can be combated by helping the client practice getting up very slowly from a lying or seated position. Sensitivity to sunburn responds well to sunscreens and avoiding peak sun exposure.

For some physical side effects, such as hormonal changes, tremors, and rashes, there are usually no quick solutions. Other side effects, such as agranulocytosis, aplastic anemia, acute dystonias, and neuroleptic malignant syndrome, demand immediate medical attention.

Tardive dyskinesia (TD) has created the most controversy to date about side effects, with the possible exception of concern over fluoxetine (see Chapter 9). Critiques of psychiatry, for example, have speculated that "resistance and incomplete recognition" of TD has a long history and relates to issues of client subordinance, professional dominance, and the overreliance on drug treatments in general (Brown & Funk, 1986, p. 116). At the center of the controversy lie questions about true prevalence and the availability of effective treatment. Estimates of the prevalence of TD vary widely. Feltner and Hertzman (1993) estimate that about 20% of those who receive long-term treatment with neuroleptics will develop TD. Most cases will be "mild but persistent," but "some may be irreversible" (p. 25). They also note that a 1992 report concludes that there are no safe and effective treatments for TD. Such treatments have included vitamin E, calcium channel blockers, dopamine agonists, lithium, and benzodiazapines. Apparently, the best advice offered by psychiatrists is still to discontinue the drug or reduce the dosage. Feltner and Hertzman report that 40% of the clients in their own studies who did this achieved a 50% reduction of TD symptoms. They also acknowledge that because reducing or stopping medication is quite difficult for some individuals with TD, social workers may need to make a careful assessment and review of risks and benefits. Clearly, social workers can and should participate in these important decision-making processes.

Besides monitoring physical side effects, both clients and social workers should monitor the psychological, emotional, and social side effects of taking medication. In addition to regularly inquiring and helping clients articulate and reflect on these issues, depending on their level of functioning or interest, social workers might also encourage clients to keep a journal of their reactions or express their feelings in art. Though no art therapy program to date explicitly aims to help people monitor and cope with their own responses and side effects to medications, such therapy has helped people with such disorders as depression, bipolar disorder, and schizophrenia (e.g., Buchalter-Katz, 1985; Green, Wehing, & Talesk, 1987; Wadeson, 1987). In the field of social work, Potocky (1993) describes the use of an art therapy group in a residential facility to help residents increase their social skills through self-expression and social interaction. Admittedly, these approaches for encouraging expression, ventilation, and developing insight are intuitively appealing but in general untested and might best be thought of as potentially useful adjuncts to more traditional supportive techniques (Lisenbee, 1994).

It is hard to imagine techniques more relevant and useful to medication management than traditional social work strategies such as empathetic listening, support, reflective discussion, and interpretation. This is evident when helping clients manage the differences between their expectations of a drug's effect versus the actual effect. For example, clozapine has often been associated with dramatic improvements as shown in the movie *Awakenings*. Though some individuals, formerly unable to complete logical sentences or participate fully in daily activities, are now holding excellent jobs and are rediscovering the world, these success stories are by no means a universal or even typical response to clozapine. Without the same results, others using the same drug can experience overwhelming disappointment or despair. We suspect that this scenario is played out on a smaller scale in the lives of our clients all the time. Obviously, social workers can and should offer the warmth, empathy, support, and genuine concern that is needed in these situations, because both outcomes may require huge adjustments in emotional functioning, self-concept, and lifestyle.

Decision Making and Problem Solving in Medication Management

One could argue that problem solving is the heart of social work practice. As such, most texts on social work present various models of the problem-solving process and direct practitioners to work collaboratively through the steps with their clients as systematically as possible. Newer texts include substantial content on how to teach clients the problem-solving process and apply it to concerns and decisions that arise in everyday life (e.g., Hepworth & Larsen, 1993). Other helping professions also value such training for clients as an avenue for increased social competence. For example, D'zurilla (1986) looks at the effectiveness of problem-solving training across a wide variety of target groups, including people with alcohol dependency or psychiatric problems, depression, agoraphobia, stress, weight problems, marital and family problems, vocational indecision, and problems with academic achievement. He concludes that very promising support for using problem-solving training as a clinical intervention can help clinicians move away from defect models of psychopathology. Problem solving, then, becomes a portable self-management technique and coping strategy that serves as a buffer against future problems.

You can easily find specific examples of successful problem-solving training programs for people with mental illness and emotional distress. These are often presented as the backbone of family psychoeducation programs (e.g., Barrowclough & Tarrier, 1992; Falloon et al., 1984; Mueser & Gingerich, 1994). Positive outcomes range from increased problem-solving knowledge and problem-solving behaviors to more global measures of outcome such as increased social functioning and decreased depression.

Falloon et al. (1984), in examining the problem-solving sessions of their behavioral family management project, show that "coping with illness" was the most frequent topic chosen, representing the content of 17% of all problem-solving sessions. Rather than being raised mostly at the beginning of their intervention project, as might be expected, the "coping with illness" concerns were evenly distributed throughout the two years, highlighting the need for social workers to continue to address and respond to medication, side effects, and symptoms over the long run.

Problem-solving training involves reviewing the six steps of the problem-solving process and then applying them to real decisions, problems, or questions. We have taken the following steps from Hepworth and Larsen (1993), Falloon et al. (1984), and Mueser and Gingerich (1994) and have provided an example for each.

1. *Define the problem*—The first, most important, and most difficult step in problem solving involves determining what exactly the problem is. This is achieved through discussing the problem openly and sharing perspectives either in a group or with a provider; clients may also define problems by themselves using the learned steps outside clinical supervision. Mueser and Gingerich (1994) suggest providing a "Defining Problems Exercise" to help clients and families understand the challenges in defining problems. That is, they suggest offering a case vignette with which clients and families could "practice" every step of the process before working with their own problems.
2. *Generate possible solutions*—In this step, participants share their ideas for solutions to the agreed-upon problem in a nonevaluative environment.

With such brainstorming, everyone should be encouraged to participate. Even outrageous ideas for solutions should be made welcome. Falloon et al. (1984) suggest that at least five or six solutions be identified and that great care be taken at this point to avoid evaluative comments, such as "That's a crazy idea" or "Yes let's do that!"

3. *Evaluate the pros and cons of each solution*—This step involves evaluating the positive and negative aspects of each brainstormed idea. Mueser and Gingerich (1994) suggest moving through this step rather quickly by highlighting only main strengths and weaknesses. Falloon et al. (1984) also suggest avoiding lengthy debates but emphasizing that each idea has merits.
4. *Choose the "best" solution*—This step involves coming to consensus on a solution or some combination of solutions based on the evaluation. It calls for clear communication and a willingness to negotiate and compromise.
5. *Plan how to carry out the solution*—Even the best of solutions cannot be implemented without some plan of action. In this step, plans are broken down into manageable tasks; assigned to participants according to interest, time, resources, and ability; and included with a time frame for completion. Discussion that anticipates potential negative consequences may also help. Participants should practice steps that require some overt skill or activity. Mueser and Gingerich (1994) provide a suggested "Action Planning Worksheet," much like a typical social work contract, that specifies the task, the person assigned to carry it out, the target date for completion, and a column to be checkmarked upon completion of the task. Clients might want to place this worksheet on the refrigerator as a reminder. Falloon et al. (1984) suggest that someone in the family or group (when relevant) be elected as coordinator.
6. *Review implementation and praise ALL efforts*—At some future time, mutually agreed on, the group will evaluate the progress of task completion in particular and problem solving in general. Social workers should lavishly praise all efforts. In cases in which individual clients use the process on their own, they should be encouraged to reward all accomplishments. It may be necessary to return to other steps in the process, particularly if the tasks were completed but the problem remains. The cyclical nature of problem solving should be stressed. *Partial success* is a useful way to describe the most common outcomes of problem solving. Failure should be reserved for those rare occasions when no efforts are made to achieve progress.

It may help to consider how such problem-solving efforts might help in an actual case taken from Chapter 1. Darlene is a 22-year-old single woman, unemployed and currently living with her sister in an apartment, but financially supported by her parents, who were very involved in her treatment planning and care. Darlene suffers from bipolar disorder, which has required a number of hospitalizations in the last 3 years. Though stable on a combination of antipsychotic and mood-stabilizing drugs, Darlene stopped taking them. Her parents became furious with the social worker and the agency when they found they did not know about it. Darlene finally revealed that she hadn't been honest about her adherence and was actually intentionally trying to prompt a regression out of her own fears of increasing responsibility. However, it was too late. The family decided to terminate care from this agency.

In this case, the client and family might have come together to solve a number of problems to prevent the impending relapse and the major disruption in service to Darlene. For example, they could have examined Darlene's worsening symptoms, her covert noncompliance, her fears of independence, the family's anger at the agency, or even continuous care for Darlene in the transition to a new provider. In discussing Darlene's worsening symptoms, joint problem solving would have afforded opportunities for the group to "define the problem" from each perspective, to express their feelings and disappointments, and to offer important reassurances. Darlene's nonadherence and her fears about becoming more independent would likely have surfaced. Brainstorming possible solutions might have yielded ideas such as increasing responsibility more slowly, adding psychosocial supports, arranging for additional counseling about her fears, learning more about medication, and adding tangible rewards for adherence. Each person in the group could help evaluate alternatives and select and monitor a solution or combination of solutions.

Hepworth and Larsen (1993) offer much guidance on how to prepare clients effectively for problem solving, how to introduce the process to them, and how to manage interaction during the sessions. These guidelines stress laying the groundwork for problem solving early in the intervention phase; maintaining a positive, collaborative stance; and being sure to praise and highlight connections between problem-solving efforts and goal attainment. As with skills training, problem-solving training begins with providing clients and families a rationale for the skill, which in this case is the use of a step-by-step process. Being specific when discussing problems and solutions, focusing on the present, breaking a problem into smaller parts (partialization), and listening actively are all keys to successful use of problem solving.

Because both teaching and problem solving work well in large audiences, many problem-solving training programs focus on families, groups of clients in clinics, support groups, clubhouses, or residential facilities as the targets of intervention. Nevertheless, social workers can readily teach problem-solving skills to individuals. Though the content of training programs is remarkably similar, usually a review of the six steps just summarized, the suggested format often varies. For example, D'zurilla (1986) describes different methods of presentation for teaching problem solving, including didactic presentations, slides, video demonstrations and taped practice, specially created games, and group exercises. Role playing and homework are always crucial components of such programs.

Foxx and Bittle (1989) have developed a program that specifically addresses problem solving for medication issues. They present a curriculum for teaching people with mental illness what they call assertive problem solving, with similar curriculums for people with developmental disabilities, brain injuries, and adolescents. Curriculum materials include trainee score-recording forms, a facilitator's scoring guide, and evaluation forms to make precise tracking of progress possible. Participants are taught to use a problem-solving "cue card," which provides guiding questions for the participants to solve case scenarios. By applying the following questions to each problem situation, participants build problem-solving competence:

1. When will the problem be solved?
2. Where would you (or a friend) look for help?
3. Whom would you talk to?
4. What would you say? (p. 6)

Participants receive 48 problem-situation cards with cases that deal with many topics such as obtaining professional help, stating one's rights, interpersonal issues, authority figures, community resources, and medication. Here are some examples of the problem situations that relate to medication, adapted from Foxx and Bittle (1989):

1. Every time you take your medication you become very fidgety and can't concentrate on one thing very long. What should you do?
2. A friend of yours has been taken off her medication for some time and doesn't understand why her doctor has placed her back on it. She is thinking of not filling the prescription and not letting her doctor know. How would you help?
3. You feel the treatment you've been receiving at the community mental health center is not helping. What should you do? (pp. 7, 10)

In example one, the answers to the "cue card" questions might be

1. The problem will be solved when I am not fidgety and stop losing my concentration after taking my medication.
2. I could look up my doctor or pharmacy in the phone book.
3. I could talk to my pharmacist, doctor, or social worker.
4. I could say, "Whenever I take my medication, I get fidgety and can't concentrate. I am taking [name of medication]. What should I do?"

Social workers could easily adapt or expand not only the case scenarios but also the answers to the questions for use with other medication-related problems. These might include the ambiguity some clients feel about the rationale for medication use, the impact of medication on the client's sense of self, compliance issues, the client's concerns about his or her relationship with the prescribing physician, and any agency policy that precludes effective psychopharmacology practice.

Negotiating Medication Issues with Health Care Providers

Clients and families need certain communication skills to discuss medication-related concerns with the client's providers. Similarly, as a foundation for a productive partnership, social workers must also have the knowledge and skills to negotiate with clients, families, and physicians and other health care providers. As presented in Chapter 6, a few psychoeducation programs include "how to negotiate" with mental health providers. For example, Collins-Colon (1990) stresses five principles of negotiation in her medication-management protocol. She suggests teaching clients to remain calm during all communication, to jot down questions about their medications to bring to their appointments, to write down the answers and repeat them back to insure clarity, to make sure all information is clearly understood before they leave, and to teach clients to be assertive, not aggressive.

In fact, assertiveness provides a base for the communication skills needed to effectively negotiate with health care providers. Galassi, Galassi, and Vedder (1981) review a number of definitions of assertiveness and conclude that it means being able to communicate one's desires and feelings directly. This includes being able to say "no"; to ask for favors or make requests of others; to express positive and negative feelings; to initiate, continue, and terminate conversations; to accept and give compliments; to express personal opinions; and to stand up for one's rights. Thus, assertiveness is a necessary precondition to effective negotiation. One can see how clients would need to be able to say "No, I don't want to discontinue medication until after I start my new job" or "Please change my medication to one that does not increase my appetite, because I already have a weight problem" or "Dr. Smith, I'd really like to clarify your availability after-hours" or even "I don't think the medication is helping."

Focused discussions with clients and families of assertiveness versus aggressiveness and nonassertiveness may serve as a helpful precursor to more specifically directed communication skills training. Clients can help articulate the differences in these three interactive styles and how their own and others' behaviors reflect them. Hepworth and Larsen (1993), for example, note that assertive communication is characterized by a relaxed posture and direct eye contact with appropriately varied eye contact and moderately expressive gestures. On the other hand, aggressive communication is characterized by a glaring stare, pursed lips, rigid posture, and loud and sarcastic speech. Nonassertive communication is characterized by evasive eye contact, nervousness, and soft, whiny, and hesitant speech. Social workers can also help clients and families explore the feelings that each style elicits. How does it feel when someone points a finger and raises his or her voice? To understand how these differences relate to medication management, clients can generate examples, or social workers can create case scenarios based on their experience, of aggressive or passive behavior preventing some desired outcome, such as getting a timely appointment with the prescribing physician or getting the physician to agree to reduce dosage. Examples can also be shared of assertive behavior helping to reach a goal, such as getting a "drug holiday" or trying one of the newer generation of antidepressants.

Liberman, Kane, Vaccaro, & Wirshing (1987) detail how to teach clients the microskills of negotiating with their health care providers, one of the four "skill areas" in their Medication Management Module (see Chapter 6). They provide 11 specific requisite behaviors for "Negotiating with Health Care Providers," which look remarkably like those needed for assertiveness. Effective negotiation means that clients should be able to

- pleasantly greet the provider
- describe their problem specifically
- tell the length of its occurrence
- describe the extent of their discomfort
- specifically request some action
- repeat or clarify the doctor's advice
- ask about the expected time frame of effect
- thank the provider for assistance
- establish and maintain good eye contact
- maintain good posture
- speak audibly and clearly (adapted from Eckman & Liberman, 1990; Eckman et al., 1990, 1992).

These skills can be taught using a structured skills-training process. We have summarized this process as six steps conducive to working with individuals, groups, or families.

1. *Discuss the rationale for the skill*—The first step involves engaging the clients in the training process by building together a motivating rationale for learning the skill and each behavior required to perform the skill. Clients need to see, for example, the connections among effectively asking questions of physicians, understanding the physician's dosage rationale, and a generally greater knowledge of and motivation for using the psychotropic medication.
2. *Identify the components of the skill*—Every skill can and should be broken down into manageable components or steps, which the client can help articulate. Thus, for example, clients who try to get clarification of medication orders perform at least three steps: (1) Looking at the physician/health care provider, (2) Telling the provider what they heard her or him say about the medication orders, saying "I understood you to say ________" or "Did you say that ________," and (3) Directly asking for feedback, such as "Is that right?" The extent to which components of any given skill are broken down depends on the functioning level of the client or family member.

3. *Model the skill*—In this step, the social worker actually demonstrates each of the components outlined in the previous step. The client or another group member can play the part of the physician. Given what is known about the power of observational learning, this step is crucial. It also reinforces a partnership model of practice. The social worker might begin by saying, "If *I* were to ask for clarification of the dosage levels, I would sit up straight, look at Dr. Jones, and say, 'I hear you saying you are going to increase my dose because you want to see if it will lower my anxiety level faster so that I can get some better sleep, is that right?' Now, if you were the physician, you would say, 'Yes that's right, you haven't had any really bothersome side effects yet, so we'll try this and see how it goes.'"
4. *Role play each component*—This is where the client walks through the components in a role-play exercise. Clients can help set the stage by providing examples from their own lives of situations where the skill might have been useful, obviously providing greater relevance.
5. *Evaluate the role play*—Next, the social worker offers much positive feedback that is behaviorally specific, then some corrective feedback. The social worker then encourages the client to practice the role play again, incorporating the feedback received. Feedback should attend to both verbal and nonverbal behaviors, and participants should receive an opportunity to share their feelings about the role play.
6. *Apply the skill in real life*—Hepworth and Larsen (1993) call this step the "ultimate test of the skill training effort" (p. 457). In this step, the client actually uses the skill in a real-life situation. Because this task usually entails some preparation, problem solving is almost always a useful and important adjunct to skills training. As in problem solving, social workers can help clients find the internal and external resources (that is, the courage, the time, the money, the telephone) to carry out the skill. Anticipating problems and disappointments is also important preparation. What will the client do if the physician ignores her requests for clarification? What if the physician belittles him? Debriefing and booster sessions can help consolidate learning and insure proper credit. Praise is offered for successes, no matter how small.

Liberman's modules, as described in Chapter 6, often rely on videotaped case scenarios as part of the modeling step of skills training. Videotape can also be used to provide effective feedback. These tools may become much more widely available in the future. In addition, more interactive and individualized computer-assisted instruction, video discs, and the like are being developed.

Liberman et al. (1987), in their guidelines for *providers* negotiating with clients and families about medication, echo the principles we've emphasized throughout the book, especially those discussed in relation to medication adherence and refusal. They suggest that all mental health providers

1. Employ effective communication, including active listening, and acknowledge the client and family as "experts"; reinforce mutual collaboration and encourage the expression of goals, needs, and wishes
2. Acknowledge the rights and responsibilities of clients and families concerned about and actively involved in medication-related dilemmas
3. Solicit their reactions and suggestions about medication management
4. Maintain a nonpunitive stance
5. Recognize and accept that not all treatment decisions will be accepted
6. Be prepared for difficult negotiations

Difficult situations may require compromise; restating your position while acknowledging the client's or family member's position; ignoring provocation, criticism, and threats; focusing on benefits; and, when all else fails, politely terminating the interaction. *All* suggested responses begin with listening empathetically to clients and their families and exploring their reactions to medication issues. Docherty (1986) reiterates, saying that "negotiation and collaborative decision-making" is an essential component of all client-provider relationships with "the rights and responsibilities of both made clear" (p. 124).

Advocacy in Medication Management

It has been said that "the history of the social work profession has in large measure been based on the premise of client advocacy" and yet "putting this rhetoric into practice techniques has been underutilized" (Lurie, 1982, p. 77). The underutilization of advocacy as an intervention technique in psychopharmacology is no doubt related to issues of status and power in interdisciplinary teams and to a lack of clear roles in medication management. Connaway (1975) and Mailick and Ashley (1981) were among the first to ask questions about how advocacy and interdisciplinary collaboration fit (or don't fit) together. For example, they both note that while *collaboration* calls up notions of cooperation and cohesion, *advocacy* implies subtle coercion and potential conflict. Thus, a healthy dose of political acumen can help a social worker make judgments about when and how to advocate.

In defining the social workers' role of advocacy, Gerhart writes that they "monitor the rights and entitlements of their clients" and "focus on influencing decision makers." Encouraging social workers not to equate routine brokering or linking services with advocacy, she describes true advocacy as simply making persistent demands to decision makers on behalf of clients and families in cases where services have been "refused, resisted or inadequately offered" (1990, pp. 271, 272; see also Gerhart & Brooks, 1983).

Here are some examples of situations that might call for either social worker advocacy or client self-advocacy:

- A clinician refuses to refer clients for medication screening.
- An agency structures all medication-review appointments during the daylight hours on weekdays.
- A psychiatrist seems to be overmedicating a client.
- A family physician will not adjust the medication in response to continuing concerns about side effects.
- A hospital administrator opts not to participate in a free clozapine trial program.
- A treatment team will not allow a trial program of intermittent medication.
- An agency discontinues its medication education program when a key staff person resigns.
- An agency will not allow use of a certain drug reported to be effective.
- An insurance company differentially reimburses cost of the drug depending on diagnosis.

As can be seen, advocacy is closely linked with client and family rights, particularly regarding access to quality treatment. In all mental health settings, clients' rights have long been a concern; certainly, regarding medication, these issues are even more pronounced (see Chapter 7). A statement of our views of client rights, adapted from "Everyperson's Bill of Rights" (anonymous, undated), may be useful.

Mental Health Client's Medication Rights

1. The right to be treated as competent health care clients
2. The right to ask questions about the medication and its effects
3. The right to express one's own opinions about medication
4. The right to be listened to by the prescribing physician
5. The right to be educated about one's medication
6. The right to participate in psychopharmacological treatment planning and decision making
7. The right to make mistakes and to change one's mind
8. The right to choose not to assert oneself

Social workers perform two essential tasks that relate to medication management and their historic and ethical mandate to advocate for clients: (1) advocate directly for clients and families (see Chapter 1) and (2) empower and facilitate clients to advocate for themselves. Willetts (1980) pointed out quite a while ago that clients themselves are often the most effective advocates because of their unique legitimacy and sensitivity to the issues. The rise of the mental health client and family movements over the past 15 years has proven that point. All advocates, whether social workers or clients and families, should have a general knowledge of psychopharmacology, mental illness, and mental health law, as well as an awareness of the interdisciplinary and sociopolitical challenges that emerge in the advocacy arena. Advocates must also have a foundation of good communication skills, some level of assertiveness, and a planned guide for action.

Shulman (1992) cautions that when helping a client advocate within a system, social workers often make a crucial error. Though social workers can apparently tolerate and forgive all sorts of behaviors on the part of the client and have little trouble finding strengths, they are often harsh on those with whom the client is trying to negotiate. Social workers can thus put clients at greater risk of being cut off by the system. To be an effective medium between the client and the mental health (or other) system, the social worker must first recognize and deal with his or her own feelings about other professionals until he or she can respond empathetically to them.

Gerhart (1990) outlines in detail the steps social workers should take on behalf of clients. We have adapted these guidelines for use by clients and families. Bentley has used them extensively at mental health client conferences and workshops.

Self-Advocacy Steps for Mental Health Clients

1. *Identify the complaint*—Think about your complaint: identify the facts and your feelings about them. Decide if this issue is worth fighting for. Forgive yourself if you decide it isn't. Psychologically prepare if you decide it is. Congratulate yourself no matter what you decide.
2. *Identify and minimize your risks*—Try to anticipate the consequences of your advocacy efforts without exaggerating or minimizing them. Look for allies in friends, organizations, providers.
3. *Identify the appropriate decision maker*—In general, go to the first-line authority first. With medication management issues, most often the "decision makers" are physicians, treatment teams, medical directors, commissioners, or even legislative bodies. Who is the person who really made the decision, and who has the power to change it?
4. *Prepare your requests*—Write an outline of your anticipated presentation to the decision maker, including any available information and a consideration of objections they are likely to have.
5. *Practice your presentation*—Rehearse the presentation of your claim/request either in the mirror, with a friend, or with your social worker, paying close attention to your demeanor. Calmness, politeness, and strength of conviction will make you seem the most credible. Always try to *request* rather than *demand.*
6. *Present your request*—Make an appointment with the decision maker and present your claim as practiced. Use negotiation, compromise, expression of feelings, and other communication skills to achieve the best outcome possible. Advocates should be prepared to pursue decision makers persistently and assertively, in a manner that doesn't generate unnecessary hostility. They must "marshal data carefully," emphasizing their needs, desires, and values and their relationship to the specific requested changes (Gerhart & Brooks, 1983, p. 457).

This plan of action is particularly relevant for "case advocacy," or advocacy on behalf of an individual client or situation, such as approaching a psychiatrist about changing to an intermittent regimen of medication. It is also useful for "cause advocacy." Hepworth and Larsen (1993) provide a list of adjunct techniques needed for advocacy and social action at a more global level, to use either in conjunction with the direct approach or when this approach fails, that includes the following: initiating legal action (e.g., suing for not referring for medication in the case of severe depression), forming interagency committees (e.g., for improving the quality of psychopharmacological care in a state hospital), providing expert testimony (e.g., on the psychosocial impact of long-term medication use), developing petitions (e.g., to request longer medication clinic hours), and contacting public officials (e.g., for insuring that new effective medications will be covered by Medicaid). Because we believe many of the medication-related needs and dilemmas of the clients we serve too often go unmet, in Part Three we have offered social workers a range of psychosocial interventions and strategies to help them respond better to their clients' needs.

PART FOUR

FUTURE DIRECTIONS

CHAPTER 9

FUTURE DIRECTIONS IN PSYCHOPHARMACOLOGY: IMPLICATIONS FOR SOCIAL WORKERS

CHAPTER 9

Future Directions in Psychopharmacology: Implications for Social Workers

Right now, a number of scientific, social, and political issues are emerging in psychopharmacology that will likely affect the role of the social worker and the future of the profession at large. These include the rapid appearance of new drug treatments; creative new delivery routes or treatment philosophies; the growing debate about expanding prescription privileges among non-physician mental health care providers, such as psychologists, pharmacists, nurses, and social workers; and, finally, the increased public scrutiny on psychotropic medications, particularly the loud call for more attention to the negative impact of these medications, as well as persistent questions about how drug companies, advertising agencies, and new models of health care financing will influence drug availability and use. Because increased scrutiny has caused increasing concern among professionals about liability and malpractice claims, we will discuss the implications of these developments for social workers.

New Treatments

As the 21st century approaches, optimism pervades the pharmaceutical industry (Lader & Herrington, 1990). In spite of the fact that advances in drug treatment often occur by serendipity, huge amounts of money are being invested in the discovery of new compounds, new derivatives, and new uses for existing drugs, as well as in using such complementary treatments as vitamins, either alone or in combination with other psychotropic medications (Yudofsky et al., 1991). Advances in molecular biology, particularly continuing research into neurotransmission and central receptor subtypes, should lead to greater pharmacological specificity in the coming years (Langer, Arbilla, & Graham, 1991). The field, then, is moving toward discovering and refining drugs that affect some aspect of neurotransmission precisely where needed, but *not* where it is not needed, leading to drugs that produce desired therapeutic effects without unwanted side effects.

Hollister (1994) reviews new psychotropic drugs coming on the market in each of the four classes of medication discussed in this book. Research into new antipsychotics, for example, seeks a "narrower spectrum of action" (p. 54), explaining enthusiasm over risperidone, a drug known for its ability to improve both positive and negative symptoms while having a low potential for inducing EPS (Chouinard & Arnott, 1993). Similarly, such not-yet-available drugs as amisulpiride, melperone, and flupenthixol, respectively related to clozapine, haloperidol, and fluphenazine, all supposedly have fewer side effects than their counterparts. The newsletter for the National Alliance for Research on Schizophrenia and Depression touts dibenzothiazepine (Seroquel), olanzapine (Lanzac), serindole, and ziprasidone as promising antipsychotics in various stages of clinical trials or the application/approval process with the FDA (Promising medications on the horizon, 1994).

Current research with antidepressant medications is quite varied. It includes, for example, the development of new MAO inhibitors, such as moclobemide, which is different in chemical structure from currently available inhibitors and offers a lower risk of hypertensive crises related to tyramine consumption, thus requiring fewer dietary restrictions. A new generation of heterocyclics, such as mirtazapine (Remeron), is said to be on its way to market. Further development in the atypical antidepressants is seen in the selective serotonin reuptake inhibitors (SSRIs) and even the development of completely new types of antidepressants, such as nefazodone hydrochloride (Serzone), which is pharmacologically distinct from the heterocyclics, the MAO inhibitors, and the SSRIs (Promising medication on the horizon, 1994). Refinements center on finding precise compounds that fit various individual symptom profiles that also might include obsessive-compulsive symptoms, panic, and anxiety.

The mood stabilizer valproate, or divalproex sodium (Depakote), has emerged as a promising alternative to lithium and is particularly important because approximately 30% of persons diagnosed with bipolar disorder do not respond to lithium (Promising medication on the horizon, 1994). New research on anti-anxiety medications includes the testing of compounds similar in structure to buspirone, attempting again to find a drug that reduces anxiety without causing sedation and withdrawal (Hollister, 1994).

In addition to new medications, innovations in the administration of psychotropic medications have been developed. For example, drugs that can be placed under the tongue, much like nitroglycerine in the treatment of angina, may soon become available, which would be an obvious breakthrough for people who suffer from panic (Yudofsky, et al., 1991). In the 21st century, small external or internal pumps may inject drugs into the brain, or electrical devices may be transplanted into precise regions of the brain, all to stimulate specific chemical reactions. Dose sequencing and the intermittent administration of medications may come to respond to individual profiles and experiences even more quickly than implants.

Clearly, to most effectively fulfill their roles as educators, consultant/collaborators, and monitors, social workers need to stay abreast of these developments through reading, in-service training, conferences, and collaborative discussions with colleagues and clients. Professional social work organizations can help by sponsoring training and increasing the coverage of such topics in their workshops, journals, newsletters, and brochures. Schools of social work may have a special obligation and opportunity to respond to the need for more psychopharmacological content. In ever more settings, social workers can and should expand their roles as researchers by participating in the design and implementation of clinical outcome studies. They have a tremendous unfulfilled potential to increase knowledge of how combined medication and psychosocial treatments affect client functioning.

Expanding Prescription-Writing Privileges

Other professions have debated for years about who should and who should not be able to prescribe psychotropic medications. DeLeon, Fox, and Graham (1991) note the gradually increasing support of efforts to obtain prescription privileges for psychologists. They suggest that in spite of organized medicine's claim that this is a public health hazard, objective studies seem to support just the opposite. In fact, on a small scale in such service agencies as the Indian Health Service and the Department of Veteran Affairs, psychologists are already writing prescriptions. Pilot training projects with the Department of Defense have looked toward allowing psychologists certain privileges. The rationale for expansion is often tied to the underavailability of psychiatrists and the lack of psychopharmacological training of regular physicians, who write between 50% and 70% of psychotropic drug prescriptions in the United States (Olfson & Klerman, 1993; Wiggins, 1994). In 1990, the American Psychological Association convention voted, 118–2, to establish a task force to study this issue. While some psychologists describe their field as deeply split over this issue, citing a survey that shows that 34% of psychologists *strongly* support the notion, while 27% *strongly* oppose it (DeLeon et al., 1991), others contend that the field's support is probably underestimated (Wiggins, 1994).

One of the biggest concerns of psychologists is whether gaining prescription-writing privileges will somehow hurt the credibility of their profession and obscure their distinction from psychiatry (Boswell & Litwin, 1992). Nevertheless, as the debate continues, it will likely focus less on whether or not psychologists should seek this privilege and more on the conditions under which it should be allowed: Should privileges be completely unlimited or limited to certain settings, circumstances, or specific medications? Should psychologists be permitted to act independently or be required to have physician oversight and supervision?

Psychologists do not stand alone in their quest for prescription privileges. In fact, 28 states already allow nurse practitioners certain privileges (DeLeon et al., 1991) and some pharmacists, especially Pharm.D.s, are beginning to stir. One group of researchers, for example, describe a program in a

San Diego veteran's hospital where three specially trained pharmacists acquired prescription-writing privileges in a clozapine program. The pharmacists had to extensively screen patients, enroll them in the tracking system, and actually initiate the medication treatment. The pharmacist then worked in close collaboration with a psychiatric resident in weekly evaluations and other consultations as needed and recommended any dose adjustments or side-effect medications. In the outpatient part of this program, pharmacists distributed the medication and were formally responsible for the monitoring (Dishman, Ellenor, Lacro, & Lohr, 1994).

While acknowledging the expertise of Pharm.D.s in psychopharmacology, Sovner and Bailey (1993) argue that psychiatric nurse clinical-specialists also have sufficient training for prescription privileges. They note that nurses' training is more comprehensive than the Pharm.D.s and includes content on the "psychological aspects" of prescribing, including the meaning of medication to the patient (p. 396).

The early literature on social work and psychopharmacology (e.g., Brodsky, Fisher, & Weinstein, 1964; Hankoff & Galvin, 1968) rarely put forth the idea that social workers should seek training toward writing prescriptions. These articles mainly advanced the perspective that psychotropic medications represent a positive aspect of treatment for many people with mental illness and emotional distress, and that social workers needed to develop their ability to participate actively in the monitoring process as physicians' helpers. In the sole exception to this general position, Abroms and Greenfield (1973) suggested that social workers begin to work toward acquiring prescription privileges. They argued that this was a logical next step given social workers' person-in-environment perspective, the new emphasis on medication in the field of mental health, and the increasing complexity of cases faced by social workers. Elliot and Kintzer (1973) responded by arguing against this recommendation with two still relevant concerns: (1) that adding content on pharmacology to the social work curriculum would broaden an already overly general educational experience and (2) that it actually might work against the maintenance of a psychosocial intervention framework. Interestingly, physicians call on many social workers to dispense medication or write prescriptions to be later signed by the physician (Miller et al., 1980).

DeLeon and Pies (1994) argue each side of this debate as it relates to nonphysician providers in general. DeLeon argues that adding prescription writing to any list of potential nonphysician activities among the helping professions would fill a desperate need for more holistic care, especially for those who have limited access to physicians. With improved curriculum and ongoing training and credentialing, this is a realistic goal. On the other hand, Pies disagrees, claiming that performance of a sound differential diagnosis with implications for treatment with psychotropic medication is a complex issue that goes well beyond the mere addition of course work in pharmacology.

Although we have made the case that expanding their knowledge base in psychopharmacology will help social workers respond well to their clients, we do not embrace prescription writing as either feasible or desirable. The

2-year MSW curriculum is simply too packed as it is, with subjects including basic practice theory and skills, advanced human behavior, cultural diversity, social policy and services, and single-case research. In addition, clients seem best served by productive interdisciplinary relationships, which stand the best chance of emerging when both parties genuinely respect and legitimize each other's expertise and acknowledge their own professional boundaries or limitations. Even though social work has recognized biological issues as a crucial aspect of the biopsychosocial perspective, prescription writing would probably only serve to confuse and blur their roles and responsibilities. The absence of any swell of support for prescription privileges among social workers supports this view.

It is clear that all professions, including social work, that consider expanding their professional domain need to consider accountability issues, including liability concerns. Even though we do not advocate seeking prescription privileges, we do support expanded knowledge and roles in medication management for social workers or, at the very least, expanded application of existing skills to clients' concerns about psychotropic medication. But are social workers thus setting themselves up for increased liability risks? Will they be held liable for a failure to properly educate a client about missed doses, for example, or a failure to adequately monitor the side effects of medication, or coercing ambivalent clients into taking powerful medications with serious side effects? Even with the social worker's and the client's input, the physician still clearly makes the final decision about medications. In most cases, a nurse or pharmacist still distributes the medication.

We have stressed our role as consultants and collaborators with clients and other providers, and have emphasized our role in helping clients gain new knowledge and skills, and making informed decisions. Social workers are accountable for their own actions and ought to strive to achieve the highest standards of their *own* profession. For instance, one of the most difficult situations arises when social workers must decide what to do when faced with incompetence or inadequate care on the part of other providers. Though we discussed specific advocacy steps in Chapter 8, we recognize they do not offer solutions for all real-world circumstances. Social workers every day have to weigh the consequences to themselves and others of "whistleblowing" against the consequences of remaining silent.

Increased Public Scrutiny of Psychotropic Medications

Keshavan and Kennedy (1992) devote an entire edited volume to dysfunction related to the use of psychotropic medications. Topics include overdosing, problematic interactions, drug-induced neuropsychiatric symptoms (dystonias, parkinsonism, TD, NMS, akathesia), abuse of and dependence on benzodiazepines and anticholinergics, and drug-induced systemic syndromes such as cardiovascular problems, sexual dysfunctions, and immunological problems. However, the controversies surrounding the use of psychotropic medication are moving beyond scholarly journals, medical books, and college classrooms and toward newspapers and the popular press. Perhaps the best-known example of this is Prozac, the best-selling antidepressant. Between 10 and 15 million people have received prescriptions for Prozac since its introduction in 1986. Some tout its wonders to treat depression, help reduce anxiety in people with panic, and decrease the intrusive thoughts and rituals in people diagnosed with obsessive-compulsive symptoms. Others are amazed by its ability to improve concentration and productivity even in asymptomatic persons. In his best-selling book, *Listening to Prozac,* Kramer (1993) enthusiastically endorses the medication, claiming that it carries more power to change peoples's behavior than long-term psychological treatments.

On the other hand, Barondes (1994) writes that he is disturbed by such support for Prozac and wonders if it is really just an expensive placebo. He asks just how long lasting the changes are and how long someone has to take it. Others have tried to link Prozac to suicide or other acts of violence or aggression. In late 1994, over 160 cases had been filed against Eli Lilly, the makers of Prozac, with 92 already dismissed (Dowling, 1994). The first case to go to trial involved a disgruntled worker who killed 8 and wounded 13 during a shooting spree in a Louisville printing plant after being on Prozac for about a month. After a 47-day hearing, the jury took five hours to rule in favor of the drug company, which then in turn claimed complete vindication.

Breggin (1987, 1991) also harshly criticizes psychiatry in general and the use of psychotropic medications in particular. He attacks the overreliance on chemical imbalances to explain commonplace human problems and urges his readers to see medications *not* as miracles but as chemical lobotomies. While strongly urging the use of psychosocial approaches, he also argues that "all of life is an alternative to drugs . . . The whole spectrum of secular and religious philosophy is better than biopsychiatry" (1991, p. 375).

This debate grows particularly active regarding the medication of children. It often comes up in agency and facility philosophies and policies, as well as families. New clinicians usually take little time to determine on which side of the falsely dichotomous "medication fence" a certain child mental health facility falls: behavior management or medication? One concern arises that by medicating, clinicians may avoid proper focus on the "true" genesis (such as physical, sexual, or emotional abuse) of children's disorders. Widespread concern exists about overmedicating children, especially those diagnosed with attention deficit disorders or learning disabilities. In fact, public controversy surrounding Ritalin is probably second only to that of Prozac.

However, others worry more about an *under*medicated society. What about all the adults and children who suffer from treatable illnesses but receive insufficient treatment or no treatment at all (Bernstein, 1988)? What about those who receive inadequate dosages or an inadequate trial? What about people who receive some type of psychotherapy alone when a combination of medication and psychotherapy or psychosocial intervention would be best? For instance, Dr. Osheroff, a physician, sued Chestnut Lodge for failing to provide him with adequate treatment (medication) for his severe depression, instead providing long-term intensive insight-oriented psychotherapy on an inpatient basis. Over the course of many months, he deteriorated to such a poor physical and mental state that his family, worried about his survival, had him discharged and arranged for alternative treatment, which included medication. In a relatively short time, he was back working in his medical practice and resuming his life. Although the case was settled out of court and thus set no legal precedent, it spurred an important debate about the future of psychodynamic approaches for disorders and illnesses known to respond to medication (see Klerman, 1990; Stone, 1990).

As in the cases of Prozac and Dr. Osheroff, increased public attention on psychotropic medication and warnings about overreliance or underreliance have numerous legal and ethical implications. In fact, improper medication management is the most common legal claim against psychiatrists (Wettstein, 1992). Most complaints relate to negligence and lack of informed consent, such as failing to take an adequate history, prescribing an improper dose, prescribing a drug without proper indicators, failing to recognize or treat side effects and interactions, and failing to discuss the benefits, risks, and alternatives. Thus far, the courts have been unwilling to hold manufacturers liable for failing to warn consumers about the risks and side effects of *prescription* medication because of a "learned intermediary" rule, which says that since physicians decide which medication will be prescribed and how much, injury is best avoided by a direct warning from the physician (Walsh, 1993). Walsh, however, describes the case of a woman who sued Upjohn, claiming that Halcion (triazolam) was responsible for her severe anxiety, sleeplessness, decreased appetite, and suicidal ideation. In this case, the court looked at not only the warnings the physician had given his patient, but also the warning given by the pharmaceutical representative to the physician. The case record reports that a reasonable warning is one that

> not only conveys a fair indication of the nature of the dangers involved, but also warns with a degree of intensity demanded by the nature of the risk. A warning may be found to be unreasonable in that it was unduly delayed, reluctant in tone, or lacking in a sense of urgency (Walsh, 1993, p. 68).

Because the costs of medication affect availability and use, they have clear ethical dimensions. For example, tremendous controversy centers on the availability of clozapine in public settings. Even though research strongly supports the efficacy of the drug with persons diagnosed with treatment-resistant schizophrenia, the drug itself and the required blood-monitoring system make the cost prohibitive for many community mental health centers and state hospitals. Though the drug has been on the market for several years, those who might really benefit from it have very limited access to it (Reid et al., 1993). The National Alliance for the Mentally Ill (NAMI) has fought long and hard on moral grounds alone for making the drug more widely available. Risperidone has sparked similar activities. At one time NAMI actually began legal action against Sandoz, the maker of Clozaril (clozapine), claiming unreasonable price fixing, because the drug was available in Europe for thousands of dollars less (per year) than in the United States.

Clearly, some of these issues have implications for the types of advocacy in which social workers become involved. Developing clearer ethical guidelines around psychopharmacology issues may also help clarify the advocacy role. For example, what should the relationship be between social workers' organizations and drug companies? Should drug companies be allowed or even encouraged to set up booths at social workers' national conferences, as they do at conferences sponsored by the American Psychiatric Association? Why or why not? Because the pharmaceutical industry invests up to 40% of its revenue on promotional activities, such as advertising, direct mail, and sales representatives, concerns have arisen about the relationships between this industry and physicians (Caudill, Lurie, & Rich, 1992). Neill notes that "a complex ideological and financial relationship exists between the drug industry and the prescribing psychiatrist, the vendor and the consumer, which has yet to be explored" (1989, p. 333). For example, after reviewing hundreds of drug advertisements in medical journals, Neill notes that even as drug companies exploit and manipulate physicians, drug advertisements minister to the psychological needs of physicians for prestige, identity, potency, and self-satisfaction. Although drug companies do not currently court social workers, if their role in medication management continues to expand, such subtle influences on autonomy may need to be confronted.

Unfortunately, drug advertisements apparently reinforce medical concepts of illness that tend to locate pathology in individuals, deemphasizing the social context and competing psychosocial interventions. "Alternative remedies," such as psychosocial rehabilitation, improvements in housing, education, and jobs, "are totally beyond the pale" (Kleinman & Cohen, 1991, p. 868). Social workers are thus challenged to maintain their psychosocial emphasis and perspective even as they take on roles traditionally ascribed to the medical sphere.

Health care professionals are still a long way from understanding how new modes of financing health and mental health services, such as managed care, will affect psychopharmacology practice. Should they worry that it may lead to even greater reliance on medications because of their sheer efficiency? Will people be "treated only from the neck up" (Flynn, 1994, p. 16)? Or should they be hopeful that the rhetoric of managed care, which supports empirically validated treatments such as combined psychotherapeutic or rehabilitative approaches, will finally be realized? Similarly, what will changes in Medicare and Medicaid coverage, which will most likely be reduced, do to psychopharmacology practices?

Poulson (1992) urges health care providers to consider not only increasing providers who will either prescribe medications themselves or take leadership roles in medication management, but also looking for other changes in health care, which include the shift in decision-making authority from physicians to outside reviewers, the persistent demand for cost controls, the growing importance of the voice of the consumer, and increasing competition from drug companies.

Final Words

In this chapter, we have tried to summarize how social workers might respond to new treatments, expanded prescription privileges among related professions, increased public scrutiny of psychotropic medications, and concerns about liability. In spite of many unanswered questions, we still envision social workers who hold fast to the principles of partnership, balance, and integration. We still see social workers who strive to fulfill their unique mission while working side by side with clients, families, and providers, who also make major contributions to client care. We still see a profession that isn't afraid to pose difficult ethical questions, wrestle with the most complex cases, and confront its own future with vigor and pride.

References

Abramowitz, I. A., & Coursey, P. D. (1989). Impact of an educational support group on family participants who take care of their schizophrenic relatives. *Journal of Consulting & Clinical Psychology, 57,* 232–236.

Abroms, G., & Greenfield, N. (1973). Drug-prescribing and the nonmedical therapist. *Clinical Social Work Journal, 1,* 132–134.

Adams, S. G., & Howe, J. T. (1993). Predicting medication compliance in a psychotic population. *Journal of Nervous and Mental Disease, 181,* 558–560.

Adebimpe, V. R. (1994). Race, racism, and epidemiological surveys. *Hospital & Community Psychiatry, 45,* 27–31.

Adelman, G. (Ed.). (1987). *Encyclopedia of neuroscience.* Boston: Birkhaeuser.

American Psychiatric Association. (1994). *Diagnostic and statistical manual of mental disorders* (4th ed.). Washington, DC: Author.

Anderson, C., Reiss, D., & Hogarty, G. (1986). *Schizophrenia and the family: A practitioner's guide to psychoeducation and management.* New York: The Guilford Press.

Anthony, W. A. (1993). Recovery from mental illness: The guiding vision of the mental health service system in the 1990s. *Psychosocial Rehabilitation Journal, 16,* 11–23.

Appelbaum, P., & Guteil, T. (1979). "Rotting with their rights on": Constitutional theory and clinical reality in drug refusal by psychiatric patients. *Bulletin of the American Academy of Psychiatry and the Law, 7,* 306–315.

Arana, G. W., & Hyman, S. E. (1991). *Handbook of psychiatric drug therapy* (2nd ed.). Boston: Little, Brown.

Ascher-Svanum, H. A., & Krause, A.A. (1991). *Psychoeducational groups for patients with schizophrenia: A guide for practitioners.* Gaithersburg, MD: Aspen.

Aspler, R., & Rothman, E. (1984). Correlates of compliance with psychoactive prescriptions. *Journal of Psychoactive Drugs, 16,* 193–199.

Awad, A. G. (1992). Quality of life of schizophrenic patients on medications and implications for new drug trials. *Hospital & Community Psychiatry, 43,* 262–265.

Bachur, J. A. (1986). A social work perspective. *The Gerontologist, 26,* 614–617.

Baker, F. M. (1994). Psychiatric treatment of older African Americans. *Hospital & Community Psychiatry, 45,* 32–37.

Barondes, S. H. (1994). Thinking about Prozac. *Science, 263*(5150), 1102–1103.

Barrowclough, C., & Tarrier, N. (1992). *Families of schizophrenic patients: Cognitive behavioral intervention.* New York: Chapman & Hall.

Batey, S. R., & Ledbetter, J. E. (1982). Medication education for patients in a partial hospitalization program. *Journal of Psychosocial Nursing and Mental Health Services, 20*(7), 7–15.

Beitman, B. D., & Klerman, G. L. (Eds.). (1991). *Integrating pharmacotherapy and psychotherapy.* Washington, DC: American Psychiatric Press.

Belcher, J. R., & Ephross, P. H. (1989). Toward an effective practice model for the homeless mentally ill. *Social Casework, 70,* 421–427.

Bentley, K. J. (1991). Voluntary recruitment of psychiatric patients for clinical research. *International Journal of Mental Health, 20,* 94–107.

Bentley, K. J. (1993). The right of psychiatric patients to refuse medications: Where should social workers stand? *Social Work, 38*, 101–106.

Bentley, K. J., Farmer, R. L., & Phillips, M. E. (1991). Student knowledge of and attitudes toward psychotropic drugs. *Journal of Social Work Education, 27*, 279–289.

Bentley, K. J., & Harrison, D. F. (1989). Behavioral, psychoeducational, and skills training approaches to family management of schizophrenia. In B. A. Thyer (Ed.), *Behavioral family therapy* (pp. 147–168). Springfield, IL: Charles C. Thomas.

Bentley, K. J., & Reeves, J. (1992). Integrating psychopharmacology into social work curriculum: Suggested content and resources. *Journal of Teaching in Social Work, 6*, 41–48.

Bentley, K. J., Rosenson, M., & Zito, J. (1990). Promoting medication compliance: Strategies for working with families of mentally ill people. *Social Work, 35*, 274–277.

Berg, W. E., & Wallace, M. (1987). Effect of treatment setting on social workers' knowledge of psychotropic drugs. *Health and Social Work, 12*, 144–152.

Bernheim, K. F., & Lehman, A. (1985). *Working with families of the mentally ill.* New York: Norton.

Bernheim, K. F., & Switalski, T. (1988). Mental health staff and patients' relatives: How they view each other. *Hospital & Community Psychiatry, 39*, 63–68.

Bernstein, J. G. (1988). *Handbook of drug therapy in psychiatry* (2nd ed.). Littleton, MA: PSG Publishing Company.

Bisbee, C. (1988, October). *Psychiatric patient education: Teaching patients about illness, treatment, and role.* Paper presented at the 40th Institute on Hospital and Community Psychiatry, New Orleans, LA.

Biegon, A., & Gruener, N. (1992). Age-related changes in serotonin $5HT_2$ receptors on human blood platelets. *Psychopharmacology, 108*, 210–212.

Blackwell, B. (1979). The drug regimen and treatment compliance. In R. B. Haynes, D. W. Taylor, & D. L. Sackett (Eds.), *Compliance in health care* (pp. 144–156). Baltimore: Johns Hopkins University Press.

Blanchard, R. J., Yudko, E. B., Rodgers, R. J., & Blanchard, D. C. (1993). Defense system psychopharmacology: An ethological approach to the pharmacology of fear and anxiety. *Behavioral Brain Research, 58*, 155–165.

Boczknowski, J. A., Zeichner, A., & DeSanto, N. (1985). Neuroleptic compliance among chronic schizophrenic outpatients: An intervention outcome report. *Journal of Consulting & Clinical Psychology, 53*, 666–671.

Booker, W., Brenner, H. D., Gerstner, G., Keller, F., Muller, J., & Spichtig, L. (1984). Self-healing strategies among schizophrenics: Attempts at compensation for basic disorders. *Acta Psychiatricia Scandivania, 69*, 373–378.

Boswell, D. L., & Litwin, W. J. (1992). Limited prescription privileges for psychologists: A 1-year follow-up. *Professional Psychology, 23*(2), 108–113.

Bradley, S. (1990). Non-physician psychotherapist—physician pharmacotherapist: A new model for concurrent treatment. *Psychiatric Clinics of North America, 13*(2), 307–322.

Breggin, P. R. (1987). *Psychiatric drugs: Hazards to the brain.* New York: Springer.

Breggin, P. R. (1991). *Toxic psychiatry.* New York: St. Martin's Press.

Brodsky, C., Fisher, A., & Weinstein, M. (1964). Modern treatment of psychosis: New tasks for social therapies. *Social Work, 9*, 71–78.

Brooks, A. (1987). The right to refuse medication: Law and policy. *Rutgers Law Review, 39*, 339–376.

Brown, C. S., Wright, R. G., & Christenson, O. B. (1987). Association between type of medication, instruction and patient's knowledge, side effects and compliance. *Hospital & Community Psychiatry, 38,* 55–60.

Brown, P. (1985). *The transfer of care: Psychiatric deinstitutionalization and its aftermath.* Boston: Routledge & Kegan Paul.

Brown, P., & Funk, S. C. (1986). Tardive dyskinesia: Barriers to the professional recognition of an iatrogenic disease. *Journal of Health & Social Behavior, 27,* 116–132.

Buchalter-Katz, S. (1985). Observations concerning the art productions of depressed patients in a short-term psychiatric facility. *Arts in Psychotherapy, 12*(1), 35–38.

Buckalew, L., & Sallis, R. (1986). Patient compliance and medication perception. *Journal of Clinical Psychology, 42,* 49–53.

Buckwalter, K. C., & Kerfoot, K. M. (1982). Teaching patients self-care: A critical aspect of psychiatric discharge planning. *Journal of Psychosocial Nursing and Mental Health Services, 20*(4), 15–20.

Busch, F. N., & Gould, E. (1993). Treatment by a psychotherapist and a psychopharmacologist: Transference and countertransference issues. *Hospital & Community Psychiatry, 44,* 772–774.

Butler, R. N., Lewis, M. I., & Sunderland, T. (1991). *Aging and mental health: Positive psychosocial and biomedical approaches* (4th ed.). New York: Macmillan.

Callicutt, J. (1983). Contemporary settings and the rise of the profession in mental health. In J. Callicutt & P. Lecca (Eds.), *Social work and mental health* (pp. 30–41). New York: Free Press.

Campbell (1981). *Psychiatric dictionary* (5th ed.). New York: Oxford University Press.

Caplan, R. B. (1969). *Psychiatry and the community in nineteenth century America.* New York: Basic Books.

Carpenter, W. T., & Heinrichs, D. W. (1983). Early intervention, time-limited, targeted pharmacotherapy of schizophrenia. *Schizophrenia Bulletin, 9,* 533–542.

Carrion, P. G., Swann, A., Kellert-Cecil, H., & Barber, M. (1993). Compliance with clinic attendance by outpatients with schizophrenia. *Hospital & Community Psychiatry, 44,* 764–767.

Caudill, T. S., Lurie, N., & Rich, E. (1992). The influence of pharmaceutical industry advertising on physician prescribing. *Journal of Drug Issues, 22*(2), 331–338.

Chouinard, G., & Arnott, W. (1993). Clinical review of risperidone. *Canadian Journal of Psychiatry, 38* S89–S95.

Ciccone, R., Tokoli, J. F., Gift, T. E., & Clements, C. D. (1993). Medication refusal and judicial activism: A reexamination of the effects of the Rivers decision. *Hospital & Community Psychiatry, 44,* 555–560.

Clements, M. (1993, October 31). What we say about mental illness. *Parade Magazine,* pp. 4–6.

Cohen, D. (1988). Social work and psychotropic drug treatments. *Social Service Review, 62,* 576–599.

Cohen, D., & McCubbin, M. (1990). The political economy of tardive dyskinesia: Asymmetries in power and responsibility. *The Journal of Mind and Behavior, 11,* 465–488.

Cohen, N. L. (1993). Stigmatization and the "noncompliant" recidivist. *Hospital & Community Psychiatry, 44,* 1029.

Cole, R. (1982). Patient's rights vs. doctor's rights: Which should take precedence? In A. E. Doudera & J. P. Swazey (Eds.), *Refusing treatment in mental institutions:*

Values in conflicts (pp. 56–71). Washington, DC: Association of University Programs in Health Administration.

Collins-Colon, T. (1990). Do it yourself: Medication management for community-based clients. *Journal of Psychosocial Nursing and Mental Health Services, 28*(6), 25–29.

Connaway, R. S. (1975). Teamwork and social worker advocacy: Conflicts and possibilities. *Community Mental Health Journal, 11,* 381–388.

Conrad, P. (1985). The meaning of medications: Another look at compliance. *Social Science and Medicine, 20,* 29–37.

Cordoba, O., Wilson, W., & Orten, J. (1983). Psychotropic medications for children. *Social Work, 28,* 448–453.

Corrigan, P. W., Liberman, R. P., & Engel, J. D. (1990). From noncompliance to collaboration in the treatment of schizophrenia. *Hospital & Community Psychiatry, 41,* 1203–1211.

Corty, E., Lehman, A. F., & Myers, C. P. (1993). Influence of psychoactive substance use on reliability of psychiatric diagnosis. *Journal of Counseling and Clinical Psychology, 61,* 165–170.

Coudreaut-Quinn, E. A., Emmons, M. A., & McMorrow, M. J. (1992). Adherence and accuracy: Self-medication during inpatient psychiatric treatment. *Journal of Psychosocial Nursing and Mental Health Services, 30*(12), 32–36.

Cournoyer, D. E., & Johnson, H. C. (1991). Measuring parents' perception of mental health professionals. *Research on Social Work Practice, 1,* 399–415.

Cowles, L. A., & Lefcowitz, M. (1992). Interdisciplinary expectations of the medical social worker in the hospital setting. *Health & Social Work, 17*(1), 57–65.

Cubine, T., Bentley, K. J., Poe, J., & McCafferty, P. (1995). *The MESA model of family-professional education: Virginia's experience in enhancing collaboration.* Manuscript under review.

Daley, D. C., Bowler, K., Cahalane, H. (1992). Approaches to patient and family education with affective disorders. *Patient Education and Counseling, 19,* 163–174.

Dane, B. O., & Simon, B. L. (1991). Resident guests: Social workers in host settings. *Social Work, 36,* 208–213.

Davidhizar, R. E., & McBridge, A. B. (1985). Teaching the client with schizophrenia about medication. *Patient Education and Counseling, 7,* 137–145.

Davidson, M., & Jamison, P. (1983). The clinical social worker and current psychiatric drugs: Some introductory principles. *Clinical Social Work Journal, 11,* 139–150.

Davis v. Hubbard, 506 F. Supp. 915 (1980).

Dawson, D., Blum, H., & Bartolucci, G. (1983). *Schizophrenia in focus.* New York: Human Sciences Press.

DeChillo, N. (1993). Collaboration between social workers and the families of the mentally ill. *Families in Society, 74,* 104–115.

Deegan, P. E. (1992). The independent living movement and people with psychiatric disabilities: Taking back control over our own lives. *Psychosocial Rehabilitation Journal, 15*(3), 3–19.

DeGeest, S., Abraham, I., Gemoets, H., & Evers, G. (1994). Development of the long-term medication behavior self-efficacy scale: Qualitative study for item development. *Journal of Advanced Nursing, 19*(2), 233–238.

DeLeon, P. H., Fox, R. E., & Graham, S. R. (1991). Prescription privileges: Psychology's next frontier? *American Psychologist, 46,* 384–393.

DeLeon, P. H., & Pies, R. W. (1994). Should non-physician mental health professionals be allowed to prescribe medicine? In S. A. Kirk & S. D. Einbinder (Eds.), *Controversial issues in mental health* (pp. 177–188). Boston: Allyn & Bacon.

Devane, C. L. (1990). *Fundamentals of monitoring psychoactive drug therapy.* Baltimore: Williams & Wilkins.

Dewan, M. J. (1992). Adding medications to ongoing psychotherapy: Indications and pitfalls. *American Journal of Psychotherapy, 46,* 102–110.

Dewan, M. J., & Koss, M. (1989). The clinical impact of the side effects of psychotropic drugs. In S. Fisher & R. P. Greenberg (Eds.), *The limits of biological treatments for psychological distress* (pp. 189–234). Hillsdale, NJ: Lawrence Earlbaum Associates.

Diamond, R. (1983). Enhancing medication use in schizophrenic patients. *Journal of Clinical Psychiatry, 44*(6, no. 2), 7–14.

DiMatteo, M. R., & DiNicola, D. D. (1982). *Achieving patient compliance: The psychology of the medical practitioner's role.* New York: Pergamon Press.

Dishman, B. R., Ellenor, G. L., Lacro, J. P., & Lohr, J. B. (1994). Pharmacists' role in clozapine therapy at a Veterans Affairs Medical Center. *American Journal of Hospital Pharmacy, 51,* 899–901.

Docherty, J. P. (1986). Psychopharmacology evaluation: Psychosocial issues. In D. C. Jimerson & J. P. Docherty (Eds.), *Psychopharmacology consultation* (pp. 118–129). Washington, DC: American Psychiatric Press.

Dowling, C. (1994, December 13). Prozac not to blame in slayings, jury says. *USA Today,* p. 3A.

Draine, J., & Solomon, P. (1994). Explaining attitudes toward medication compliance among a seriously mentally ill population. *Journal of Nervous and Mental Disease, 182,* 50–54.

Duchin, S. P., & Brown, S. A. (1990). Patients should participate in designing diabetes educational content. *Patient Education and Counseling, 16,* 255–267.

Dulcan, M. K. (1992). Information for parents and youth on psychotropic medications. *Journal of Child and Adolescent Psychopharmacology, 2,* 81–101.

Dunbar, J., Marshall, G., & Hovell, M. (1979). Behavioral strategies for improving compliance. In R. B. Haynes, D. W. Taylor, & D. Sackett (Eds.), *Compliance in health care* (pp. 174–190). Baltimore: Johns Hopkins University Press.

D'zurilla, T. J. (1986). *Problem-solving therapy: A social competence approach to clinical intervention.* New York: Springer.

Eckman, T. A., & Liberman, R. P. (1990). A large-scale field test of a medication management skills training program for people with schizophrenia. *Psychosocial Rehabilitation Journal, 13,* 31–35.

Eckman, T. A., Liberman, R. P., Phipps, C. C., & Blair, K. E. (1990). Teaching medication management skills to schizophrenic patients. *Journal of Clinical Psychopharmacology, 10*(1), 33–38.

Eckman, T. A., Wirshing, W. C., Marder, S. R., Liberman, R. P., Johnston-Cronk, K., Zimmerman, K., & Mintz, J. (1992). Technique for training schizophrenic patients in illness self-management: A controlled trial. *American Journal of Psychiatry, 149,* 1549–1555.

Eisenberg, G., Hilliard, J., & Gutheil, T. (1981). The ethical aspects of the right to refuse medication: A clinicolegal dilemma for the psychiatrist and patient. *Psychiatric Quarterly, 53,* 93–99.

Elliot, C., & Kintzer, C. (1973). No prescription pads for social workers. *Clinical Social Work Journal, 1,* 134–136.

Estroff, S. E. (1981). *Making it crazy: An ethnography of psychiatric clients in an American community.* Berkeley: University of California Press.

Everett, B., & Nelson, A. (1992). We're not cases and you're not managers: An account of a client-professional partnership developed in response to the "borderline" diagnosis. *Psychosocial Rehabilitation Journal, 15*(4), 49–60.

Falloon, I., Boyd, J., & McGill, C. (1984). *Family care of schizophrenia: A problem-solving approach to the treatment of mental illness.* New York: The Guilford Press.

Feltner, D. E., & Hertzman, M. (1993). Progress in the treatment of tardive dyskinesia: Theory and practice. *Hospital & Community Psychiatry, 44,* 25–33.

Flynn, L. M. (1994). The impact of managed care. *Advocate* (newsletter of the National Alliance for the Mentally Ill), *16*(2), 1, 16, 23.

Ford, M. (1980). The psychiatrist's double bind: The right to refuse medication. *American Journal of Psychiatry, 137,* 332–339.

Foxx, R. M., & Bittle, R. G. (1989). *Thinking it through: Teaching a problem-solving strategy for community living—curriculum for individuals with chronic mental illness.* Champaign, IL: Research Press.

Frank, E., & Kupfer, D. J. (1986). Psychotherapeutic approaches to treatment of recurrent unipolar depression: Working progress. *Psychopharmacology Bulletin, 22,* 558–563.

Frank, E., Perel, J. M., Mallinger, A. G., Thase, M. E., & Kupfer, D. J. (1992). Relationship of pharmacologic compliance to long-term prophylaxis in recurrent depression. *Psychopharmacology Bulletin, 28,* 231–235.

Frank, J. (1974). *Persuasion and healing* (Rev. ed.). New York: Shocken Books.

French, L. M. (1940). *Psychiatric social work.* New York: The Commonwealth Fund.

Freund, P. D. (1993). Professional role(s) in the empowerment process: "Working with" mental health consumers. *Psychosocial Rehabilitation Journal, 16*(3), 65–73.

Gadow, K. D. (1991). Clinical issues in child and adolescent psychopharmacology. *Journal of Counseling and Clinical Psychology, 59*(6), 842–852.

Galassi, J. P., Galassi, M. D., & Vedder, M. J. (1981). Perspectives on assertion as a social skills model. In J. D. Wine & M. D. Smye (Eds.), *Social competence* (pp. 287–345). New York: Guilford.

Garrity, T. F., & Lawson, E. J. (1989). Patient-physician communication as a determinant of medication misuse in older, minority women. *The Journal of Drug Issues, 19*(2), 245–249.

Gelenberg, A. J., Bassuk, E. L., & Schoonover, S. C. (1990). *The practitioner's guide to psychoactive drugs* (3rd ed.). New York: Plenum Medical Books.

Geller, J. L. (1982). State hospital patients and their medication—Do they know what to take? *American Journal of Psychiatry, 139,* 112–113.

Gerhart, U., & Brooks, A. (1983). The social work practitioner and anti-psychotic medication. *Social Work, 28,* 454–459.

Gerhart, U. C. (1990). *Caring for the chronic mentally ill.* Itasca, IL: F. E. Peacock.

Gibelman, M. (1993). School social workers, counselors, and psychologists in collaboration: A shared agenda. *Social Work in Education, 15*(1), 45–51.

Gitlin, M. J., Cochran, S. D., & Jamison, K. R. (1989). Maintenance lithium treatment: Side effects and compliance. *Journal of Clinical Psychiatry, 50,* 127–131.

Glazer, W. M., Morgenstern, H., & Doucette, J. (1994). Race and tardive dyskinesia among outpatients at a CMHC. *Hospital & Community Psychiatry, 45*(1), 38–42.

Glick, I. D., Burti, L., Suzuki, K., & Sacks, M. (1992). Effectiveness in psychiatric core IV: Achieving effective medication management for major affective disorders. *Psychopharmacology Bulletin, 28,* 257–259.

Goldberg, R. S., Riba, M., & Tasman, A. (1991). Psychiatrists' attitudes toward prescribing medication for patients treated by nonmedical psychotherapists. *Hospital & Community Psychiatry, 42,* 276–280.

Goldman, C., & Quinn, F. (1988). Effects of a patient education program in the treatment of schizophrenia. *Hospital & Community Psychiatry, 39,* 282–286.

Goldwyn, R. M. (1988). Educating the patient and family about depression. *Medical Clinics of North America, 72,* 887–896.

Grabowski, J., & VandenBos, G. R. (1992). *Psychopharmacology: Basic mechanisms and applied interventions.* Washington, DC: American Psychological Association.

Green, B., Wehing, C., & Talesk, C. (1987). Group art therapy as an adjunct to treatment for chronic outpatients. *Hospital & Community Psychiatry, 38*(9), 988–994.

Greenberg, L., Fine, S. B., Cohen, C., & Larson, K. (1988). An interdisciplinary psychoeducation program for schizophrenic patients and their families in an acute care setting. *Hospital & Community Psychiatry, 39,* 277–282.

Greenhill, L. L., & Setterberg, S. (1993). Pharmacotherapy of disorders of adolescents. *Psychiatric Clinics of North America, 16*(4), 793–810.

Greenwald, B. S., Kremen, N., & Aupperle, P. (1992). Tailoring of adult psychiatric practices to the field of geriatrics. *Psychiatric Quarterly, 63*(4), 343–364.

Halford, W. K., & Hayes, R. (1991). Psychological rehabilitation of chronic schizophrenic patients: Recent findings on social skills training and family psychoeducation. *Clinical Psychology Review, 11,* 23–44.

Hankoff, L., & Galvin, J. (1968). Psychopharmacological treatment and its implications for social work. *Social Work, 13,* 40–47.

Harmon, R. B., & Tratnack, S. A. (1992). Teaching hospitalized patients with serious, persistent mental illness. *Journal of Psychosocial Nursing and Mental Health Services, 30*(7), 33–36.

Harrison, W. D., Drolen, C. S., & Atherton, C. R. (1989). Role discrepancies in state hospital social work. *Social Casework, 70,* 622–626.

Hatfield, A. B. (1981). Self-help groups for families of the mentally ill. *Social Work, 26,* 408–413.

Hayes, R., & Gantt, A. (1992). Patient psychoeducation: The therapeutic use of knowledge for the mentally ill. *Social Work in Health Care, 17*(11), 53–67.

Hays, R. D., & DiMatteo, M. R. (1987). Key issues and suggestions for patient compliance assessment: Sources of information, focus of measures, and nature of response option. *Journal of Compliance in Health Care, 2,* 37–53.

Heinrichs, D. W., Cohen, B. P., & Carpenter, W. T. (1985). Early insight and the management of schizophrenic decompensation. *Journal of Nervous and Mental Disease, 173,* 133–138.

Hepworth, D. H., & Larsen, J. A. (1993). *Direct social work practice: Theory and skills* (4th ed.). Pacific Grove, CA: Brooks/Cole Publishing.

Herz, M. I. (1984). Recognizing and preventing relapse in patients with schizophrenia. *Hospital & Community Psychiatry, 35,* 344–349.

Heszen-Klemens, I. (1987). Patients' noncompliance and how doctors manage this. *Social Science & Medicine, 24,* 409–416.

Heyduk, L. J. (1991). Medication education: Increasing patient compliance. *Journal of Psychosocial Nursing and Mental Health Services, 29*(12), 32–35.

Higgins, P. B. (1995). Clozapine and the treatment of schizophrenia: Implications for social work practice. *Health and Social Work, 20,* 124–132.

Hoffman, J. S. (1990). Integrating biologic and psychologic treatment: The need for a unitary model. *Psychiatric Clinics of North America, 13*(2), 369–372.

Hogan, T. P., Awad, A. G., & Eastwood, R. (1983). A self-report scale predictive of drug compliance in schizophrenics: Reliability and discriminative validity. *Psychological Medicine, 13,* 177–183.

Hogarty, G. E. (1984). Depot neuroleptics: The relevance of psychosocial factors. *Journal of Clincal Psychiatry, 45*(Supp. 2), 36–42.

Hogarty, G. E. (1991). Social work practice research on severe mental illness: Charting a future. *Research on Social Work Practice, 1*(1), 5–31.

Hogarty, G. E., Anderson, C. M., Reiss, D. J., Kornblith, S. J., Greenwald, D. P., Ulrich, R. F., & Carter, M. (1991). Family psychoeducation, social skills training, and maintenance chemotherapy in the aftercare treatment of schizophrenia II. Two year effects of a controlled study on relapse and adjustment. *Archives of General Psychiatry, 48,* 340–347.

Hogarty, G. E., Goldberg, S., & Schooler, N. R. (1974). Drug and sociotherapy in the aftercare treatment of schizophrenia: II. Two year relapse rates. *Archives of General Psychiatry, 31,* 603–608.

Hollister, L. E. (1994). New psychotherapeutic drugs. *Journal of Clinical Psychopharmacology, 14,* 50–73.

Howard, K., Rickels, K., Mock, J., Lipman, R., Covi, L., & Baumm, N. (1970). Therapeutic style and attrition rate from psychiatric drug treatment. *Journal of Nervous and Mental Disease, 150,* 102–110.

Isaac, L. M., Tamblyn, R. M., & McGill-Calgary Drug Research Team. (1993). Compliance and cognitive function: A methodological approach to measuring unintentional errors in medication compliance in the elderly. *The Gerontologist, 33,* 772–781.

Ivanoff, A., & Stern, S. B. (1992). Self-management in health and mental health settings: Evidence of maintenance and generalization. *Social Work Research & Abstracts, 28*(4), 32–38.

Jacobsen, F. M. (1994). Psychopharmacology. In L. C. Comez-Diaz & B. Greene (Eds.), *Women of color: Integrating ethnic and gender identities in psychotherapy* (pp. 319–336). New York: Guilford Press.

Jamison, K., Gerner, R., & Goodwin, F. (1979). Patient and physician attitudes toward lithium. *Archives of General Psychiatry, 36,* 866–869.

Jamison, K. R., & Akiskal, H. S. (1983). Medication compliance in patients with bipolar disorder. *Psychiatric Clinic of North America, 6,* 175–192.

Janicak, P. G., Davis, J. M., Preskorn, S. H., & Ayd, F. J. (1993). *Principles and practice of psychopharmacotherapy.* Baltimore: Williams & Wilkins.

Jeste, D. V., & Caligiuri, M. P. (1993). Tardive dyskinesia. *Schizophrenia Bulletin, 19,* 303–312.

Johnson, A. B. (1990). *Out of bedlam: The truth about deinstitutionalization.* New York: Basic Books.

Johnson, H. (1989). Resisting the evil empire: Comments on "Social work and psychotropic drug treatments." *Social Service Review, 63,* 657–660.

Jones, R. E. (1976). Franklin and Rush: American psychiatry's two revolutionaries. *Hospital & Community Psychiatry, 27*(7), 461–463.

Kabat-Zinn, J., Massion, A. O., Kristeller, J., Peterson, L. G., Fletcher, K. E., Phert, L., Lenderking, W. R., & Santorelli, S. F. (1992). Effectiveness of a meditation-based stress reduction program in the treatment of anxiety disorders. *American Journal of Psychiatry, 149,* 936–943.

Kail, B. L. (1989). Drugs, gender, and ethnicity: Is the older minority woman at risk? *The Journal of Drug Issues, 19*(2), 171–189.

Kane, J. M. (1983). Problems of compliance in the outpatient treatment of schizophrenia. *Journal of Clinical Psychiatry, 44*(6), 3–6.

Kanter, J. (1989). Clinical case management: Definition, principles, components. *Hospital & Community Psychiatry, 40*, 361–368.

Kaplan, H. I., & Sadock, B. J. (1993). *Pocket handbook of psychiatric drug treatment.* Baltimore: Williams & Wilkins.

Kassis, J. P., Boothroyd, P., & Ben-Dror, R. (1992). The family support group: Families and professionals in partnership. *Psychosocial Rehabilitation Journal, 15*, 91–96.

Kelly, G. R., Scott, J. E., and Mamon, J. (1990). Medication compliance and health education among outpatients with chronic mental disorders. *Medical Care, 28*(12), 1181–1197.

Kelly, K. V. (1992). Parallel treatment: Therapy with one clinician and medication with another. *Hospital & Community Psychiatry, 43*, 778–780.

Keshavan, M. S., & Kennedy, J. S. (1992). *Drug-induced dysfunction in psychiatry.* New York: Hemisphere Publishing.

Kisthardt, W. E. (1992). A strengths model of case management: The principles and functions of a helping partnership with persons with persistent mental illness. In D. Saleeby (Ed.), *The strengths perspective in social work* (p. 59–83). New York: Longman.

Kleinman, D. L., & Cohen, L. J. (1991). The decontextualization of mental illness: The portrayal of work in psychiatric drug advertisements. *Social Science and Medicine, 32*(8), 867–874.

Klerman, G. L. (1984). Ideologic conflicts in combined treatment. In B. D. Beitman & G. L. Klerman (Eds.), *Combining psychotherapy and drug therapy in clinical practice* (pp. 17–39). Jamaica, NY: Spectrum Publications.

Klerman, G. L. (1990). The psychiatric patient's right to effective treatment: Implications of Osheroff v. Chestnut Lodge. *American Journal of Psychiatry, 147*, 409–418.

Kopp, J. (1988). Self-monitoring: A literature review of research and practice. *Social Work Research & Abstracts, 4*(4), 8–20.

Kramer, P. D. (1993). *Listening to prozac: A psychiatrist explores antidepressant drugs and the remaking of self.* New York: Viking.

Kucera-Bozarth, K., Beck, N. C., & Lyss, L. (1982). Compliance with lithium regimens. *Journal of Psychosocial Nursing and Mental Health Services, 20*(7), 11–15.

Lader, M., & Herrington, R. (1990). *Biological treatments in psychiatry.* New York: Oxford University Press.

Langer, S. Z., Arbilla, S., & Graham, D. (1991). Current developments in preclinical neuropharmacology which will impact on pharmacotherapy of major mental illness. In H. Y. Meltzer & D. Nerozzi (Eds.), *Current practices and future developments in the pharmacotherapy of mental disorders* (pp. 3–10). Amsterdam: Excerpta Medica.

Lantz, J. (1987). Guilt and restitution: A ghetto healer's approach. *Voices, 23*, 42–45.

Lawson, G., & Cooperrider, C. (1988). *Clinical psychopharmacology: A practical reference for the non-medical psychotherapist.* Rockville, MD: Aspen.

Lawson, W. B. (1986). Chronic mental illness and the black family. *American Journal of Social Psychiatry, 37*, 50–54.

Lee, J. A. B. (1994). *The empowerment approach to social work practice.* New York: Columbia University Press.

Lefley, H. P. (1993). Involuntary treatment: Concerns of consumers, families and society. *Innovations and Research, 2*, 7–9.

Lehman, A. F., Herron, J. D., Schwartz, R. P., & Myers, C. P. (1993). Rehabilitation for adults with severe mental illness and substance use disorders: A clinical trial. *Journal of Nervous and Mental Disease, 181,* 86–91.

Leventhal, H., Diefenbach, M., & Leventhal, E. A. (1992). Illness cognition: Using common sense to understand treatment adherence and affect cognition interactions. *Cognitive Therapy and Research, 16,* 143–163.

Levy, R. (1978). Facilitating patient compliance and medical programs: An area for social work research and intervention. In N. Bracht (Ed.), *Social work in health care: A guide to professional practice* (pp. 281–292). New York: Haworth Press.

Libassi, M. F. (1992). The chronically mentally ill: A practice approach. In S. M. Rose (Ed.), *Case management and social work practice* (pp. 77–90). New York: Longman.

Liberman, R., Kane, J., Vaccaro, J., & Wirshing, W. (1987, October). *Negotiating medication issues with schizophrenic patients.* Workshop conducted at the Institute on Hospital & Community Psychiatry, Boston, MA.

Liberman, R. P. (1988a). Behavioral family management. In R. P. Liberman (Ed.), *Psychiatric rehabilitation of chronic mental patients* (pp. 199–244). Washington, DC: American Psychiatric Press.

Liberman, R. P. (1988b). Coping with chronic mental disorders: A framework for hope. In R. P. Liberman (Ed.), *Psychiatric rehabilitation of chronic mental patients* (pp. 1–28). Washington, DC: American Psychiatric Press.

Lin, I. F., Spiga, R., & Fortsch, W. (1979). Insight and adherence to medication in chronic schizophrenics. *Journal of Clinical Psychiatry, 40,* 430–432.

Lin, K., Poland, R. E., Smith, M. W., Strickland, T. L., & Mendoza, R. (1991). Pharmacokinetic and other related factors affecting psychotropic responses in Asians. *Psychopharmacology Bulletin, 27*(4), 427–436.

Lin, K., & Shen, W. W. (1991). Pharmacology for southeast Asian psychiatric patients. *The Journal of Nervous and Mental Disease, 179*(6), 346–350.

Lisenbee, K. (1994). *Art therapy: An effective treatment for consumers diagnosed with a long-term mental illness?* Unpublished manuscript, School of Social Work, Virginia Commonwealth University, Richmond.

Littrell, J., & Ashford, J. B. (1994). The duty of social workers to refer for medications: A study of field instructors. *Social Work Research, 18*(2), 123–128.

Lubove, R. (1965). *The professional altruist: The emergence of social work as a career 1880–1930.* Cambridge, MA: Harvard University Press.

Lukoff, D., Liberman, R. P., & Nuechterlein, K. H. (1986). Symptom monitoring in the rehabilitation of schizophrenic patients. *Schizophrenia Bulletin, 12,* 578–593.

Lurie, A. (1982). The social work advocacy role in discharge planning. *Social Work in Health Care, 8*(2), 75–85.

MacPherson, R., Double, D. B., Rowlands, R. P., & Harrison, D. M. (1993). Long-term psychiatric patients' understanding of neuroleptic medication. *Hospital & Community Psychiatry, 44,* 71–73.

Mailick, D., & Ashley, A. (1981). Politics of interprofessional collaboration: Challenge to advocacy. *Social Casework, 65,* 131–137.

Mailick, M. D., & Jordan, D. (1977). A multimodel approach to collaborative practice in health care settings. *Social Work in Health Care, 2,* 445–457.

Mancuso, L., & Emrey, B. (Eds.). (1991). Special issue: Serving persons with dual disorders of mental illness and substance abuse. *Psychosocial Rehabilitation Journal, 15.*

Manderscheid, R. W., & Sonnenschein, M. A. (1990). *Mental health, United States, 1990.* Rockville, MD: National Institute of Mental Health, Division of Biometry and Applied Sciences, U.S. Department of Health and Human Services.

Manheimer, D., Davidson, S. T., Balter, M. B., Mellinger, G. D., Cisin, I. H., & Parry, H. J. (1973). Popular attitudes and beliefs about tranquilizers. *American Journal of Psychiatry, 130,* 1246–1253.

McCandless-Glimcher, L., McKnight, S., Hamera, E., Smith, B. L., Peterson, K. A., & Plumlee, M. N. (1986). Use of symptoms by schizophrenics to monitor and regulate their illness. *Hospital & Community Psychiatry, 37,* 929–933.

McCollum, A., Margolin, C., & Lieb, J. (1978). Consultation on psychoactive medication. *Health & Social Work, 3*(4), 72–98.

McEntee, W. J., & Crook, T. H. (1991). Serotonin, memory, and the aging brain. *Psychopharmacology, 103,* 143–149.

McGill, C., Falloon, I., Boyd, J., & Wood-Siverio, C. (1983). Family educational intervention in the treatment of schizophrenia. *Hospital & Community Psychiatry, 34,* 934–938.

Mendoza, R., Smith, M. W., Poland, R. E., Lin, K., & Strickland, T. L. (1991). Ethnic psychopharmacology: The Hispanic and Native American Perspective. *Psychopharmacology Bulletin, 27*(4), 448–458.

Miller, R., Wiedeman, G., & Linn, G. (1980). Prescribing psychotropic drugs: Whose responsibility? *Social Work in Health Care, 6*(1), 51–61.

Mizrahi, T., & Abramson, J. (1985). Sources of strain between physicians and social workers. Implications for social workers in health care settings. *Social Work in Health Care, 10*(3), 33–51.

Morris, L. S., & Schulz, R. M. (1993). Medication compliance: The patient's perspective. *Clinical Therapeutics, 15*(3), 593–606.

Morris, L. S., & Schulz, R. M. (1992). Patient compliance—An overview. *Journal of Clinical Pharmacy and Therapeutics, 17*(5), 283–295.

Morse, E. V., Simon, P. M., & Balson, P. M. (1993). Using experiential training to enhance health care professionals' awareness of patient compliance issues. *Academic Medicine, 68*(9), 693–697.

Mosher, L. R., & Burti, M. (1992). Relationships in rehabilitation: When technology fails. *Psychosocial Rehabilitation Journal, 15*(4), 11–17.

Moxley, D. P., & Freddolino, P. P. (1990). A model of advocacy for promoting client self-determination in psychosocial rehabilitation. *Psychosocial Rehabilitation Journal, 14*(2), 69–82.

Mueser, K. T., Bellack, A. S., Wade, J. H., Sayers, S. L., & Rosenthal, C. K. (1992). An assessment of the educational needs of chronic psychiatric patients and their relatives. *British Journal of Psychiatry, 160,* 674–680.

Mueser, K. T., & Gingerich, S. (1994). *Coping with schizophrenia: A guide for families.* Oakland, CA: New Harbinger Publications.

National Association of Social Workers. (1980). *Code of Ethics.* Washington, DC: Author.

Neill, J. R. (1989). A social history of psychotropic drug advertisements. *Social Science and Medicine, 28*(4), 333–338.

Olfson, M., & Klerman, O. (1993). Trends in the prescription of psychotropic medications: The role of the physician speciality. *Medical Care, 31*(6), 559–564.

O'Shea, M., Bicknell, L., & Whatley, D. (1991). Brief multifamily psychoeducation programs for schizophrenia. Strategies for implementation and management. *American Journal of Family Therapy, 19*(1), 33–44.

Pakes, G. (1979). Group medication counseling conducted by a pharmacist for severely disturbed clients. *Hospital & Community Psychiatry, 28,* 125–127.

Parrish, J. (1993). Involuntary use of interventions: Pros & cons. *Innovations and Research, 2,* 15–22.

Pilette, W. L. (1988). The rise of three-party treatment relationships. *Psychotherapy, 25,* 420–423.

Pirodsky, D. M., & Cohen, J. S. (1992). *Clinical primer of psychopharmacology: A practical guide* (2nd ed.). New York: McGraw-Hill.

Posner, C. M., Wilson, K. G., Kral, M. J., Lander, S., & McIlwraith, R. D. (1992). Family psychoeducational support groups in schizophrenia. *American Journal of Orthopsychiatry, 62,* 206–218.

Potocky, M. (1993). An art therapy group for clients with chronic schizophrenia. *Social Work with Groups, 16*(3), 73–82.

Poulsen, R. L. (1992). Some current factors influencing the prescribing and use of psychotropic drugs. *Public Health Reports, 107*(1), 47–53.

Powell, B. J., Ekkehard, O., & Sinkhard, C. (1977). Pharmacological aftercare for homogeneous groups of patients. *Hospital & Community Psychiatry, 28,* 125–127.

Pray, J. E. (1991). Responding to psychosocial needs: Physician perceptions of their referral practices for hospitalized patients. *Health & Social Work, 16*(3), 184–192.

Promising medications on the horizon. (1994, Summer). *NARSAD Research Newsletter,* pp. 5–11.

Raffoul, P. R., & Haney, C. A. (1989). Interdisciplinary treatment of drug misuse among older people of color: Ethnic considerations for social work practice. *The Journal of Drug Issues, 19*(2), 297–313.

Rapp, C. A. (1992). The strengths perspective of case management with persons suffering from severe mental illness. In D. Saleebey (Ed.), *The strengths perspective in social work practice* (pp. 45–58) New York: Longman.

Ravid, R., & Menon, S. (1993). Guidelines for disclosure of patient information under the Americans with Disabilities Act. *Hospital & Community Psychiatry, 44,* 280–281.

Reamer, F. G. (1987). Informed consent in social work. *Social Work, 32,* 425–429.

Reid, W. H., Pham, V. A., & Rago, W. (1993). Clozapine use by state programs: Public mental health systems respond to a new medication. *Hospital & Community Psychiatry, 44,* 739–743.

Remler, M., & Cohen, D. (1992). Should the right of mental patients to refuse treatment with psychotropic drugs be severely curtailed? In E. Gambrill & R. Pruger (Eds.), *Controversial issues in social work* (pp. 301–315). Boston: Allyn & Bacon.

Ries, R. K. (1993). The dually diagnosed patient with psychotic symptoms. *Journal of Addictive Diseases, 12,* 103–122.

Robbins, C., & Clayton, R. R. (1989). Gender-related differences in psychoactive drug use among older adults. *The Journal of Drug Issues, 19*(2), 207–219.

Robinson, G., Gilbertson, A., & Litwak, L. (1986). The effects of psychiatric patient education to medication program on post-discharge compliance. *Psychiatric Quarterly, 58,* 113–118.

Rodenhauser, P., Schwenker, C. E., & Khamis, H. J. (1987). Factors related to drug treatment refusal in a forensic hospital. *Hospital & Community Psychiatry, 38,* 631–637.

Rodin, J., & Ickovics, J. R. (1990). Women's health: Review and research agenda as we approach the 21st century. *American Psychologist, 45*(9), 1018–1034.

Rose, S. M. (1990). Advocacy/empowerment: An approach to clinical practice for social work. *Journal of Sociology and Social Welfare, 17*(2), 41–52.

Rosenson, M., & Kasten, A. M. (1991). Another view of autonomy: Arranging for consent in advance. *Hospital & Community Psychiatry, 17,* 1–7.

Rosenson, M. K. (1993). Social work and the right of psychiatric patients to refuse medication: A family advocate's response. *Social Work, 38,* 107–112.

Roth, L., Meisel, A., & Lidz, C. (1977). Tests of competence to consent to treatment. *American Journal of Psychiatry, 134,* 279–284.

Rothman, J. (1989). Client self-determination: Untangling the knot. *Social Service Review, 63*(4), 598–612.

Runyan, C. L., & Faria, G. (1992). Community support for the long-term mentally ill. *Social Work in Health Care, 16*(4), 37–53.

Saleeby, D. (1985). In clinical social work is the body politic? *Social Service Review, 59,* 578–592.

Saleeby, D. (1992). Introduction: Beginnings of a strength approach to practice. In D. Saleeby (Ed.), *The strengths perspective in social work practice* (pp. 41–44). New York: Longman.

Sands, R. (1989). The social worker joins the team: A look at the socialization process. *Social Work in Health Care, 14*(2), 1–14.

Schwartz, H., Vingiano, W., & Perez, C. (1988). Autonomy and the right to refuse treatment: Patients' attitudes after involuntary medication. *Hospital & Community Psychiatry, 39,* 1049–1054.

Sclafani, M. (1977). Medication classes for the emotionally ill. *Journal of Psychiatric Nursing, 15*(4), 13–16.

Sclar, D. A. (1991). Improving medication compliance: A review of selected issues. *Clinical Therapeutics, 13*(4), 436–440.

Segal, S. P., Cohen, D., & Marder, S. R. (1992). Neuroleptic medication and prescription practices with sheltered-care residents: A 12-year perspective. *American Journal of Public Health, 82,* 846–852.

Seltzer, A., Roncari, I., & Garfinkel, P. (1980). Effect of patient education on medical compliance. *Canadian Journal of Psychiatry, 25,* 638–645.

Seltzer, M. M., Litchfield, L., Kapust, L. R., & Mayer, J. B. (1992). Professional and family collaboration in case management: A hospital based replication of a community-based study. *Social Work in Health Care, 17*(1), 1–22.

Sheline, Y., & Beatti, M. (1992). Effects of the right to refuse medication in an emergency psychiatric service. *Hospital & Community Psychiatry, 43,* 640–642.

Shulman, L. (1992). *The skills of helping individuals, families and groups* (3rd ed.). Itasca, IL: F. E. Peacock Publishers.

Silverstone, T., & Turner, P. (1988). *Drug treatment in psychiatry* (4th ed.). New York: Routledge.

Simon, B. L. (1994). *The empowerment tradition in American social work: A history.* New York: Columbia University Press.

Solomon, P. (1992). The efficacy of case management services for severely mentally disabled clients. *Community Mental Health Journal, 28*(3), 163–180.

Solomon, P., & Marcenko, M. O. (1992). Families of adults with severe mental illness: Their satisfaction with inpatient and outpatient treatment. *Psychosocial Rehabilitation Journal, 16*(1), 121–134.

Sovner, R., & Bailey, K. P. (1993). Nurse clinical specialists as nonphysician prescribers: Reply. *Journal of Clinical Psychiatry, 54*(10), 396.

Southard, E. E., & Jarret, M. C. (1922). *The kingdom of evils.* New York: Macmillan.

Soyer, D. (1963). The right to fail. *Social Work, 8*(3), 72–78.

Spaniol, L., Zipple, A., & FitzGerald, S. (1984). How professionals can share power with families: Practical approaches to working with families of the mentally ill. *Psychosocial Rehabilitation Journal, 8*(2), 77–84.

Spiegel, D., & Wissler, T. (1987). Using family consultation on psychiatric aftercare for schizophrenic patients. *Hospital & Community Psychiatry, 38,* 1096–1099.

Steiner, D., & Marcopulos, B. (1991). Depression in the elderly: Characteristics and clinical management. *Nursing Clinics of North America, 26*(3), 585–596.

Stimson, G. V. (1974). Obeying doctor's orders: A view from the other side. *Social Science and Medicine, 8,* 97–104.

Stone, A. (1981). The right to refuse treatment: Why psychiatrists should and can make it work. *Archives of General Psychiatry, 38,* 351–354.

Stone, A. A. (1990). Law, science, and psychiatric malpractice: A response to Klerman's indictment of psychoanalytic psychiatry. *American Journal of Psychiatry, 147,* 419–427.

Sullivan, G., Wells, K. B., & Leake, B. (1992). Clinical factors associated with better quality of life in a seriously mentally ill population. *Hospital & Community Psychiatry, 43,* 794–798.

Sullivan, W. P. (1992). Reclaiming the community: The strengths perspective and deinstitutionalization. *Social Work, 37,* 204–209.

Swezey, R. L., & Swezey, A. M. (1976). Educational theory as a basis for patient education. *Journal of Chronic Diseases, 29,* 417–422.

Sylvester, C. (1993). Psychopharmacology of disorders in children. *Psychiatric Clinics of North America, 16*(4), 779–788.

Szasz, T. (1994). *Cruel compassion: Psychiatric control of society's unwanted.* New York: John Wiley.

Test, M. A., Wallisch, L. S., Allness, D. J., & Ripp, K. (1989). Substance use in young adults with schizophrenic disorders. *Schizophrenia Bulletin, 15,* 465–476.

Thale, T. (1973). Effects of medication on the caseworker-client relationship. *Social Casework, 54,* 27–36.

Thompson, R., & Weisberg, S. (1990). Families as educational consumers: What do they want? What do they receive? *Health and Social Work, 15,* 221–227.

Tobias, M. (1990). Validator: A key role in empowering the chronically mentally ill. *Social Work, 35,* 357–359.

Torrey, E. F. (1986). *Witchdoctors and psychiatrists.* Northvale, NJ: J. Aronson.

Toseland, R., Zaneles-Palmer, J., & Chapman, D. (1986). Teamwork in psychiatric settings. *Social Work, 31,* 46–52.

Turk, D., Salovey, P., & Litt, M. (1986). Adherence: A cognitive-behavioral perspective. In K. Gerber & A. Nehemkis (Eds.), *Compliance: The dilemma of the chronically ill* (pp. 44–72). New York: Springer.

Valenstein, E. T. (1986). *Great and desperate cures: The rise and decline of psychosurgery and other radical treatments for mental illness.* New York: Basic Books.

Van Putten, T. (1974). Why do schizophrenic patients refuse to take their drugs? *Archives of General Psychiatry, 31,* 67–72.

Van Putten, T., Crumpton, E., & Yale, C. (1976). Drug refusal in schizophrenia and the wish to be crazy. *Archives of General Psychiatry, 33,* 1443–1446.

Veeninga, A. T., Westenberg, H. G. M., & Weusten, J. T. N. (1990). Fluvoxamine in the treatment of menstrually related mood disorders. *Psychopharmacology, 102,* 414–416.

Wadeson, H. (1987). *The dynamic of art psychotherapy.* New York: Wiley.

Waller, D. A., & Altshuler, K. Z. (1986). Perspectives on patient noncompliance. *Hospital & Community Psychiatry, 37,* 490–492.

Walsh, C. B. (1993). This prescription may be hazardous to your health: Who is accountable to the patient? *Journal of Clinical Psychopharmacology, 13*(1), 68–70.

Walsh, J. (1987). The family education and support group: A psychoeducational aftercare program. *Psychosocial Rehabilitation Journal, 10,* 51–61.

Walsh, J. (1989). Treatment of the bipolar client: Clinical social work contributions. *Clinical Social Work Journal, 17,* 367–381.

Weick, A., & Pope, L. (1988). Knowing what's best: A new look at self-determination. *Social Casework, 69,* 10–16.

Weick, A., Rapp, C., Sullivan, W. P., & Kisthardt, W. (1989). A strengths perspective for social work practice. *Social Work, 34,* 350–354.

Weiden, P., Rapkin, B., Mott, T., Zygmut, A., Goldman, D., Horvitz-Lennon, M., & Frances, A. (1994). Rating of medication influences (ROMS) scale in schizophrenia. *Schizophrenia Bulletin, 20,* 297–307.

Weil, M. (1982). Research on issues in collaboration between social workers and lawyers. *Social Service Review, 56,* 393–405.

Weiner, B. (1985). Treatment rights. In S. Brakel, J. Parry, & B. Weiner (Eds.), *The mentally disabled and the law* (pp. 327–367). Chicago: American Bar Association.

Weissman, M. (1972). Casework and pharmacotherapy in the treatment of depression. *Social Casework, 53,* 38–44.

Wettstein, R. M. (1992). Legal aspects of prescribing. In M. S. Keshavan & J. S. Kennedy (Eds.), *Drug-induced dysfunction in psychiatry* (pp. 9–19). New York: Hemisphere Publishing.

Whiteside, S. E., Harris, A., & Whiteside, H. (1983). Patient education: Effectiveness of medication programs for psychiatric clients. *Journal of Psychosocial Nursing and Mental Health Services, 21*(10), 16–21.

Wiggins, J. G. (1994). Would you want your child to be a psychologist? *American Psychologist, 49,* 485–492.

Wilk, R. J. (1994). Are the rights of people with mental illness still important? *Social Work, 39,* 167–177.

Willetts, R. (1980). Advocacy and the mentally ill. *Social Work, 25,* 372–377.

Wilson, W. H., & Claussen, A. M. (1993). New antipsychotic medications: Hope for the future. *Innovations & Research, 2,* 3–11.

Winslade, W. (1981). Ethical issues. In E. A. Serafetinides (Ed.), *Psychiatric research in practice: Biobehavioral terms* (pp. 227–240). New York: Grune & Stratton.

Wise, M. G., & Tierney, J. (1992). Psychopharmacology in the elderly. *Journal of the Louisiana State Medical Society, 144*(10), 471–476.

Wittlin, B. (1988). Practical psychopharmacology. In R. P. Liberman (Ed.), *Psychiatric rehabilitation of chronic mental patients* (pp. 117–145). Washington, DC: American Psychiatric Press.

Wolpe, P. R., Gorton, G., Serota, R., & Sanford, B. (1993). Predicting compliance of dual diagnosis inpatients with aftercare treatment. *Hospital & Community Psychiatry, 44,* 45–53.

Yank, G. R., Bentley, K. J., & Hargrove, D. S. (1993). The vulnerability-stress model of schizophrenia: Advances in psychosocial treatment. *American Journal of Orthopsychiatry, 63*(1), 55–69.

Youssef, F. (1984). Adherence to therapy in psychiatric patients: An empirical investigation of the impact of patient education. *International Journal of Nursing Studies, 21,* 51–57.

Yudofsky, S. C., Hales, R. E., & Ferguson, T. (1991). *What you need to know about psychiatric drugs.* New York: Ballantine Books.

Ziedonis, D. M., Rayford, B. S., Bryant, K. J., & Rounsaville, B. J. (1994). Psychiatric comorbidity in white and African-American cocaine addicts seeking substance abuse treatment. *Hospital & Community Psychiatry, 45*(1), 43–48.

Zind, R. (1991). Mental health care and illness knowledge among chronic schizophrenics. *Military Medicine, 156,* 159–166.

Zind, R., Furlong, C., & Stebbins, M. (1992). Educating patients about missed medication doses. *Journal of Psychosocial Nursing and Mental Health Services, 30,* 10–14.

Zipple, A. M., Langle, S., Spaniol, L., & Fisher, H. (1990). Client confidentiality and the family's need to know: Strategies for resolving the conflict. *Community Mental Health Journal, 26,* 533–545.

Zito, J. M., Routt, W. W., Mitchell, J. E., & Roering, J. C. (1985). Clinical characteristics of hospitalized psychotic patients who refuse antipsychotic drug therapy. *American Journal of Psychiatry, 142,* 822–826.

GLOSSARY

(Indexed terms are in bold italics. Pronunciations and trade names are provided for some terms.)

Absorption The process by which the bloodstream takes in a drug, most commonly through passive diffusion into the bowel wall. Absorption efficiency is affected by the chemical nature of the drug, its method of delivery, and the time of day, as well as the client's gender and physiology. Intravenous injection provides the most rapid form of drug absorption, followed by intramuscular injection and oral administration.

Acetylcholine (ah-SEAT-till-CO-leen) A type of ***neurotransmitter*** released by all neurons that controls the activity of the skeletal muscles, heart beat, some glandular functions, mood, sleep, and memory. It is essential to the transmission of brain/spinal-cord messages.

Adherence The degree to which the client follows the prescribed course of medication administration. It is used as an alternative term to "compliance," which has overtones of client passivity and obedience, and "noncompliance," which has overtones of deviancy.

Adjustment disorder According to the DSM-IV, an excessive and maladaptive response, lasting 6 months or less, to an identifiable external stressor. Psychosocial functioning of the individual is impaired beyond what would be expected given the known stressors. It may include symptoms of depression and/or anxiety, such as fearfulness and feelings of hopelessness.

Advocacy role The role in which the social worker uses knowledge of law, mental illness, and advocacy to help represent the wishes of the client(s) to the decision-making authorities in hopes of achieving changes in practice and/or policy related to access to care or services.

Aftercare A term commonly used in the 1960s and 1970s, but now outdated, which refers to all mental health services provided to people with mental illness after they have been discharged from a psychiatric hospital or other inpatient facility and focused on coping, personal growth, skill building, and community adaptation. Terms more commonly used at present include ***psychosocial rehabilitation,*** case management, and ***community care.***

Agoraphobia (ah-GORE-ah-FO-bee-ah) According to the DSM-IV, a type of ***panic disorder*** that arises when an individual becomes anxious about being alone outside the home to the extent of experiencing an incapacitating fear. The individual suffering from agoraphobia also fears having an unexpected panic attack in a public setting where withdrawal is difficult or embarrassing.

Agranulocytosis (ah-GRAN-you-low-sigh-TOE-sis) A dramatic decrease in the number of infection-fighting white blood cells. Agranulocytosis is a very rare ***side effect*** of ***antipsychotic drugs,*** most notably of ***clozapine.*** Even in the case of clozapine, it is said to afflict only 1–2% of users, and the ill effects of this disease can be reversed if it is identified early, and the drug discontinued.

Akathesia (ack-ah-THEE-zsha) Experience of extreme internal restlessness accompanied by muscle discomfort. Akathesia is an ***extrapyramidal side effect*** of ***antipsychotic drugs.***

Alprazolam (al-PRAZ-oh-lam) (Xanax) A ***benzodiazepine*** with a rapid onset of effects, which makes it effective in dealing with episodic bursts of anxiety.

Amitriptyline (am-ah-TRIP-til-een) (Elavil, Endep) A commonly prescribed ***heterocyclic antidepressant drug.***

Anorexia (an-or-EX-ee-ah) The condition called anorexia nervosa, an eating disorder characterized by self-imposed, deliberate restriction of food intake regardless of appetite and/or nutritional needs, leading to pronounced and physically harmful weight loss, possibly requiring hospitalization.

Anti-anxiety drugs Any of the ***benzodiazepines, beta-blockers,*** or ***buspirone,*** which are used to treat anxiety symptoms or disorders, for the purpose of lowering the client's experience of symptoms to levels that do not significantly interfere with desired social functioning.

Anticholinergic (ann-tie-koh-lin-URR-jick) **(Side) Effects (ACEs)** Adverse effects that result from the suppressive action of certain ***antipsychotic*** and ***antidepressant*** medications on the action of ***acetylcholine*** in the brain and ***peripheral nervous system.*** The actual side effects include dry mouth, blurred vision, constipation, and urinary hesitancy.

Antidepressant drugs A major class of ***psychotropic drugs*** with diverse chemical configurations including the ***Monoamine Oxidase Inhibitors (MAOIs),*** the ***heterocyclic drugs*** (composed of mono-, di-, tri- and hetracyclics), and the ***serotonin reuptake inhibitors (fluoxetine, paroxetine, sertraline, trazodone,*** and venlafaxine), which, along with ***bupropion*** are more recent innovations. Antidepressants usually must be taken for several weeks to have the desired effect and have a low ***therapeutic index,*** so they must be closely monitored.

Antihistamine A class of drugs that can impede the effects of naturally occurring chemical compounds in the body called histamines, which can dilate capillaries, produce headaches, and decrease blood pressure. Antihistamines may be employed for their ***sedative*** and ***hypnotic*** properties, and to treat ***extrapyramidal symptoms.***

Antipsychotic drugs A major class of ***psychotropic drugs,*** most of which are ***dopamine receptor antagonists*** (with the exception of ***clozapine*** and ***risperidone***). Many antipsychotic ***metabolites*** also act as dopamine receptor antagonists. Antipsychotics have a high ***therapeutic index.***

Anxiety The presence of high levels of physiological and psychological distress unconnected to any immediate threats in the environment. It is distinguished from fear by the fact that the threat is not known and by its serious and negative impact on psychosocial functioning. Anxiety is manifested in feelings of helplessness, self-doubt, self-absorption, and excessive preoccupation with perceived threats in the environment. It may also be expressed as a variety of somatic complaints and symptoms, such as headaches and false "heart attacks," for which no organic cause can be found.

Aplastic (ay-PLASS-tick) **anemia** A condition in which the body cannot produce a normal number of red blood cells or cannot correct a deficiency in hemoglobin. It ordinarily occurs when a drug, a toxic agent, radiation, or disease acts to inhibit the production of red blood cells.

Arrhythmia (ah-RITH-mee-ah) Variation in the normal rhythm of heartbeats, which is normally between 60 and 90 beats per minute in adults. At the high end (above 100 beats per minute) the arrhythmia is termed ***tachycardia.*** At the low end (below 60 beats per minute) it is termed *bradycardia.* Tachycardia or bradycardia may indicate heart disease or a drug ***side effect.***

Autonomic (ought-oh-NAW-mick) **nervous system** Regulates the involuntary processes of the internal organs and blood vessels. Many of the functions controlled by the **autonomic nervous system** are self-regulating or autonomous. It is comprised of two primary subsystems: the ***sympathetic*** and ***parasympathetic systems,*** which sometimes work in cooperation but other times are antagonistic in their contrasting roles of "arousal" and "rest."

Autoreceptors ***Receptors*** on the presynaptic neurons that regulate the release of ***neurotransmitters.***

Axon A nerve-fiber projection from the ***neuron*** that serves to transmit signals to adjacent neurons. ***Neurotransmitter*** substances are contained within an axon. The axon terminal (or end) is also the site of the neurotransmitter release.

Balanced perspective The maintenance of a balance between competing and sometimes conflicting needs, rights, and aspirations of the individual, family, and society. Although the client's perspective should be preeminent, the effective collaboration needed for positive outcomes depends on balancing the perspectives of all stakeholders and participants.

Basal ganglia (BAY-zill-GANG-lee-ah) Structures located on both sides of the limbic system, involved in the regulation and initiation of movement and in a variety of neuropsychiatric symptoms, including dementia, ***major depression,*** and psychosis. They may be inadvertently affected by certain ***psychotropic drugs,*** resulting in adverse ***side effects.***

Behavior disturbances Marked changes in a person's behavior patterns, typical of ***psychotic disorders.*** The disturbances are reflected by withdrawal, apathy, and bizarre actions.

Benzodiazepines (bens-oh-dye-AZ-eh-peens) A class of drugs used both as ***antianxiety drugs*** and as ***sedatives.*** They are not associated with as much euphoric effect as other tranquilizing drugs. Common benzodiazepines include ***chlordiazepoxide*** (Librium) and ***diazepam*** (Valium).

Beta-blockers (BAY-ta) Refers to a class of drugs that reduces the physiological analogs of anxiety by blocking the beta receptors in the ***autonomic nervous system.*** They block those receptors that stimulate heart beat and those that dilate blood vessels and air channels in the lungs. They are as strong as ***benzodiazepines,*** despite the greater dosages needed, and they are not addicting. They are, however, short-acting and do not remain long in the client's system. They are most effective for specific situations of unmanageable anxiety.

Bioavailability The amount of drug that reaches the bloodstream without being metabolized, or chemically changed.

Biogenic amines (bye-oh-JEN-ick AH-meens) ***Neurotransmitters*** synthesized in the nerve terminals, as opposed to the cell body, that affect nerve functioning through the chemical synapses. The ***catecholamines*** and the ***indoleamines*** are included in this group.

Bipolar disorder A recurring illness of elevated mood that impairs psychosocial functioning (a manic episode), and depressed affect that also impairs psychosocial functioning (an episode of depression). The DSM-IV identifies three types of bipolar disorders: bipolar/depressed, bipolar/manic, and bipolar/mixed. Most clients will experience both ***depression*** and ***mania,*** although some 10–20% will experience only mania.

Blood-brain barrier A semipermeable barrier between the blood vessels and the brain. For medications and other compounds to pass through the tightly constricted capillary parts of the barrier, they must be ***fat-soluble.*** In areas where capillaries are not so tightly constricted, water-soluble substances may pass through.

Blood level The measure of a drug's presence in the plasma at a given time.

Borderline personality disorder A type of personality disorder characterized by emotional instability, ***narcissism,*** controlling behavior, identity diffusion, feelings of loneliness and abandonment, and troubled interpersonal relationships.

Bromides (BROH-mides) Sedative medications introduced into the practice of mental health treatments in the second half of the 19th century. The chief result of such medications seems to have been the quieting of the psychiatric wards rather than the improvement of clients' mental and emotional conditions. This situation continued through the 1940s, when nonspecific sedative drugs were still promoted in medical textbooks.

Bupropion (byu-PROH-pee-on) (Wellbutrin) An ***antidepressant drug*** known to induce seizures in certain cases and therefore administered with specific recommendations on dose ranges. It should not be administered with ***MAOIs.***

Buspirone (byu-SPYE-rohn) (BuSpar) An ***anti-anxiety drug*** that is not often associated with abuse because of the absence of withdrawal phenomena, cognitive impairment, and ***sedation.*** It has a short half-life and must be taken several times daily to maintain a therapeutic level.

Carbamazepine (kar-bah-MAH-zeh-peen) (Epitol, Tegretol) Originally developed as an anticonvulsant, along with ***valproic acid,*** and effective in treating some mood disorders (acute mania and bipolar disorders). It is thought to retard the electrochemical ***kindling process*** in the nervous system that can help set off either convulsions or manic episodes.

Catecholamines (kat-ah-KOH-la-meens) A group of ***biogenic amines,*** belonging to the catechol group, that play an important role in nervous-system functioning, particularly regarding sleep, mood states, sexual behavior, and aggressiveness. This group includes the ***neurotransmitters dopamine, norepinephrine,*** and epinephrine.

Cell body Central area of the ***neuron*** where cell metabolism takes place.

Cell membrane A barrier that separates the contents of the cell from the fluid enveloping it.

Central nervous system The system of ***neurons*** comprising the brain and ***spinal cord,*** which serves as the body's major nerve control system, directing and regulating all parts of the body in receiving stimuli from external and internal environments, interpreting those stimuli, and causing the body to react.

Cerebellum Located in the ***hindbrain,*** the cerebellum controls bodily functions that operate below the level of consciousness, including posture, balance, and movement through space. It receives information directly from sense organs, muscles, and joints.

Cerebral cortex The folded, outermost region of the ***cerebrum,*** responsible for primary sensory functioning, visual processing, long-term memory, motor and perceptual coordination and integration, language, thinking, and problem-solving. It is entirely made up of the so-called "gray matter." These functions are managed by the four lobes, each with a distinct function: the ***frontal lobe,*** the ***temporal lobe,*** the ***parietal lobe,*** and the ***occipital lobe.***

Cerebrum Physically the largest and most imposing structure of the brain, it is, along with the ***cerebral cortex,*** the locus of higher mental functions such as memory, reasoning, language, judgment, and abstract thought.

Chloral hydrate A generic sedative popular among hospital psychiatrists during the late 19th century for its expediency in producing more manageable clients despite grave side effects, including poisoning and paralysis of the respiratory system.

Chlordiazepoxide (klor-dye-ayz-eh-POX-eyed) (Librium) The first ***benzodiazepine*** (***anti-anxiety drug***), introduced in 1960. It is also considered a sedative-hypnotic because it reduces daytime activity and helps induce sleep, and has been used for anxiety reduction with clients about to undergo surgery.

Chlorpromazine (klor-PROH-mah-zeen) (Thorazine) An ***antipsychotic drug*** with low potency, used sometimes to treat severe psychotic symptoms in children.

Clearance The measure of the amount of a drug excreted through pores and bodily secretions (such as saliva), in a given amount of time.

Client system The person or persons for whom the social worker provides services. The client system may be an individual client, a family, a couple, a group, or any combination thereof. The worker contracts with the client system to provide specified treatment, ideally through a **collaborative partnership.**

Clinical depression Severely depressed affect accompanied by psychomotor difficulties (such as slower reaction times or excessive physical activity) and difficulties in thinking, planning, and goal setting. Sometimes this term is used interchangeably with ***major depression.***

Clomipramine (kloh-MIP-rah-meen) (Anafranil) A ***heterocyclic antidepressant drug*** that is also effective in the treatment of obsessive-compulsive disorder.

Clorazepate (klor-AY-zeh-payt) (Tranxene) A ***benzodiazepine*** and long-acting ***antidepressant*** sometimes used to treat acute alcohol withdrawal and convulsive disorders.

Clozapine (KLOH-zah-peen) (Clozaril) An ***antipsychotic drug*** found effective in treating severe and persistent ***schizophrenia.*** It is not used as a first-line antipsychotic drug because it produces a small risk of ***agranulocytosis,*** a depletion of white blood cells that can be fatal if not monitored. Clozapine has demonstrated effectiveness in treating both the positive and negative symptoms of schizophrenia.

Community care The range of treatment and support services available to clients outside of institutions, usually a less intensive or restricted level of care than that offered by institutions. Medication management may be an important part of community care, inasmuch as it helps the client function more independently in the community.

Consultant/collaborator role The role in which the social worker helps to evaluate the client's need for medication, makes physician referrals, monitors the effect of medications, and consults with the psychiatrist/physician on treatment issues as needed. In this role, the worker avoids taking either adversarial or advocacy stances with respect to client medication adherence.

Continuity of care The continuous provision of needed services and support for clients moving from one setting, or care provider, to another, including client and care-provider collaboration in relocation, discharge contacts, and planning and follow-up. Despite being a nearly century-old notion (beginning with the work of the New York State Charities Aid Association and aftercare agent Edith

Horton in 1904), many states and agencies are still struggling to provide organized continuity of care.

Cyclothymia (SIGH-kloh-THIGH-mee-ah) According to the DSM-IV, it is characterized by the manifestation of several ***hypomanic episodes*** and periods of depressed mood, which do not meet the full criteria for ***mania*** or ***major depression. Psychotic symptoms*** are absent in cyclothymia.

Deinstitutionalization The mass release of institutionalized persons to the community over the course of three decades (from the 1950s to the 1980s). Deinstitutionalization specifically refers to the reduced census at state hospitals.

Delusion A "false belief," or a belief strongly held despite contrary evidence of a different social (commonly agreed-on) reality. Common types are persecutory delusions (belief of threat/harm from others), delusions of grandeur (inflated sense of self), delusions of being controlled (external agents impose thoughts/feelings), and delusions of reference (external events are significant/reflective of self).

Dendrite (DEN-dright) The short extension of the neuron that is the neuron's "receiving end" for signals sent from other cells, it is located close to the ***axons*** of other cells but separated by a short distance from the ***synaptic cleft.***

Depression A state of low mood that interferes to some degree with one's ability to manage tasks of daily living effectively. Unlike ***clinical depression,*** it occurs at times to all people and may or may not signify a problem requiring medication or any other form of professional intervention.

Desipramine (dez-IP-rah-meen) (Norpramin, Pertofrane) A ***tricyclic antidepressant*** sometimes prescribed because it is thought to have the least ***anticholinergic effects*** of the ***heterocyclic drug*** class.

Diazepam (dye-AY-zeh-pam) (Valium) A ***benzodiazepine*** used to treat ***anxiety,*** which also may act as a ***sedative.*** It provides short-term relief for mild to moderate anxiety and is used to treat epileptic and alcohol withdrawal symptoms.

Diphenhydramine (dye-fen-HIGH-drah-meen) (Allerdyl, Benadryl) An ***antihistamine,*** sometimes used as a ***hypnotic drug,*** but ordinarily prescribed to combat ***extrapyramidal symptoms,*** and as an antiparkinsonian medication.

Distribution The process by which the drug travels from the blood stream to its target site by one of two routes: dissolving in blood plasma, which is relatively efficient in getting drugs to the target brain site, and attaching to proteins in the blood plasma, which is problematic because of individual differences in protein-binding rates. Only the unbound portion of the drug can cross into the brain. Most ***psychotropic drugs*** have a fairly high ***protein binding*** rate.

Dopamine (DOPE-ah-meen) A type of ***neurotransmitter*** thought to be involved in disorders of cognition (such as ***schizophrenia***), motor control systems, and limbic activity (emotional behavior).

Dose response The measure of therapeutic effect as a function of dosage.

Doxepin (DOCKS-ah-pin) (Sinequan, Adapin) A commonly prescribed ***heterocyclic antidepressant drug.*** It is also occasionally prescribed for the treatment of ***anxiety.***

Drug agonist (AG-un-ist) A drug that acts to facilitate or enhance the effect of another drug.

Drug antagonist A drug that acts against or hinders the effect of another drug.

Drug half-life The time it takes for the concentration of a drug within the body to fall to 50% of its previous (peak) level.

Dysthymia (diss-THIGH-mee-ah) A depression that is chronic (most of the day, most days) but not acute, and lasts for at least 2 years, according to the DSM-IV. Symptoms resemble those of ***major depression***—including sleep disturbances, low energy levels, depressed self-esteem, concentration problems, and general lack of energy—but are generally milder and last longer.

Dystonias (diss-TONE-ee-ahz) Uncoordinated, involuntary twisting movements of the jaw, tongue, or entire body, produced by sustained muscle spasms.

Educator role The social worker's role of helping clients and their families understand the reasons for medication and treatment, the benefits and risks of such treatment, and the various options available to them.

Efferent Nerve impulse conduction from the ***central nervous system*** outward to the periphery (muscles and glands).

Electroconvulsive therapy (ECT) A procedure used in the treatment of severe depression in which an electric current is very briefly applied through electrodes to one or both sides of the brain. Temporary side effects may include convulsions, unconsciousness, and temporary memory loss.

Elimination All bodily processes that act to lower the concentration of a drug in the body. ***Metabolism, excretion*** (e.g., bodily wastes), and secretion (e.g., tears) are processes that help sustain elimination.

Enzymes Proteins in the body that cause chemical changes but do not become part of those changes. They are important catalysts for bodily functions such as ***metabolism,*** which in turn can affect drug ***potency*** and the rate of drug ***absorption.***

Euthymic (you-THIGH-mick) **mood state** A generally positive mood state, or state of emotional wellness, marked by the absence of chronic or serious ***mood disorders,*** which might affect social functioning negatively.

Excretion (x-KREE-shun) The process following ***metabolism*** in which the body eliminates a drug, generally through the bile, feces, urine, sweat, saliva, tears, or milk.

Extrapyramidal pathways (EX-stra-peer-AM-id-ill) Long nerve pathways stretching from the ***cerebral cortex*** to the ***spinal cord*** and used by motor nerves, the other pathways being ***pyramidal.*** This diffuse set of neural structures influences movement, coordination, and posture.

Extrapyramidal symptoms (EPS) The side effects of ***antipsychotic drugs*** and the ***heterocyclic antidepressants.*** These effects include ***akathisia, dystonias,*** and ***parkinsonian effects.***

Fat-soluble drugs Drugs that dissolve only in body tissues that absorb fat. Other drugs dissolve in the body's water content. This means that the concentration of fat-soluble drugs varies in proportion to the ratio of fat to water in the body. Individuals with proportionately more fat to water will have lower concentrations of fat-soluble drugs than those with proportionately more water. Increased age is associated with higher fat-to-water ratios, and women tend to have greater fat-to-water ratios than men. Virtually all ***antipsychotic drugs*** are fat-soluble.

"First pass" metabolism The initial, rather extensive breakdown of the drug within the liver before the drug reaches the circulatory system. This substantially reduces the amount of drug available for the target site.

Fluoxetine (flew-OX-ah-teen) (Prozac) One of the new class of "atypical" ***antidepressant drugs,*** which functions as a ***serotonin-reuptake inhibitor*** in producing a therapeutic effect.

Fluphenazine (flew-FEN-ah-zeen) (Prolixin, Permitil) A high-potency ***antipsychotic drug*** used for the treatment of disorganized and psychotic thinking, as well as delusions and hallucinations.

Forebrain The last of the three parts of the brain to evolve in embryonic development. The forebrain is highly specialized in many areas; it also contains the limbic system, which is responsible for emotions and homeostasis of bodily functions, and which is a target of many ***psychotropic medications.*** The ***cerebrum*** and the ***cerebral cortex,*** centers of higher functioning processes, such as reasoning, decision making, and abstract thought, are also located in the forebrain.

Frontal lobe One of four major hemispheres in the ***cerebrum*** of the human brain. It is located behind the forehead and controls the functions of speech, thought, and consciousness.

GABA (GAB-ah) **(gama aminobutyric acid)** An amino acid and ***neurotransmitter,*** found throughout the ***central nervous system,*** that has a vital dampening effect on the excitability of nerve cells.

Generalized anxiety According to the DSM-IV, excessive and pervasive worrying that is difficult to control and that leads to restlessness, lack of focus, ***tachycardia,*** irritability, motor tension, heightened apprehension, and vigilance.

Glial (GLEE-ahl) **cells** A class of cells in the nervous system that support neuron functioning and may play an important role in neuronal activity in their contribution to the ***blood-brain barrier*** permeability of compounds both entering and leaving the brain and ***central nervous system.***

Hallucinations "False" sense perceptions of "external objects" that do not exist. Common types are auditory (hearing), visual (sight), tactile (touch), somatic (internal organs), olfactory (smell), and hypersensitivity (hyperacute sight, sound, smell).

Haloperidol (HAH-low-PAIR-ih-dohl) (Haldol) A high-potency ***antipsychotic drug*** used for the treatment of ***schizophrenia*** and Tourette's syndrome.

Health belief model Postulates that individuals will choose a course of action based on their motivational investment in the goal of action and the perceived relevance of that goal to a recommended/requisite behavior. Medication education or any other change-based intervention will be effective insofar as it taps into a personal goal that the learner is strongly motivated to achieve. For instance, a client may be motivated to take medications enabling him or her to work a steady job, which in turn makes it possible to sustain independent living.

Heterocyclic (het-ur-oh-SIGH-click) **drugs** A group of ***antidepressant drugs*** that takes its name from the varying number of chemical rings that determine the drugs' structure and includes hetracyclic, ***tricyclic,*** dicyclic, and monocyclic drugs. Most have long enough half-lives that they need to be taken just once daily.

Hindbrain The first part of the brain to evolve in embroyonic development, the hindbrain consists of the brain stem, ***reticular formation,*** and ***cerebellum,*** which regulate vital bodily functions (such as breathing rate and heart beat), posture, balance, kinesthetic motion, and rudimentary memory functions, among other functions.

Hippocampus (hip-po-CAM-pus) A brain structure that is part of the ***limbic system*** and thus concerned with emotion and motivation. It appears to be important to learning and long-term memory. It extends ***efferent neuron*** pathways (conduits for nerve impulses) to the ***hypothalamus.***

Hypertension High, life-threatening blood pressure possibly due to hereditary predisposition and/or lifestyle (stress levels), health habits (smoking, overeating, food choices), and emotional habits (expressed and repressed hostility), along with other emotions.

Hyperthymia (HIGH-per-THIGH-mee-ah) An affective state characterized by heightened activity and emotional responses that exceed the norm but fall short of ***manic*** proportions.

Hypnotic drugs Drugs that can induce calmness when administered in low doses. Properly administered, hypnotic drugs do not induce sleep.

Hypomania (HIGH-po-MAIN-ee-ah) An episode of manic symptoms that does not attain the full DSM-IV criteria for a ***manic episode.*** The episode is characterized by mood elevation and possibly irritability that interfere with social functioning. It may also describe symptoms displayed by people who formerly had a depressive episode and now manifest a mild form of ***mania.***

Hypothalamus (HIGH-poh-THAL-ah-muss) A peanut-sized structure at the base of the brain that is ultimately involved in the regulation of temperature, balance, appetite, fundamental emotional states, and sexual arousal.

Iatrogenic effects (eye-ah-tro-JEN-ik) Harmful effects presumed to be caused (inadvertently) by the treatment itself.

Imipramine (im-IHP-rah-meen) (Tofranil) A ***heterocyclic antidepressant*** ordinarily prescribed to treat panic attacks, but also sometimes administered to help with cocaine addiction withdrawal.

Impotence (IM-poe-tents) The inability of a man to perform sexual intercourse, usually because of an inability to achieve erection or experience ejaculation. This is a ***side effect*** of some medications but can also exist as a psychological problem.

Indoleamines (in-DOLE-ee-ah-meens) A class of ***neurotransmitter*** characterized by a particular chemical structure, of which ***serotonin*** is a member. Indoleamine is also a ***biogenic amine.*** Tryptophan is an essential amino acid utilized by the body in the synthesis of this substance.

Individual dignity A fundamental value of the social work profession, arising from the notion that all people are intrinsically equal, regardless of status, income, religion, creed, color, language/dialect, ethnic group, ability, sexual orientation, etc.

Kindling process Much as the burning of kindling (wood and other flammables) enables a beginning fire to take hold, the electrophysiological process of kindling generates an action potential (electrochemical "fire") in a ***neuron*** following repeated stimulation below the threshold level.

Lag time The amount of time required for a drug to have its desired effect, depending on factors such as the body's ***tolerance*** of the drug; the drug's ***absorption, protein binding,*** and ***metabolizing rate;*** and individual differences in the client's physiology.

Lithium (carbonate) The most commonly used mood-stabilizing drug, lithium is both naturally occurring and relatively inexpensive. With a shorter half-life than most ***antipsychotics*** and ***antidepressants,*** it must generally be taken more than once a day. As a rule, it is the drug of choice for treating ***bipolar disorder.*** There is a narrow band of effective dosage above which toxicity occurs and below which there is no effect.

Lobotomy (prefrontal) A surgical procedure in which certain nerve tracts in the frontal lobe area are severed to produce a reduction in the tension and ***psychotic*** symptoms of the client. Today, prefrontal lobotomies are seldom performed because of the irreversible apathy, decision-making impairments, and seizures that result from this procedure.

Lorazepam (lor-AS-uh-pam) (Ativan) An ***anti-anxiety drug,*** used as a ***sedative*** or ***hypnotic.*** It is a member of the ***benzodiazepine*** drug class.

Manic episode According to the DSM-IV, a mood state that features euphoria, irritability, and lack of inhibition. It is often accompanied by substance abuse. There is a distinct period of consistently elevated or irritable mood followed by significant problems in psychosocial functioning that may require hospitalization.

MAO inhibitors See ***Monoamine oxidase inhibitors***

Major depression A severely depressed mood state featuring a total loss of interest and/or pleasure in life, with a significant change in the usual quality of life functioning. Characteristic symptoms include marked weight changes, daily psychomotor disturbances, sleep disturbances, loss of concentration, loss of energy, and recurring thoughts of death or suicide. A DSM-IV diagnosis of major depression requires two or more major depressive episodes, separated by at least 2 months of ordinary functioning.

Mania (MANE-ee-uh) A physiological and emotional state in which the person's predominant mood is elevated, expansive, or irritable to a degree that seriously impairs reality testing, relationships, and occupational or social functioning. The condition may persist for a time ranging from several days to several months.

Medication education programs Programs that provide clients and their families with information on drug dosages and uses, as well as potential physical, psychological, and social side effects associated with the use of psychotropic medication.

Mental hygiene movement One of several social reform movements in the early 20th century concerned with public education, research, and prevention services. It was begun with the efforts of Clifford Beers, a Yale-educated psychiatric client, who helped found the National Committee on Mental Hygiene in 1909.

Mesoridazine (mez-oh-RID-ah-zeen) (Serentil) An ***antipsychotic drug*** with a fairly strong ***sedating*** effect that may calm persons who feel highly agitated or violent.

Metabolism The process by which the body breaks down a drug into its chemical derivatives, which can then be eliminated from the body. The metabolic process is usually carried out by enzymes in the liver.

Metabolites (meh-TAB-oh-lights) The chemical by-products of drug ***metabolism*** that can still serve to maintain a therapeutic effect on cognition or affect because they can themselves be psychopharmacologically active, despite having been altered.

Midbrain The second portion of the brain to evolve in embryonic development, the midbrain integrates and monitors many sensory functions and is the center for visual and auditory stimulation. Certain cells in the midbrain serve as relays for information passing from the sense organs to more sophisticated levels of the brain.

Monitor role The role in which the social worker continues to help determine the outcomes, both positive and negative, of medication on social, psychological, and physical functioning through ongoing ***client system*** contact.

Monoamine oxidase (MAHN-oh-AH-meen OX-id-ace) **(MAO) inhibitors** A class of drugs developed as the first ***antidepressants.*** They differ from more recent antidepressants in that they inhibit action on enzymes that metabolize ***norepinephrine*** and ***serotonin*** in the nervous system. They are not widely used today because of the strict dietary regimes that they require. They have, however, been shown to relieve some depressions that are not responsive to other antidepressant drugs.

Monoamines (MAHN-oh-AH-meens) ***Biogenic amines*** with a single amine (organic compound), this group includes ***dopamine, norepinephrine,*** epinephrine (the ***catecholamines***), ***acetylcholine*** (a so-called quaternary amine) and ***serotonin*** (an ***indoleamine***).

Mood disorders Characterized by disturbances in affect, typical of ***psychotic disorders*** and ***depression.*** The disturbances in mood are reflected by severely flattened affect and by extreme emotional ambivalence.

Mood-stabilizing drugs Drugs that feature actions aimed at keeping mood within a stable range, particularly effective in lowering moods from a ***manic*** state. Included in this grouping are the ***tricyclics, MAOIs*** (for ***depression***) and ***lithium*** (for ***bipolar disorders***). The mood stabilizers work to keep moods from extremes of either pole. Because of individual variations in the timing and amplitude of mood swings, mood stabilizers as a class may be used in conjunction with other drugs in keeping with the specific nature of the disorder.

Moral treatment (of mental illness) The predominant mental illness treatment model in America for the first half of the 19th century, based upon the notion that active rehabilitation and a structured life would help to steady uncontrolled thoughts and "problematic" emotions. Structured activities commonly included occupational therapy, religious exercises, sports, amusements, and reading. The typical time frame for such treatment was 6 weeks to 3 months.

Narcissism Egocentrism, or self-centeredness, and self-preoccupation of excessive proportions. The ego and the id are undifferentiated for the narcissistic individual.

Narcissistic injury Occurs when an individual interprets a situation or event as a personal attack or a condemnation that insults or wounds his or her core being. An individual with a mental illness who interprets the prescription of ***antipsychotic drugs*** as proof that "I must be sicker than I thought I was" has suffered a narcissistic injury.

Negative symptoms of psychosis The absence of affective experiences ordinarily present in a person's "normal" experience. Symptoms include apathy, withdrawal, and poverty of thought.

Neonatal (NEE-oh-NATE-al) **withdrawal syndrome** Drug withdrawal symptoms experienced by a newborn child because of drug exposure and addiction in utero. Symptoms include insomnia, increased respiratory efforts and heart rate, and spontaneous body tremors. Behaviors that mark neonatal drug withdrawal symptoms can be recorded using the Neonatal Abstinence Score Tool (NAST).

Nervous system The body's information-processing unit consisting of 100 billion nerve cells and the "action site" for psychotropic medications. It is the entire system of neurons and their supporting material. The nervous system is commonly divided into three branches: the ***central nervous system*** (brain and ***spinal cord***), the ***peripheral nervous system*** (cranial, spinal nerves, and peripheral ganglia), and the ***autonomic nervous system*** (internal organs), which includes the ***sympathetic*** and the ***parasympathetic*** subsystems.

Neurohormones (NEW-row-hoar-moans) Neuromessengers (chemicals) that are released into the bloodstream. They can be chemically indistinguishable from ***neurotransmitters.***

Neuroleptic (new-row-LEHP-tick) **malignant syndrome** A potentially fatal but rare toxic complication of antipsychotic drug treatment that usually occurs within 2 weeks of drug initiation. Typical symptoms include high fever, muscle rigidity, instability of the ***autonomic nervous system*** (e.g., rapid heart beat), and alternating levels of consciousness (from confusion to coma).

Neuron (NEW-rahn) A nerve cell, consisting of a ***cell body*** (nucleus and cytoplasm) as well as a single ***axon*** and several shorter, branched ***dendrites.***

Neurotransmitter A chemical found in the nerve cells that acts as a "neuromessenger" by carrying electrical impulses between cells. Some of the principle neurotransmitters in the nervous system include ***GABA, dopamine, serotonin, norepinephrine,*** and ***acetylcholine.***

Norepinephrine (nor-epp-in-EH-frin) A type of ***neurotransmitter,*** secreted by the adrenal glands in response to arousal-provoking events such as stress. It influences affective behavior, alertness, anxiety, and tension.

Nortriptyline (nor-TRIP-tih-leen) (Pamelor) A ***heterocyclic antidepressant*** with moderate sedation effects and of great benefit for persons with major depression.

Occipital (ox-SIP-i-tahl) **lobes** A physically distinct area of the ***cerebral cortex*** that serves as the foremost processing center for visual signals.

Orgasmic (oar-GAZ-mick) **dysfunction** The inability of a woman to achieve orgasm, because of decreased libido or the inability to experience sexual stimulation. This is a ***side effect*** of some medications but can also exist as a psychological problem.

Orthostatic hypotension An abrupt lowering of blood pressure that can cause fainting, dizziness upon standing, falling, or other injuries, particularly if the client is elderly. Most commonly a side effect of ***chlorpromazine*** and ***thioridazine,*** or high intramuscular doses of low-potency ***antipsychotics.*** It usually occurs during the early phase of treatment, before the body has had time to develop a tolerance.

Oxazepam (ox-AZ-ip-am) (Serax) A drug used primarily to treat ***anxiety,*** and also alcohol withdrawal, which is prescribed for its ***sedative*** and anticonvulsant effects. It is a member of the ***benzodiazepine*** drug class.

Panic disorder A condition in which panic attacks are experienced, followed by 1 month or longer of persistent concerns about having another attack, concerns about the implications or consequences of the attack, or significant behavioral changes related to the attack. A panic attack is characterized by a period of intense fear or physiological discomfort with sudden onset and rapid build to a peak (usually within 10 minutes). It is often accompanied by a sense of imminent danger or impending doom and an urge to escape the situation.

Paranoid ideation The mistaken belief that one is being persecuted, followed, discussed, or observed. It may be related to a mental disorder, such as a delusional disorder, ***schizophrenia,*** or a personality disorder.

Parasympathetic (PAIR-ah-SIMP-ah-THEH-tick) **system** That part of the ***autonomic nervous system*** which functions to support the at-rest bodily processes, such as digestion. It is prominent in the body's conservation of energy reserves.

Parietal (purr-EYE-it-ahl) **lobe** A physically distinct area of the ***cerebral cortex*** responsible for the intellectual processing of sensory information (visual, tactile, auditory) and also responsible for verbal and visual-spatial processing.

Parkinsonian (PARK-in-SO-nee-an) **effects** Drug-induced effects resulting from antipsychotic medications that mirror classical Parkinson's disease symptoms, such as reduction in motor abilities and coordination, shuffling gait, drooling, muscle rigidity, and tremors. Ordinarily the effect occurs within 5 to 90 days of drug initiation.

Paroxetine (pair-OX-ah-teen) (Paxil) One of the new class of "atypical" ***antidepressant drugs,*** which functions as a ***serotonin-reuptake inhibitor*** in producing a therapeutic effect.

Partnership model of practice A model of clinical practice with clients and families in which the worker forges a nonthreatening alliance with the client/family that validates and respects their perspectives, concerns, strengths, and aspirations and that features a mutual, collaborative action-oriented helping process. It is ultimately client-centered in its focus and in its goals, advocating for and representing the client system's needs, wants, and aspirations.

Peripheral (purr-IF-ur-all) **nervous system** The system of ***neurons*** branching from the ***central nervous system*** into the body from the lower brain and ***spinal cord.*** These nerves influence such sensations and actions as sight, smell, chewing and swallowing, and muscle movement.

Pharmacodynamics (farm-ah-co-dye-NAM-icks) The study of the effects of a drug on the body. On the cellular level, the drug works at the nerve cell ***receptor site.*** The interaction between drug and nerve cell chemicals over time leads to effects such as tolerance (gradual lessening of drug effectiveness) and withdrawal (effects of ceasing use of a drug on which the individual is dependent). Factors affecting the interaction and, ultimately, the effect of the drug include client age, gender, physical characteristics, and organic pathologies.

Pharmacokinetics (farm-ah-co-kin-ET-icks) How the body handles a drug, and in particular, the blood plasma concentration of a drug. Specifically, this refers to the ***absorption, distribution, metabolism*** and ***excretion*** of the medication.

Phenothiazine (FEE-no-THIGH-ah-zeen) A type of ***antipsychotic drug*** used in the treatment of ***schizophrenia*** and other ***psychotic disorders.***

Physician's assistant role The traditional role that social workers played most often in the past when collaborating with physicians/psychiatrists. The social worker prepares the client for referral to the physician and enforces the directives of the physician with the client.

Polypharmacy (Pah-lee-FARM-ah-see) The use of more than one drug for treatment of the same ailment. This includes the concurrent administration of several ***psychotropic drugs.***

Positive symptoms of psychosis The presence of bizarre and frequently affect-laden experiences ordinarily absent from a person's "normal" experience. Symptoms include ***hallucinations, delusions,*** and bizarre thinking and behavior.

Postpartum psychosis A psychotic episode of the mother following childbirth. It is sometimes referred to as puerperal psychosis. Postpartum psychosis afflicts mothers within 1 month of delivery, and its causes are thought to include personality factors, the degree to which childbearing was voluntary, life stressors, and endocrinological factors.

Postsynaptic (post-sin-AP-tick) **membrane** The wall of the ***dendrite*** cell body, located at the opposite side of the ***synaptic cleft*** from the ***axon,*** on which ***receptor*** sites are located to receive ***neurotransmitter*** input and pass the impulse through the rest of the cell.

Potency The drug's relative strength in standard units of measure (e.g., milligrams). Low-potency drugs, such as ***chlorpromazine,*** are given in high milligram amounts, while high-potency drugs, such as ***haloperidol,*** are given in low milligram doses.

Presynaptic (pree-sin-AP-tick) **terminal** ***Axon*** endings extending to the ***synapse*** and containing ***neurotransmitters,*** which are released into the ***synaptic cleft*** during neuron activation.

Prodromal (pro-DRO-mull) **phase** The phase during which a deteriorating state of health is recognized that later culminates in full-blown illness. During the deterioration phase, there are subtle warning signs of the impending illness, such as withdrawal, bizarre thoughts, or other behaviors recognized as precursors of a ***psychotic*** episode.

Progressivism An early 20th-century middle-class movement of mainly social reforms aimed at promoting harmony among social classes and races. Progressivism was a response to social change that threatened the upheaval of middle class values such as rationality, efficiency, and incremental upward mobility. Social work is, in part, an outgrowth of progressivism, given the profession's roots in "friendly visitors" to the urban poor who promoted self-improvement and social harmony.

Protein binding One of the routes of drug transport in the bloodstream, involving the attachment of the drug to plasma proteins in the blood. Drug bound to the plasma is essentially lost, because only the unbound portion of the drug can pass into the brain. The protein-binding rate of drugs differs and has a corresponding effect on the amount of drug available for action over time.

Psychiatric social work A term to describe a specialized area of social work practice, first developed in the early 20th century, that focuses on practice with people who have a mental illness or who suffer severe emotional distress.

Psychological side effects The negative impact of taking medication on clients' beliefs about themselves.

Psychopathic hospitals A term used at the beginning of the 20th century to describe short-term, acute-care facilities that also provided outpatient care and educational services to the community.

Psychopharmacology The study of drugs that affect thinking, emotion, and behavior.

Psychosocial rehabilitation A global term that refers to the notion of restoring the client to a level of functioning that will permit him or her to resume life in the community. It operates on the premise that the best way to help clients progress toward greater self-sufficiency is to help them develop skills and competencies simultaneously on individual, interpersonal, and social levels. Clients participate in structured activities aimed at improving emotional and cognitive resources, often including vocational training and counseling.

Psychotic disorders A major group of mental disorders characterized in part by ***delusions,*** catatonic or grossly disorganized behavior, and ***hallucinations.*** Psychotic disorders are identified in the DSM-IV as falling into two broad categories: ***schizophrenia*** and other psychotic disorders. The category of other psychotic disorders includes ***schizoaffective disorders, schizophreniform disorder, delusional*** disorder, brief psychotic disorder, shared psychotic disorder, psychotic disorder due to a general medical condition, and substance-induced psychotic disorder.

Psychotropic drugs Drugs that alter psychological functioning and/or mood, thoughts, motor abilities, balance, movement, and coordination.

Pyramidal (peer-RAM-id-ahl) **nerve pathways** Long nerve pathways stretching from the ***cerebral cortex*** to the ***spinal cord.*** These are one of the two pathways taken by motor nerves, the other being ***extrapyramidal.*** Pyramidal pathways carry messages to and from the ***central nervous system*** that control groups of muscles that contract simultaneously, such as those involved in gripping a pen.

Receptors Special receiving areas in the ***dendrite,*** composed of nerve cell membranes partially exposed to the extracellular fluid that recognize neuromessengers.

Researcher role The role of the social worker in documenting how medications affect the lives of clients and their families and in expanding the existing knowledge base. This role also encompasses collaborations with researchers in other disciplines.

Reticular (reh-TICK-you-lar) **formation** Also known as the reticular activating system, it is a diffuse network of ***neurons*** that trace the midline of the brain stem, sending impulses up the brain stem ultimately to the ***cerebral cortex.*** It can activate the cortex into a state of alert wakefulness and transmits information about the environment. Some psychiatric motivational and arousal disorders can be attributed to problems in this area.

Reuptake The process by which a ***neuron*** reabsorbs a ***neurotransmitter.***

Risperidone (riss-PAIR-eh-dohn) (Risperdal) A recently developed antipsychotic drug. Some recent research suggests evidence of the safety and efficacy of risperidone as it acts on both positive and negative symptoms of ***schizophrenia.*** Risperidone is said to have a low incidence of ***extrapyramidal effects.***

Schizoaffective disorder Defined by the DSM-IV as a continuous period of illness during which there are some symptoms of ***schizophrenia,*** such as delusions, hallucinations, grossly disorganized behavior, and so on, concurrent with either a ***major depressive*** episode, a ***manic*** episode, or a mixed episode.

Schizophrenia A major mental disorder classified in the DSM-IV as lasting more than 6 months and characterized in part by ***thought disturbances,*** misinterpretations of reality, mood changes (including blunting and inappropriate moods), communication problems (poverty of speech and incoherence), and bizarre, withdrawn, or regressive behaviors. The DSM-IV identifies five different subtypes, including disorganized, catatonic, paranoid, undifferentiated, and residual.

Schizophreniform disorder Shares the symptomatology of ***schizophrenia*** but not the duration, lasting from 2 weeks to 6 months.

Sedation A common effect of ***antidepressants*** that in mild form leads to reduced excitability and anxiety and in stronger form to ***hypnotic*** (sleep-inducing) effects.

Sedative Any medication that produces a state of decreased responsiveness to usual stimuli. The state may or may not be experienced as drowsiness.

Self-determination A fundamental value of the social work profession, arising from the belief that each individual is best equipped and, except for rare instances, most competent to judge what is best for himself or herself.

Self-monitoring (drug treatment) The role of the client in noting and systematically recording the effects of drug treatment. The client's monitoring enables the client and professional to assess the impact of taking a ***psychotropic drug.*** Self-monitoring includes observations of symptoms, medication-taking times, dosage, frequency, and ***side effects.***

Serotonin (sair-ah-TONE-in) A type of ***neurotransmitter*** that impacts sensory processes, muscular activity, and cognition. It is a factor in states of consciousness, basic bodily functions, complex sensory and motor activities, and mood. Serotonin is thought to be implicated in ***mood disorders,*** aggression, and ***schizophrenia. Fluoxetine*** (Prozac) and ***clozapine*** (Clozaril) are thought to be significant effects of the serotonergic systems (those that produce serotonin).

Serotonin-reuptake inhibitors The newest group of antidepressant medications, which function by suppressing the ***reuptake*** or reabsorption of ***serotonin*** by the nerve cell and include ***fluoxetine, paroxetine, sertraline, trazodone,*** and venlafaxine. Sometimes called "atypical" drugs because of their chemical distinctiveness from other ***antidepressants,*** these drugs cause significantly less pronounced ***anticholinergic effects.*** As a result, they are more popular with many physicians and clients than other ***antidepressants.***

Sertraline (SIR-truh-leen) (Zoloft) One of the new class of "atypical" ***antidepressant drugs,*** which functions as a ***serotonin-reuptake inhibitor*** in producing a therapeutic effect.

Sexual dysfunction Reflects changes in sexual desire in men and women in addition to ***impotence*** in men and ***orgasmic dysfunction*** in women.

Side effects Any unintentional and nontherapeutic effects of a drug on the body. Side effects, also called adverse effects, are frequently due to the interaction of brain, drug, and body (see ***Pharmacodynamics***).

Social psychiatry A perspective on the practice of psychiatry developed by psychiatrist Adolf Meyer in the early 20th century. In Meyer's opinion, psychiatry needed to attend to prevention, teaching, and research in service of a comprehensive community treatment. He is said to have perceived a critical role for social workers in helping to bring about a suitable aftercare environment for clients.

Social side effects The interpersonal, community, and organizational barriers clients encounter as identified clients of ***psychotropic drugs*** (and hence deemed mentally ill).

Spinal cord A long column of neural tissue that runs from the brain stem to the base of the spine. It is part of the ***central nervous system.***

Steady state The point at which a consistent level of medication is present in the bloodstream such that the amount ingested is equal to the amount eliminated.

Stress-diathesis (dye-ATH-uh-sis) **model** A model of understanding mental illness that takes into account the interplay between biological and environmental influences. The model asserts that while the causes of mental illness seem to be associated with genetic factors as well as abnormalities in brain chemistry and structure, the course of disorders is in part related to environmental factors such as skills in coping, social competence, and social support.

Sympathetic system The part of the ***autonomic nervous system*** that functions during the expenditure of energy. The sympathetic system has been described as having an "arousal" function for the internal organs.

Synapse (SIN-aps) The bridge between one nerve cell and the next. It is across this space that ***neurotransmitters*** flow. It is not a physical structure, but rather a point of juncture marked by the ***synaptic cleft*** (or gap).

Synaptic cleft The gap between the ***axon*** of the sending ***neuron*** and the ***dendrite*** of the receiving neuron.

Tachycardia (tack-ah-CARD-ee-ah) Unusually rapid heart beat (greater than 100 beats per minute) that may result from the side effects of ***antidepressants*** acting on the ***autonomic nervous system.*** It is a form of heart ***arrhythmia.***

Tardive dyskinesia (TAR-dive diss-kin-EASE-yah) Thought to be an irreversible and serious side effect of ***antipsychotics.*** Controversy exists regarding its prevalence. The longer the client is on antipsychotics, the greater the likelihood that the client may develop tardive dyskinesia. The symptoms, coordinated but involuntary rhythmic movements, are commonly seen in facial movements, such as grimacing and lip tremors, and in finger, hand, and trunk movements.

Temazepam (tem-AZ-ah-pam) (Restoril) A ***benzodiazepine*** prescribed as an ***hypnotic*** in the treatment of anxiety or as a ***sedative.***

Temporal (TEM-pore-all) **lobe** One of four major hemispheres in the ***cerebrum*** of the human brain. It is located beneath the ***frontal lobe*** and regulates memory, smell functions, and some aspects of speech.

Thalamus A sensory relay station (for all but the olfactory senses) and an important integration and processing center for information passing from the body to the brain. It is essential to the perception of pain, helps initiate consciousness, and begins to organize sensory signals.

Therapeutic index The range of levels in which a drug is relatively safe or toxic. Drugs with a very low therapeutic index, such as ***lithium,*** must be very closely monitored.

Thioridazine (thigh-oh-RID-ah-zeen) (Mellaril) An ***antipsychotic drug*** that also has a fairly strong sedating effect. It is used for people who may be having illusions or delusions.

Thiothixene (thigh-oh-THICKS-een) (Navane) An ***antipsychotic drug*** of high-potency, used for the treatment of ***hallucinations, delusions,*** and ***psychotic*** and disorganized thinking. It is often prescribed with an ***anticholinergic drug*** to reduce movement side effects such as ***akathisia*** and ***dystonias.***

Thought disturbances Disturbances in the perception of reality that are manifest in disturbed speech and behavior. Thought disturbances are found in ***psychotic disorders,*** particularly ***schizophrenia.*** The disturbances in reality perception are reflected in ***delusions, hallucinations,*** the flight of ideas, the loosening of associations, ideas of reference (the notion that independent external events actually stand in reference to one's self), and poverty of thought.

Three-party treatment relationships The network of relationships in the treatment context including the client, prescriber (physician), and social worker.

Tolerance The reduced responsiveness of the body to a drug as a function of reduced sensitivity of the nerve ***receptors*** over time.

Trazodone (TRAYZ-oh-dohn) (Desyrel) A drug used primarily as an ***antidepressant,*** especially for major depression. Traditionally it has been a backup for ***heterocyclic drugs,*** but more recently it has served as a drug of first choice.

Tricyclic (try-SIGH-click) **antidepressants** These ***antidepressant drugs*** have a central three-ring molecular structure. This group includes ***imipramine*** (Tofranil), ***amitriptyline*** (Elavil), ***clomipramine*** (Anafranil), trimipramine (Surmontil), and ***doxepin*** (Adapin, Sinequan). Tricyclics are increasingly grouped under the larger heading of ***heterocyclic drugs.***

Trifluoperazine (try-FLEW-oh-PER-ah-zeen) (Stelazine) A high-potency ***antipsychotic drug*** used for the treatment of disorganized and psychotic thinking, as well as delusions and hallucinations.

Trihexiphenidyl (try-HEX-ih-FEN-ih-dill) (Artane, Pipanol) A type of antipsychotic drug used to provide treatment for neurological adverse effects, especially ***extrapyramidal effects.*** Feelings of euphoria have been reported from this drug, opening up the possibility of abuse.

Two-track model of treatment The treatment of mental illness proceeding along two parallel tracks; a medical track (biological) and a psychological (or psychosocial) track.

Valproic (val-PRO-ick) **acid** A medication, first used solely as an anticonvulsant drug, that has become commonly used for the treatment of ***bipolar disorder,*** and sometimes to increase the effectiveness of ***antidepressant drugs.***

Water-soluble drugs Drugs that dissolve in the water content of the body. Other drugs dissolve in the body's fatty tissue. This means that the concentration of water-soluble drugs varies in proportion to the ratio of water to fat in the body. Individuals with proportionately more fat to water will have lower concentrations of water-soluble drugs relative to those individuals with proportionately more fat. Increased age is associated with higher fat-to-water ratios, and women tend to have greater fat-to-water ratios than men. ***Lithium*** is the best example of a water-soluble ***psychotropic drug.***

Name Index

SUBJECT INDEX

Cell body, 40, 43, 45, **202**

TO THE OWNER OF THIS BOOK:

We hope that you have found *The Social Worker & Psychotropic Medication* useful. So that this book can be improved in a future edition, would you take the time to complete this sheet and return it? Thank you.

School and address: ______________________________

Department: ______________________________

Instructor's name: ______________________________

1. What I like most about this book is: ______________________________

____

____

2. What I like least about this book is: ______________________________

____

____

3. My general reaction to this book is: ______________________________

____

4. The name of the course in which I used this book is: ______________________________

____

5. Were all of the chapters of the book assigned for you to read? ______________

If not, which ones weren't? ______________________________

6. In the space below, or on a separate sheet of paper, please write specific suggestions for improving this book and anything else you'd care to share about your experience in using the book.

____

____

____

____

____

Optional:

Your name: ______________________ Date: ______________________

May Brooks/Cole quote you, either in promotion for *The Social Worker & Psychotropic Medication* or in future publishing ventures?

Yes: _________ No: ________

Sincerely,

Kia J. Bentley
Joseph Walsh

FOLD HERE

NO POSTAGE NECESSARY IF MAILED IN THE UNITED STATES

BUSINESS REPLY MAIL
FIRST CLASS PERMIT NO. 358 PACIFIC GROVE, CA

POSTAGE WILL BE PAID BY ADDRESSEE

ATT: *Kia J. Bentley and Joseph Walsh*

Brooks/Cole Publishing Company
511 Forest Lodge Road
Pacific Grove, California 93950-9968

FOLD HERE